BRITISH STEAM:
GWR COLLETT CASTLE CLASS

BRITISH STEAM: GWR COLLETT CASTLE CLASS

Keith Langston

First published in Great Britain in 2015 by
Pen & Sword Transport
An imprint of
Pen & Sword Books Ltd
47 Church Street
Barnsley
South Yorkshire
S70 2AS

Copyright © Keith Langston 2015

ISBN 978 1 47382 356 3

The right of Keith Langston to be identified as Author of this work has been asserted by him in accordance with the Copyright, Designs and Patents Act 1988.

A CIP catalogue record for this book is
available from the British Library.

All rights reserved. No part of this book may be reproduced or transmitted in any form or by any means, electronic or mechanical including photocopying, recording or by any information storage and retrieval system, without permission from the Publisher in writing.

Typeset in 11pt Minion by Mac Style Ltd, Bridlington, East Yorkshire
Printed and bound in India by Replika Press Pvt Ltd

Pen & Sword Books Ltd incorporates the imprints of Pen & Sword Archaeology, Atlas, Aviation, Battleground, Discovery, Family History, History, Maritime, Military, Naval, Politics, Railways, Select, Transport, True Crime, and Fiction, Frontline Books, Leo Cooper, Praetorian Press, Seaforth Publishing and Wharncliffe.

For a complete list of Pen & Sword titles please contact
PEN & SWORD BOOKS LIMITED
47 Church Street, Barnsley, South Yorkshire, S70 2AS, England
E-mail: enquiries@pen-and-sword.co.uk
Website: www.pen-and-sword.co.uk

CONTENTS

Acknowledgements 6

Foreword 7

Chapter 1   Introduction 9

Chapter 2   Locomotive numbers 111–4099 34

Chapter 3   Locomotive numbers 5000–5042 70

Chapter 4   Locomotive numbers 5043–5070 120

Chapter 5   Locomotive numbers 5071–5099 156

Chapter 6   Locomotive numbers 7000–7037 188

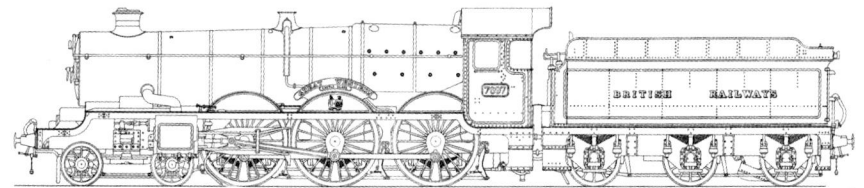

Every effort has been made in respect of ensuring that the information given is as accurate as possible regarding the details concerning locomotive withdrawal, double chimney fitting and the dates and locations of final disposal, in respect of the 171 'Castle' class engines. However, some of the previously published records do contain very minor variations in that regard, and they were understandably difficult to conclusively resolve, given the obvious passage of time.

ACKNOWLEDGEMENTS

This is a Perceptive Images 2015 © publication exclusively for Pen & Sword Books Ltd.

Additional editorial material and specific images were supplied by my good friends David Anderson and John Chalcraft, whose encouragement and shared railway knowledge was invaluable. The additional inclusion of images from the collections of a great many accomplished photographers, past and present, help to tell the 'Castle' class story. The publication of those images serves as a lasting tribute to their skills.

Keith Langston 2015

Photographic libraries whose images have been used include Author, Mike Bentley Collection, Dave Cobbe-C.R.L Coles Collection, Cresselley Photos, John Day Collection, Blenheim Duxford Limited, Bomber Command, Gordon Edgar Collection, Great Western Society, Ray Hinton Collection, J&J Collection, Mike Morant Collection, Norman Preedy Collection, Rail Photoprints Collection, R.C. Riley Collection, Royal Air Force, Royal Australian Air Force, Alan Sainty Collection, Transport Treasury and the Roy Vincent Collection.

Individual photographers whose images have been used include, Author, David Anderson, A.E. Bennett, Hugh Ballantyne, Jim Carter, John Chalcraft, J.J. Cunningham, A.E. Durrant, Clive Hanley, Willy Hermiston, Tony Hisgett, Martyn Hunt, Fred Kerr, Phil Neale, L. Nicholson, Adrian Pingstone, Malcolm Ranieri, S. Rickard, Brian Robbins, Pete Sherwood, Ian Turnbull, R.S. Wilkins, Brian Wilson, Mathew Wilson, R.A. Whitfield and Phil Vabre.

Further Research
Over many years the popular Collett 'Castle' class locomotives have featured in books and magazine articles, and now in the 21st century information is additionally available via the World Wide Web. Further research about the class can be undertaken by consulting these titles, and indeed others:

'Castles' and 'Kings' at Work – Michael Rutherford; Ian Allan Publishing 1982
Portraits of 'Castles' – Bryan Holden and Kenneth Leech; Moorland 1981
The Power of the 'Castles' – R.C Riley & Peter Walker; Oxford Publishing Co 2003
British Steam – 'Castles & Kings' – Keith Langston; Morton's Media 2010

Amongst the many websites available with 'Castle' class content are:
The Great Western Society – www.gwsmainline.org/
Tyseley Locomotive Works – www.tyseleylocoworks.co.uk/tlw/
Steam-Museum of the Great Western Railway – www.steam-museum.org.uk
Rail Info UK – www.railuk.info/steam/
BRDatabase – www.brdatabase.info/

FOREWORD

The Collett 'Castles' were the principal passenger locomotive class of the Great Western Railway and could be found working throughout the system, from top link expresses to more humble secondary services and often on fast fitted freight trains.

They were developed from Churchward's 1906 designed 4-cylinder 'Star' class 4-6-0s to cope with the company's then ever increasing volume of traffic; 155 'Castles' were built in batches between 1923 and 1950, whilst a further 15 'Star' class engines were rebuilt as 'Castles' at differing times. Famously GWR's only Pacific 'THE GREAT BEAR' was rebuilt as a 'Castle' when its boiler became due for replacement. In total 171 Collett 'Castle' class locomotive were built, all at Swindon Works.

Despite the long period of delivery, development did not stand still with improvements to the design being regularly made during the years of construction and thereafter throughout the post-nationalisation period. New boilers, fitted with Double Chimneys, were still being built in the early 1960s and but for the hasty demise of steam it is likely that the 'Castles' would have been capable of giving many more years service, in what became known as their 'final modified form'. It is fortunate that amongst the 8 Castles which have survived, there are examples of most major stages of development including No 4073 CAERPHILLY CASTLE and No 4079 PENDENNIS CASTLE, both of which are preserved in their originally introduced form.

A number of the early 'Castles' completed approximately 40 years in traffic with several clocking up a little short of 2 million miles, the outstanding example being rebuilt 'Star' class engine No 4037 THE SOUTH WALES BORDERERS, which ran a remarkable 2,429,722 miles between 1910 and 1962.

In this book, Keith Langston provides biographical details about the 'Castle' class designer Charles Benjamin Collett together with the basic history of each individual locomotive's working life. There are over 300 images included, providing a comprehensive photographic record of the class. To complete the 'Castle' story background information on the subject names which the engines carried is also included. This publication is a fact-packed reference book which will appeal to steam enthusiasts in general and in particular to those with a special interest in Great Western Railway (GWR) locomotives.

Richard Croucher Chairman
Great Western Society,
Didcot Railway Centre,
Oxon.
www.didcotrailwaycentre.org.uk/
June 2014

Preserved GWR Collett 'Castle' class 4-6-0 No 4079 PENDENNIS CASTLE is seen in Didcot shed yards prior to working a 1967 'Birkenhead Flyer' railtour.
David Anderson

In 2015 the return to steam of No 4079 PENDENNIS CASTLE was an ongoing work in progress, after the 1924 Swindon built 'Castle' was returned to the UK from Australia.

For further information on the project, or to make an offer of support please contact The Great Western Society, Didcot Railway Centre, Didcot, Oxfordshire, OX11 7NJ, England.

Tel: +44 (0) 1235 817200 or e-mail info@didcotrailwaycentre.org.uk

Chapter 1

INTRODUCTION

Castle Builder – Charles Benjamin Collett O.B.E.

In 1948 British Railways inherited some 2,288 locomotives which could be directly attributed to Charles Benjamin Collett O.B.E., almost 60% of the ex Great Western Railway total. Collett served the Great Western Railway (GWR) for the majority of his working life finally becoming Chief Mechanical Engineer (CME) of that organisation in 1922, a position which he held until his retirement in 1941. Prominent amongst his designs were the highly successful 4-cylinder 4-6-0 'Castle' class locomotives.

What follows does not purport to be a comprehensively detailed engineering-based study of the GWR 'Castle' class engines, but more a general appreciation of Collett's '4073' class during their period in service with both the GWR and British Railways Western Region. Main changes in design are highlighted as are the range of modifications in general and in particular those which depict changes in external condition between one 'Castle' locomotive and another. But first what of the man, C.B. Collett?

C.B. Collett 1871–1952. *BR*

Churchward's Heir Apparent

It is a generally held belief that Collett was an 'improver' of designs attributed to his predecessor George Jackson Churchward, indeed many considered Collett's predecessor to be the greatest of all the GWR locomotive builders. Perhaps in the full sense of the word Collett was not strictly speaking a locomotive designer, but he was undoubtedly an accomplished engineer and administrator who was well respected for his organisational abilities.

The son of a journalist, Collett was born at Paddington, London in 1871 and his formal education was at Merchant Taylors School, London and the City and Guilds College. Leaving university he went to work as an engineering pupil for Maudsley, Son & Field Ltd of Lambeth, London an established company of marine engine builders. In 1893 at the age of 22 Collett entered the hallowed portals of the GWR's Swindon Works for the first time.

Noticed as being a diligent and methodical worker he served as a junior draughtsman until 1898 when he was appointed to the position of Assistant to the Chief Draughtsman. Collett's first senior position was that of Technical Inspector Swindon Works, a post he held for just over a year. Appointed to the post of Assistant Works Manager, Swindon in 1901 Collett's not inconsiderable engineering abilities cannot have failed to come to the attention of one G. J. Churchward who was at that time Chief Assistant to the then GWR Locomotive Superintendent William Dean.

Collett served in senior positions under the aforementioned GWR locomotive engineers. He would have greatly profited from the experience he gained during his 20 years under Churchward, who was GWR Locomotive Superintendent (1902–1916) and then Chief Mechanical Engineer (1916–1921). In 1912 Collett was appointed to the post of Works Manager, Swindon. Over time it became obvious to many observers that Collett was being groomed to succeed Churchward.

Colleagues

It is interesting to note that amongst his colleagues during progress through the GWR engineering ranks was another young engineer, one William A. Stanier, later of LMS fame. Stanier joined the GWR as an apprentice in 1892 and in 1906 (during Collett's spell as Assistant Works Manager, Swindon) Stanier became Assistant to the Works Manager Swindon. In 1912 Stanier became Assistant Works Manager, Swindon as Collett became Works Manager, Swindon.

Stanier's career continued to track that of Collett and in 1922 when the latter was appointed Great Western Railway Chief Mechanical Engineer Stanier became Principal Assistant to the CME. Stanier, then aged 56 left the GWR for pastures new in 1932 after he had deduced that the signalled continuance 'in post' of Collett (then aged 61) was blocking his upward move to the CME's office. History proved Stanier to be correct as Collett continued in the job for a further 9 years. Collett and Stanier were both greatly influenced by the work of Churchward and, of course the experience they gained from working under the 'Great Man' at Swindon.

During his formative years Collett did not spend time around running sheds and on locomotive footplates, he was very much a 'works' man, thus the greater part of his later expertise lay in developing engineering practices and improving work flow methods. Before becoming CME he had spent over 20 years working to improve boiler manufacturing to great effect, and additionally rationalising rolling stock and improving locomotive repair facilities.

Great Western folklore would have it that Churchward and Collett were not necessarily the best of friends, but positive proof of that commonly held belief is hard to find. However, what is certain is the fact that they were personality-wise very different people, indeed 'chalk and cheese' would not be a misplaced appraisal of the diverse personae of the two GWR engineers. The two men did, without doubt, make a formidable team, furthermore Churchward's standard locomotive designs suited the GWR and accordingly Collett was the perfect choice of engineer to bring into being the new and improved production methods needed in order to construct 20th century steam locomotives.

Collett GWR Chief Mechanical Engineer

Churchward was a hard act to follow as he was reportedly an outgoing man with great charisma who ruled with a very firm hand, indeed the word 'domineering' has even been used to describe some aspects of his management style. By comparison Collett was perhaps a milder man and almost certainly less domineering than his predecessor but he was nevertheless a hard task master, who insisted upon top quality work from his staff and demanded their absolute loyalty. However, Collett did gain the reputation of being a very fair man and that aspect of his personality did indeed earn him the respect of colleagues. Collett did not seek to attract friends and his apparent standoffish manner meant that other members of the management team did not seek to closely associate themselves with him, on a personal level.

Soon after his appointment to the post of CME Collett got to work modernising the former Rhymney Railway Caerphilly works which he reorganised and equipped to become the maintenance and repair centre for GWR locomotives and rolling stock allocated to the Welsh valleys. Some 5 years later the workshops at Wolverhampton Stafford Road were upgraded under Collett's supervision in order to maintain all GWR locomotives in the northern area.

Much to the delight of the GWR board of directors the reorganisation of workshops and procedures instigated by Collett led to sizable reductions in manufacturing costs. Of great importance was the development of techniques associated with the optical alignment of locomotive frames, cylinders and motion using equipment supplied by the famous Zeiss Company. Swindon claimed that employing such meticulous practices turned steam locomotives into precision machines. Recorded improved 'in traffic' performances validated that claim. Collett also continued the expansion of the GWR Automatic Train Control system (ATC), which during his time was installed on almost all of the company's important routes.

Rolling Stock

Collett was associated with other GWR landmark decisions not least of which the introduction of the Laycock buckeye coupler, a move which greatly benefited the company. He also worked at improving coaching stock, and whilst his 1925 articulated suburban stock may have invited a degree of criticism other innovations and improvements were judged to be highly successful, notably his 1931 Super Saloons and 1935 Centenary coaches. We should also remember that Collett reintroduced the popular chocolate and cream livery for coaching stock.

Starting with the premise that good bogie design is paramount to the 'ride quality' of a passenger coach Collett carried out novel tests using a 7 coach consist which became known as the 'Whitewash Train'. In short each coach incorporated differently designed bogies, and in each vehicle the toilet flush box was filled with different coloured shades of colourwash. Observers, if that is the word, were posted in each WC cubicle and instructed to release wash whenever a bad lurch was experienced. Thereafter the resultant rainbow of colours observed on the ballast would indicate which bogie reacted to a particular track defect etc. Of course if all the colours had been released at one point then perchance the track was itself in need of repair! The concept of the 'Whitewash Train' was a far cry from the precision of the Zeiss Optical frame alignment system! But reportedly it was nevertheless effective.

A private man

Tragedy struck in Collett's personal life when in 1923 Ethelwyn May, his wife of 10 years standing, became seriously ill and unexpectedly died. His wife's untimely death engendered in him an interest in esoteric medicine and a linked belief in the value of dietary remedies. Indeed by employing such methods he claimed to have overcome a cancerous related illness of his own, not long after his wife's death. Always a private man, thereafter Collett became even more so, and rarely if ever attended works social functions.

Collett received an O.B.E., in 1919 in recognition of his work in the production of munitions during the First World War. There were reportedly many instances of serious friction between Collett and officials of the Ministry of Labour during that period and the whole episode had a marked effect on his future attitude to government officialdom. So much so that when at the onset of World War II the GWR were again asked to make available production facilities for the manufacture of munitions Collett was reluctant to allow such work. His objections were noted by the Paddington board members but overruled. Consequently he asked the GWR board to take note of his concerns as he feared that locomotives and rolling stock would fall into disrepair due to a resultant lack of facilities and materials. Anyone familiar with the appalling state of the railways at the end of that conflict would have to agree that Collett's caution was perfectly understandable.

Collett's name game!

Although variously described as taciturn and not overly blessed with an obvious sense of humour one particular act by Collett surely points to a hidden devilish trait! He had no time for anything which he saw as pomposity in general and in particular that facet of the character of certain directors of the Great Western Railway. A number of the GWR 'great and good' had expressed a desire to have their names carried on company locomotives. Pun certainly intended, as the saying goes 'Every dog must have his day!'

The GWR had taken the decision circa 1936/37 to combine parts of the extremely old 'Duke' and 'Bulldog' classes to form the 'Earl' or as the resultant re-builds became known 'Dukedog' class of engines. First built in the late 19th century to a design by William Dean the aging locomotives were reduced to kits of parts and then reassembled at Swindon to emerge in 1936 as a 'new' class. However even though they were fine engines no amount of re-building could disguise their obvious 19th century appearance, alongside other Swindon products of the era the 'Dukedogs' looked positively ancient.

Preserved 'Dukedog' class 4-4-0 No 9017 is seen at the Llangollen Railway in 2009.
Keith Langston

The 'new' engines were all named after earls in order to supposedly show the 'respect' which the company had for the particular directors who had asked for their names to be placed on locomotives, and perchance the titled fraternity in general. On the appointed day the GWR top brass all assembled at Paddington station to witness the arrival of the first 'new' locomotive of the 'Earl' class.

Reports from the time stated that as the mechanically sound, but nevertheless distinctly antiquated looking engine approached the welcoming party 'a deafening silence descended on the group'. Those directors etc whose names were to be allocated to the 'Dukedogs' were not amused! Collett had his moment, perchance exercising a golden opportunity to deflate what he saw as the GWR balloon of pomposity! Maybe he did have a sense of humour after all? Shortly after the Paddington event 20 intended 'Dukedog' names were instead allocated to 'Castle' class locomotives.

Collett – Swindon

Unlike other GWR officials Collett had little truck with civic affairs, but did nominally serve the town of Swindon as a Justice of the Peace from 1921 to 1928 (e.g. Gooch was MP for Cricklade and Deputy Lord Lieutenant of Berkshire whilst Churchward served a spell as Mayor of Swindon). Collett clocked up an amazing total of 48 years at Swindon Works, he retired in July 1941 in his 70th year. Other retired GWR personnel were known to regularly visit the works; not so Collett: upon retirement he virtually severed all links with the company he had served so loyally. His retirement took him to London where he died aged 81 on 5th April 1952. His funeral was from all accounts a modest affair and the attendees included his successor Frederick W. Hawksworth, former colleague Sir William A. Stanier and past GWR General Manager Sir Felix Pole.

Collett Locomotives

The GWR locomotive fleet taken into stock by BR was all the better for Collett's influence. Although most commentators pulled up short of calling Collett personally a great designer, all acknowledged his superb engineering and organisational skills. In line with most CMEs he did not necessarily hold the pencil and set square that turned new ideas into steam locomotive designs, but he firmly controlled the team that did.

Collett's first big impact on the GWR was the introduction of his 4073 'Castle' Class 7P 4-cylinder 4-6-0 locomotives which were all built at Swindon Works between 1923 and 1950. There were 171 Castles built and the total included 15 engines which were re-built from Churchward's 'Star' Class and also the rebuilt GWR Pacific No 111 THE GREAT BEAR.

Churchward's loco No 111 THE GREAT BEAR was the first Pacific locomotive ever 'steamed' in the UK and the only 4-6-2 built by the GWR. Built in 1908 this loco was considered at the time to be the company's flagship engine. The GWR Pacific had a 20ton 9cwt axle load which severely restricted its route availability. In 1924 the Pacific which had been in service for 16 years, was in need of attention and required a new boiler.

Collett decided that it should be rebuilt as a 4-cylinder 4-6-0 'Castle' not as a 4-6-2; not everyone at the GWR agreed with his decision and indeed General Manager Sir Felix Pole personally questioned Collett about it. Justifying his decision on economical grounds Collett pointed out that the engine had steaming problems which would be expensive to cure and being restricted to the London-Bristol route was, according to the CME, 'a liability not an asset'. Other critics of his decision maintained that the 'Castle' option was the easy option and suggested that Collett had missed the chance of using the 'redundant' 4-6-2 as a test bed for a completely new locomotive design.

In 1926 the London Midland and Scottish Railway took loco No 5000 LAUNCESTON CASTLE on loan and the engine was put to work on the West Coast Main Line between London and Carlisle. The locomotive performed well and as a result the LMS are said to have requested the GWR to build a batch of 'Castles' for them to use on their Anglo-Scottish express services. When the GWR declined to accept that order the LMS asked instead for a set of engineering drawings!

That request also fell upon deaf ears but although the LMS did not get the locomotives at that time they did eventually gain the services of a Swindon man who knew all about 'Castles' and 'Kings'! It is interesting to note that William A. Stanier was almost certainly 'looking over Collett's shoulder' during the development of the first 'Castle' class locomotives. Accordingly the GWR influence in Stanier's LMS designs is there for all to see.

It is a fact that 'Castles' were the backbone of GWR and later WR express services for over 40 years. They were as popular with the men who crewed them in the final years of BR steam as they were with the enginemen of the late 1920s. 'Castles' were put in charge of most of the GWR's crack express services in their heyday, and were to be seen equally at home on services to the holiday resorts of the West Country and expresses to South Wales.

In the late 1920s and early 1930s 'Castle' class 4-6-0 engines were in charge of the famous 'Cheltenham Flyer' services which called for the locos to average 66.2 mph, and allowed just 70 minutes to cover the 77.3 miles from Swindon to Paddington. By modern standards that may not seem a tall order but carried out on a daily basis it was an outstanding achievement of the time, for the locomotives and their footplatemen. There were many instances of 'Castle' class locomotives in charge of heavy trains topping the 100 mph mark, even when in their dotage.

The first of the class 4073 'CAERPHILLY CASTLE' was displayed at the 1924 British Empire Exhibition alongside the Gresley Pacific 'Flying Scotsman'.

Britain's Most Powerful Locomotive

At that time the GWR Castle 4-6-0 was the most powerful locomotive in Britain and after visiting the exhibition rival locomotive designer Nigel Gresley was reportedly 'very impressed' with the Collett locomotive. Locomotive 4073 was the first of Collett's new class to enter service; it did so on 23rd August 1923. The 4-cylinder 4-6-0 ran almost 2 million miles in service before being withdrawn in May 1960, and being initially placed on display at the Science Museum London. In 2014 the locomotive was displayed at 'Steam – The Museum of the Great Western Railway'.

When Hawksworth became GWR CME he presided over a continuing 'Castle' building programme. In 1948 BR became the builders of the remaining '4073' Class locomotives on the order books and they built numbers 7012 to 7037 (26 engines) with 7036 'TAUNTON CASTLE' and 7037 'SWINDON' being the last, both completed in August 1950. Withdrawals had started in the same year (amongst the 6 ex 'Star' re-builds) with No 100A1 LLOYDS being the first in March 1950 (formerly 'Star' class No 4009 SHOOTING STAR), the first 'Castle' 'proper' to be scrapped was No 4091 DUDLEY CASTLE (built 1925) withdrawn in January 1959, with 1,691,856 miles on the clock. The last in service was the 1950 built No 7029 'CLUN CASTLE' withdrawn in December 1965.

The first GWR 'Castle' class No 4073 CAERPHILLY CASTLE is a National Collection Engine, and it is pictured as such in 2009. *Keith Langston Collection*

Collett's Locomotive Legacy

Collett's reign as GWR CME accounted for the design of 15 new locomotive classes which over time resulted in 2,281 new locomotives being built, by both the GWR and British Railways. In the same period he supervised the rebuilding/improvement of 8 classes of locomotives totalling some 308 engines. A Collett combined total of 2,589 locomotives by any standard can be considered a formidable contribution to British steam locomotive building. As a comparison the great Sir Nigel Gresley was associated with the design and building of 1,621 locomotives, whilst Sir William A. Stanier had 2,431 locomotives attributed to him during his term as a CME.

There are a total of 138 preserved ex GWR/BR WR steam locomotives, and given the statistics quoted above it will come as no surprise to readers that 100 of those are from designs/ improvements attributable to one Charles Benjamin Collett O.B.E.(1871–1952). To many younger enthusiasts, who have only experienced GWR locomotive types on preserved railways, the name Collett is simply synonymous with the Great Western Railway!

Preserved 'Castle' class locomotives GWR/BRWR

Number	Name (s)	Introduced	Withdrawn	Status 2014
4073	CAERPHILLY CASTLE	August 1923	May 1960	Static exhibit
4079	PENDENNIS CASTLE	February 1924	May 1964	Under overhaul
5029	NUNNEY CASTLE	May 1934	December 1963	Restored to working order
5043	EARL OF MOUNT EDGCUMBE BARBURY CASTLE (03/36-09/37)	March 1936	December 1963	Restored to working order
5051	EARL BATHURST DRYSLLWYN CASTLE (05/36-08/37)	May 1936	May 1963	Static exhibit
5080	DEFIANT OGMORE CASTLE (05/39-01/41)	May 1939	April 1963	Static exhibit
7027	THORNBURY CASTLE	August 1949	December 1963	Un-restored
7029	CLUN CASTLE	May 1950	December 1965	Under overhaul

The Churchward 'Star' class 4-6-0 locomotives (built Swindon 1906–1923) were reputedly the design which inspired the Collett 'Castle' class 4-6-0 locomotives. The 'Stars' were the first in a long line of successful GWR 4-cylinder express types. There were obvious similarities in the exterior appearance of the two designs.

Preserved GWR 'Castle' class 4-6-0 No 5029 NUNNEY CASTLE is seen on main line duty with a recreated 'The Red Dragon' mainline charter at Acton Turville on 10th November 2001. *John Chalcraft/Rail Photoprints Collection*

GWR 'Star' class 4-6-0 No 4043 PRINCE HENRY, (built 1913-withdrawn 1952) is seen at Swindon Works in June 1935. *Rail Photoprints Collection*

GWR 'Star' class 4-6-0 No 4061 GLASTONBURY ABBEY (built 1922-withdrawn 1957) is seen at Gloucester in September 1955, the occasion being the Stephenson Locomotive Society (Midland Area) 'Star' Special which ran between Birmingham Snow Hill and Swindon (return). *Hugh Ballantyne/Rail Photoprints*

The first 'Castle'

C.B. Collett's first '4073' 'Castle' class 4-cylinder 4-6-0 locomotive No 4073 CAERPHILLY CASTLE was introduced to the public at Paddington Station on 23 August 1923. The new class was initially developed to handle increased traffic and heavier trains on the long non-stop runs between London Paddington and Plymouth. The class was proclaimed by the GWR as being 'Britain's most powerful express passenger locomotives', notwithstanding the fact that the Collett design was seen as a direct development of G.J. Churchward's earlier 'Star' class.

The 'Castle' class was the then new Great Western Railway Chief Mechanical Engineer's first 4-6-0 locomotive. When exhibited at the British Empire Exhibition at Wembley in 1924 it received almost unreserved acclaim. In fact No 4073 was exhibited alongside Gresley's 4-6-2 No 4472 FLYING SCOTSMAN and as a result of which trials between the two types were later held, in which the 'Castle' proved to be the superior engine.

Details of the aforementioned 1925 locomotive trials with the LNER are as follows. Locomotive No 4079 PENDENNIS CASTLE went to the LNER and worked trains on the East Coast Mainline out of Kings Cross. In a direct comparison with Gresley Pacifics No 4475 FLYING FOX and No 2545 DIAMOND JUBILEE, also LNER loco No 4474 VICTOR WILD was temporarily allocated to Old Oak Common depot in order to work 'against' No 4074 CALDICOT CASTLE on the testing Paddington – Plymouth route.

Although during the exchanges all the locomotives concerned performed their allocated tasks with credibility the GWR locomotives were judged to have been the most successful overall when taking into account coal consumption and general performance. In fairness it must be pointed out that the LNER soon after put into practice all the lessons learned from the trials, and their later built Pacifics were the better engines for it.

To celebrate CAERPHILLY CASTLE being placed on display at Wembley a jigsaw puzzle entitled 'Build the Caerphilly Castle' was put on sale by the GWR, and was very favourably received. Any person lucky enough to own one in good condition now has in their possession a very collectable item! To further promote the engine thousands of post card and cigarette card images of No 4073 were produced. Indeed a GWR 1924 publication entitled *A Book of Railway Locomotives for Boys of All Ages* featuring the 'Castle' by W.G. Chapman and priced at 1 shilling (5 new pence), incredibly sold some 60,000 copies in a couple of months (now highly valued as collectors' items).

An unusual pairing as GWR 'Castle' class 4-6-0 No 5029 NUNNEY CASTLE double heads with Standard 'Class 4' 2-6-4T No 80080 on a 'Welsh Marches Express' from Crewe to Worcester. The preserved locomotives are seen climbing to Llanvihangel summit, on 5th April 1994. *John Chalcraft/Rail Photoprints*

Power personified

The 'Castle' locomotives were in the region of 10% more powerful than the 'Star' class engines and in order to provide that power the cylinders were increased from 15 inch diameter (of the 'Star' class) to 16 inch diameter and additionally the larger 'Swindon Standard 8' boiler was developed. With working boiler pressure maintained at 225lb per square inch the 'Castle' engines could deliver a tractive effort of 31,625lb at 85% boiler pressure against the 'Star's' 27,800lb. Importantly Collett's 4-cylinder 4-6-0 design accommodated within it the maximum 20 ton axle loading (over a 14 foot 9 inch driving wheel base) demanded of him by the then in force GWR permanent way restrictions, compared with the final 'Star' class axle loading of 19.4 tons. Churchward's 'Star' class engines had driving wheels of 6 foot 8 ½ inch diameter, that dimension was also selected by Collett for his 'Castle' class.

In overall dimensions the 'Castle' class locomotives were only 12 inches longer that their predecessors but had a much better appointed cab than the 'Star' engines incorporating side windows and an extended roof, and for the driver and fireman the added luxury of tip up seats! The 'Castles' were very handsome locomotives when turned out of Swindon's famous 'A Shop' in traditional GWR Brunswick Green, with copper topped chimney, polished brass safety valve covers, polished brass splasher beadings, lined out panels and boiler bands.

GWR/BRWR 'Castle' class Build date/Lot number details

Locomotive Numbers	Build Dates	Lot Numbers
4073–4074	1923 August–December	224
4075–4082	1924 January–April	224
4083–4092	1925 May–August	232
4093–4099	1926 May–August	234
5000–5002	1926 September	234
5003–5012	1927 May–July	234
5013–5022	1932 June–August	280
5023–5032	1934 April–May	295
5033–5042	1935 May–July	296
5043–5057	1936 March–June	303
5058–5067	1937 May–August	303
5068–5077	1938 June–August	310
5078–5082	1939 May–June	310
5083–5092	See rebuilds table for dates	317
5093–5097	1939 June	324
5098–5099	1946 May	357
7000–7007	1946 May–July	357
7008–7017	1948 May–August	367
7018–7027	1949 May–August	367
7028–7037	1950 May–August	375

No 5012 BERRY POMEROY CASTLE is seen at Oxford, in July 1961. *David Anderson*

GWR 'Castle' class 4-6-0 No 5090 NEATH ABBEY, built from 'Star' class No 4070, is seen approaching Bathampton with the 10.30am Cardiff–Portsmouth service, on 19th August 1958. Note this engine was one of the 31 examples which retained 'Joggled Frames'. *Hugh Ballantyne/Rail Photoprints*

GWR 'Castle' class 4-6-0 No 5053 EARL CAIRNS at Plymouth North Road, seen on 4th July 1961. This locomotive was renamed from BISHOP'S CASTLE. *Norman Preedy Collection/Rail Photoprints*

GWR 'Castle' class 4-6-0 No 5054 EARL OF DUCIE, this locomotive was renamed from LAMPHEY CASTLE. Seen at speed (recorded at 96MPH) passing Great Somerford with the Ian Allan 'Great Western High Speed Railtour', on 9th May 1964. *Hugh Ballantyne/Rail Photoprints*

GWR 'Castle. class 4-6-0 No 5043 seen as BARBURY CASTLE the name it carried from March 1936 until renamed EARL OF MOUNT EDGCUMBE in September 1937. The engine is located on the turntable at Tyseley Locomotive Works, October 2008. *Brian Wilson*

GWR 'Castle' class 4-6-0 No 5043 seen as EARL OF MOUNT EDGCUMBE whilst passing the signal box at Abergele & Pensarn on the North Wales Coast Route with the outward train of a Tyseley – Llandudno round trip on 6th June 2009. Even in pouring rain the superbly turned out locomotive in full cry is a great sight to behold. *Pete Sherwood*

The Castle Concept

The Great Western Railway always saw itself as an industry leader, and as such was an unashamedly publicity seeking organisation. Historians have rightly commented that the organisation was in fact the most charismatic railway company, always striving to provide its customers with the very best in comfort and punctuality, whilst doing so with panache and style. Indeed the GWR's locomotive fleet was noted for its striking distinctive liveries, embracing a generous, but nevertheless tasteful use of copper embellishments. Much was made in GWR publicity of the 'Castles' roomy cab, with side windows and comfortable seats for the driver and fireman, also a canopy which extended rearwards for shelter. The GWR predilection for panache was reaffirmed when for the first time after World War 1, copper-capped chimney and matching polished brass safety-valve embellishments were reintroduced.

The 'Castle' and 'King' class 4-cylinder 4-6-0 locomotives designed by the company's Chief Mechanical Engineer (1922–1941) Charles Benjamin Collett were not only the epitome of grace and style but also express passenger locomotives of the very highest calibre. Right from the start the new engines attracted comment and publicity, firstly the 'Castle' class was introduced by the GWR publicity department as being 'Britain's Most Powerful Express Passenger Locomotive'. When the first of the class was exhibited in London it was met with almost universal approval and soon went on to prove itself worthy of the aforementioned title when trialled against similar sized locomotives manufactured by other railway companies.

Three preserved 'Castle' class engines seen adjacent to the turntable at a Tyseley Locomotive Works Open Day on 29th June 2008. Left to right No 5029 NUNNEY CASTLE, No 5043 EARL OF MOUNT EDGCUMBE and the then partly rebuilt No 7029 CLUN CASTLE. *Brian Wilson*

The detractors were quick to point out that Collett's 'Castle' class locomotives were simply a development of his predecessor G.J. Churchward's 'Star' class engines. However simply making a bigger version of something is no iron clad guarantee of success and due credit must be given to Collett for making 'his' new design 'work'. It should also be noted that the success of the class was in no small way attributable to groundbreaking new production techniques which Collett introduced at Swindon Works.

The class was produced between August 1923 and July 1946 by the GWR, and then between May 1948 and August 1950 by British Railways with all of the class being rebuilt/built at Swindon Works; boilers used were 'Swindon 8' type 'Diagrams' HA, HB, HC and HD variously. The engines were modified to good effect during their working lives with the change to varying specifications of superheated boilers and double chimneys having the most beneficial effect on performance. The GWR and then BR/WR put the 'Castle' class locomotives to good use and the type became loved and respected by railwaymen and enthusiasts alike.

Collett 'Castle' class 4-cylinder 4-6-0 locomotives, 171 engines built Swindon 1923–1950

GWR 'Castle' locomotives built from other locomotive types

Old Number	Original build year and type	Last number carried	Date to traffic as 'Castle'
111	Pacific 1908	111	September 1924
40	Star 1906	4000	November 1929
4009	Star 1907	100A1	April 1925
4016	Star 1908	4016	October 1925
4032	Star 1910	4032	April 1926
4037	Star 1910	4037*	June 1926
4063	Star 1922	5083	June 1939
4064	Star 1922	5084*	April 1937
4065	Star 1922	5085	July 1939
4066	Star 1922	5086	December 1937
4067	Star 1923	5087	November 1940
4068	Star 1923	5088*	February 1939
4069	Star 1923	5089	October 1939
4070	Star 1923	5090	April 1939
4071	Star 1923	5091	December 1938
4072	Star 1923	5092	April 1938

*New front section frames fitted

'Castle' class No 5085 EVESHAM ABBEY, built from 'Star' class No 4065, is seen passing Langley Crossing (east of Chippenham) in 1957. Note this engine was one of the 11 given new front section frames. *Rail Photoprints Collection*

In addition to new build, a batch of 5 'Star' class engines and the only GWR 'Pacific' class engine were rebuilt as 'Castle' class engines between 1924 and 1929. Other 'Star' conversions would later take place (Nos 5083–5092).

Swindon mainly built the 'Castle' class 4-6-0s in batches of 10 locomotives with the 16 rebuilt 'Star' class engines fitted in between, in no particular order but more or less as 'Stars' became due for new cylinders and boilers. The 'Star' to 'Castle' conversions required a new section to be added to the locomotives frames, behind the rear driving wheels in order to accommodate the larger 'Castle' firebox and cab, with a new boiler and cylinders also provided. Even though the old 'Star' valve gear, motion and wheels were reused, the resultant 'Castle' engines could effectively be considered as being 'new'.

There were several important differences between the 'Star' and 'Castle' designs, although the fact that the former influenced the design of the latter was never in dispute. The basic frame layout and spacing of the wheels was the same but the 4 cylinder 'Castle' design incorporated 16 inch diameter x 26 inch stroke cylinders whilst the earlier Churchward 4 cylinder 'Star' class engines had 15 inch diameter x 26 inch stroke cylinders and a GWR 'Type 1' boiler.

Both types were designed to operate with a boiler pressure of 225psi (superheated). In the early design stage Collett planned to use the Swindon 'Type 7' boiler on the 'Castle' class engines but concerns about a required 20 ton axle limit forced a rethink, accordingly the new (slightly smaller) Swindon 'Type 8' boiler was introduced. Initially the 'Number 3' Swindon superheater, used by the 'Star' class, was also selected to work with the 'Castle' boilers. The GWR pattern top feed device for introducing water to the boiler was used. In order to not loose heat the feed water was dispersed by a series of trays which caused the water to descend through the steam in a fine spray.

The 'Star' class engines tractive effort was 27,800lbf (at 85% of boiler pressure) with the 'Castle' engines being rated appreciably higher at 31,625lbf (at 85% of boiler pressure). By comparison the first Gresley Pacifics were rated at 29,838lbf (at 85% of boiler pressure).

Both designs incorporated 6 foot 8½ inch diameter driving wheels and 3 foot 2 inch diameter bogie wheels on a 'Standard' Swindon 'bar frame bogie'. The 'Castle' class grate area was 29.4 square feet in comparison to the 'Star' class grate area of 27.07 square feet. In both instances Collett chose to use Inside Walschaert valve gear with rocking shafts (piston valves).

Because of their wide route availability the 'Castles' remained the GWR/BRWR most successful express passenger locomotives during the whole of their working lives. Routes that involved the class included the West of England main line to Penzance, the South Wales route to Fishguard Harbour, the Birmingham and the North mainline to Chester, cross-country routes from Bristol via Pontypool Road and Hereford to Shrewsbury, from Birmingham via Stratford-upon-Avon, Cheltenham and over the Midland route to Bristol, and even from South Wales via Bristol and Bath to Salisbury en route (over the Southern) to Brighton and were also regular performers on the Paddington–Weymouth services. They could if required stand in for the more powerful GWR 'King' class locomotives on the hardest Paddington–Birmingham–Wolverhampton and also the Paddington–West of England turns.

The 'Castle' class GWR Power Classification was 'D' and Route Availability was Red. British Railways originally classified the engines as 6P but then reclassified them as 7P in 1951.

GWR 'Castle' class 4-6-0 No 5074 HAMPDEN (originally DENBIGH CASTLE) is seen leaving Shrewsbury with a long southbound train on the North and West route in 1956. Note the mechanical lubricator in the first position behind the modified outside steampipe. *Rail Photoprints Collection*

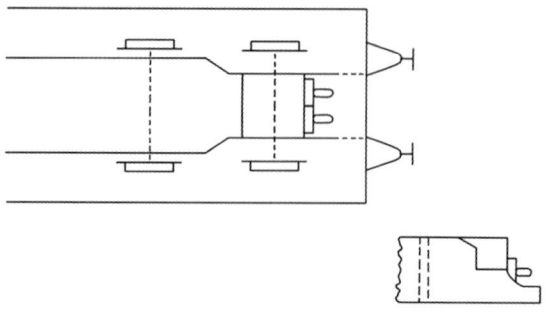

Fig 1. 'Joggled' frame set inward at the front, to clear the leading bogie wheels. Locomotives 4073–4092 and ex 'Star' rebuilds.

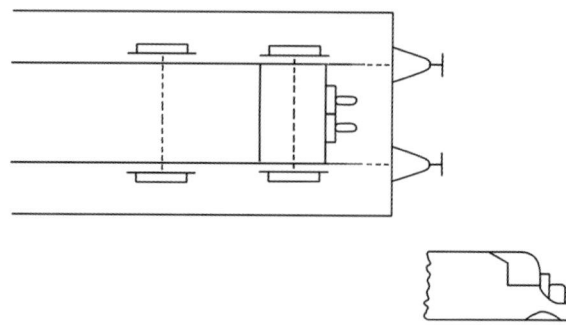

Fig 2. Straight frame with dished area, giving bogie wheel clearance. Locomotive No 4093 and all later GWR/BR 'Castles' (and rebuilds).

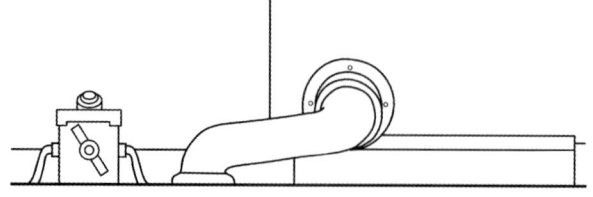

Fig 3. Original straight pattern outside steam pipe with mechanical lubricator in first position.

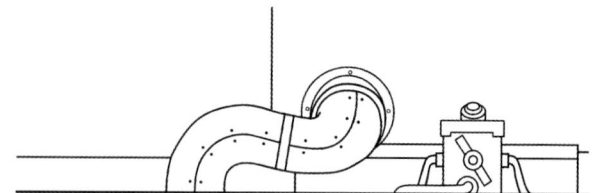

Fig 4. Modified outside steam pipe, replaced original 'straight' pattern following incidences of fractures. Mechanical lubricator in final forward position.

After the initial build of 30 'Castles', numbers 4073–4099 and 5000–5012 there followed a gap of 5 years before the next batch of locomotives were built. That batch, numbered 5013–5022, had sufficient design improvements to merit often being referred to by Swindon as the '5013' sub class. The aforementioned 1932 built locomotives had several improvements and modifications, the most obvious exterior change being the addition of a compartment to accommodate fireirons which was situated on the left hand side of the engine and located between the centre and trailing wheel splashers. That modification was first trialled on No 4085 BERKELEY CASTLE and thereafter adopted as standard, there were also changes to inside valve chest design and locomotive springing.

However, the greatest change was to the water space between the inner and outer firebox. On the original locomotives, and in order to achieve a maximum possible heating surface, the space created was narrower than that dictated by

No 4073 CAERPHILLY CASTLE seen in original condition with 'tall type' chimney, 'straight' pattern steam pipes, 'joggled' frames, curved side pattern inside cylinder casing (Nos 4073–4092, ex 'Star' rebuilds and 4093–5012 straight framed engines) and GWR pattern taper barrel buffers, circa 1930. *Rail Photoprints Collection*

No 5082 SWORDFISH seen with 'modified' outside steampipe, shorter chimney (introduced 1936) straight frames, box pattern inside cylinder casing (Nos 5013 onwards and BR straight frame rebuilds) BR pattern parallel barrel buffers and mechanical lubricator in the final forward position, circa 1961. *David Anderson*

'Castle' class 4-6-0 No 7018 DRYSLLWYN CASTLE was fitted with an experimental double chimney in May 1956, the engine is seen with a GWR 'Standard' double chimney which was fitted in April 1958. The ultimate 'Castle' class development was achieved when No 4090 DORCHESTER CASTLE became the first to be fitted with a double chimney and 4-row superheated boiler (HD 7671) in March 1957. Following that successful development a total of 65 'Castles' were eventually rebuilt with 4-row superheaters and double chimneys. Image circa 1962. *Keith Langston Collection*

previous GWR practice, but the narrowing of the gap made it hard to clean properly during boiler washouts. Thus the '5013' engines were built with the water space increased to normal standards and the grate area reduced from 30.3 square feet to 29.4 square feet, additionally the number of small tubes was reduced from 201 to 197. Reportedly the firebox/boiler alterations did not adversely affect steaming performance, probably because it was normal practice to operate the 'Castles' with a deep fire built up in 'hay-cock' style rather than pure grate area coverage. Great Western locomotives were noted for having the ability to burn coal economically, and in that regard the Collett 'Castles' were no exception. In fact the classes average coal consumption was claimed to be one of the lowest in the country being recorded at 2.83 pounds per drawbar horse power/per hour compared to a figure in the region of 4 pounds listed by other railway companies in the 1920s. The tenders originally attached to the class were of a low sided design with a coal capacity of 6 tons and 3,500 gallons of water. Later 4000 gallon and 6 ton coal capacity higher sided tenders, of Collett and Hawksworth designs, were introduced.

The compartment to accommodate fireirons, situated on the left hand side of the engines and located between the centre and trailing wheel splashers can be clearly seen in this image of No 5063 EARL BALDWIN at Paddington station. Note also the 'Box' pattern inside cylinder cover (without added step) and the taper barrel buffers. *Mike Morant Collection*

In 1935 in keeping with other railway companies, and style trends of the era, the GWR experimented with streamlining. Two locomotives were chosen for modification, they were 'King' No 6014 KING HENRY VII and 'Castle' No 5005 MANORBIER CASTLE. Fortunately the mainly unpopular experiment was a short lived affair. Partially streamlined GWR 'Castle' class 4-6-0 No 5005 MANORBIER CASTLE is seen at Newton Abbot in September 1935. Note that the front end air smoothing and cab roof extension sections of the streamlining had already been removed by that time. *R.C. Riley Collection/Transport Treasury*

The batch of locomotives which followed, numbers 5023–5032, built in 1934 were the first 'Castle' class engines to benefit from the 'Zeiss Optical Alignment' equipment which had been introduced at Swindon Works. The success, or otherwise of a locomotive's performance in service is determined by the accuracy in alignment between the frames, cylinders and axle box guides. When correctly used the GWR version of the 'Zeiss' system guaranteed absolute accuracy. The system ensured that the GWR locomotive builders could work to exacting dimensions and thus set valve gear tolerances to the absolute minimum. Observers at the time noted that the ex works 'Zeiss' aligned 'Castles' 'ran with the quietness of a sewing machine'.

The 1935 'Castle' build programme consisted of locomotive numbers 5033–5042 and for the first time the 'Castle' class engines were fitted with speedometers. That year marked the GWR 100 years celebrations, a fact which was said to have influenced the railway's directors in their decision to carry out the aforementioned streamlining experiment.

The 1936 batch of 15 engines, numbers 5043–5057 and the subsequent 1937 batch of 10 engines inherited 'Earl' names from the withdrawn 4-4-0 'Dukedog' ('Earl class') engines. In addition it was decided at this time that the last 10 members of the 'Star' class should join the list of earlier engines and be rebuilt as 'Castles'.

The 1938 batch of 10 engines, numbers 5068 to 5077 included 7 of the 12 'Castles' which were later renamed in honour of aircraft which flew in the Battle of Britain (World War 2). Five engines of the 1939 batch, numbers 5078–5082, were also renamed for the same reason, the other 5 engines in the 1939 batch were numbers 5093–5097.

Collett retired from the GWR in 1941 and the position of Swindon CME passed to F. W. Hawksworth (the last GWR CME) who after the end of WW2 and before the creation of British Railways (BR) as a part of the British Transport Commission(BTC), presided over the 1946 build of 10 engines, numbers 5098–5099 and 7000–7007, No 7007 was the last 'Castle' built by the GWR and was accordingly named GREAT WESTERN. Hawksworth introduced his design of straight sided all welded 4000 gallon water 6 ton coal capacity tenders, which were coupled with later designed 'Castles'.

The first BR built 10 locomotive batch of Hawksworth 'Castles' were introduced in 1948, numbers 7008–7017 and the latter was named in honour of G. J. Churchward.

In June 1948 locomotive numbers 4089 DONNINGTON CASTLE, 5010 RESTORMEL CASTLE, 7010 AVONDALE CASTLE, 7011 BANBURY CASTLE and 7012 BARRY CASTLE were the subject of a short lived livery change, they were painted light green with the number and nameplate backgrounds painted the same colour as the rest of the engine. Additionally the smokebox doors were fitted with brass number plates, with lettering on the tender being plain white. In 1949 a further batch of 10 engines were introduced, numbers 7018–7027, in 2014 THORNBURY CASTLE remained the only preserved member of the class not to have been rebuilt. The final batch of 10 'Castle' class engines were introduced between May and August 1950, numbers 7028–7037, the last of which was named SWINDON in honour of the world famous locomotive works. The engine's name was bestowed in a ceremony which took place during a visit to the 'Works' by HRH Princess Elizabeth on 15th November of that year.

It is generally accepted that No 7029 CLUN CASTLE was the last to remain in BR service (December 1965), although that locomotive did thereafter work special trains and on 14th October 1967 famously worked over Shap and Ais Gill.

Number of 'Castle' class locomotives listed in traffic at year end – BR era

1948	1949	1950	1951/52	1953/56	1957	1958	1959	1960	1961	1962	1963	1964
151	161	170	168	167	166	165	162	155	152	97	49	12

'Castle' class names

All of the class were given names and a great deal of 'actual' re-naming took place with 28 engines being renamed between 1936 and 1938, 12 renamed 1940/41, 2 renamed in 1954 and one loco renamed in 1957. Making up the list of 'final' names were 112 named after Castles, 21 named after Earls, 12 named after Battle of Britain aircraft, 9 named after Abbeys, 8 in honour of individuals or organisations including 3 named after Regiments, 3 named after Viscounts, 1 named after a former Queen, 1 named after a celestial star, and the last 'Castle' class engine built named after the locomotive works at Swindon.

It was considered important during the steam era to name express passenger locomotives, therefore descriptions/origins of the individual names must be considered 'as' important. Accordingly that information is included with the individual locomotive's details. Where the loco was not named after an actual Castle, a number of Castle nameplates had "Castle Class" appended below the name.

GWR 'Castle' class 4-6-0 No 5051 DRYSLLWYN CASTLE and GWR 'Hall' class 4-6-0 No 4930 KINLET HALL are seen leaving Bristol Temple Meads with the 'Great Western Limited'. Steam traction operated unaided from Bristol to 'Milepost 217' on Dainton Bank where the pair stalled, 'Class 50' diesel No 50045 ACHILLES then assisted the train up the bank, after which the 2 steam locomotives worked as far as Totnes where the tour was terminated, on the 7th July 1985. *John Chalcraft/Rail Photoprints*

Two distinctly different types of rear sandboxes were fitted, on locomotives numbers 4073–5059 and 'Star' class rebuilds. It was located below the cab floor with only the delivery pipes being visible (see No 4084 ABERYSTWYTH CASTLE). *David Anderson*

From locomotive No 5060 onwards an external box was fitted between the cab step and trailing driving wheel, and in time some of the originals were replaced with that design (see No 5082 SWORDFISH). *David Anderson*

GWR 'Castle' class 4-6-0 No 5085 EVESHAM ABBEY is seen arriving Bristol Temple Meads, note the window wiper fitted to the front cab window(s). *Rail Photoprints Collection*

Other Modifications

The majority of the modifications included for mention are those which can be discerned by examination of the locomotive's exterior appearance. Those which could not always be readily identifiable by lineside examination include the two types of frames used, i.e. joggled and straight (see Figs 1 and 2) and the particular boiler diagram, number of tubes and superheater arrangement.

It should be noted that in addition to the 3 'Star' rebuilds the following engines built with joggled frames had their frames replaced with straight ones by BR, and they were numbers 4037, 4074, 4076, 4087, 4088, 4090, 5084 and 7013 (originally 4082) i.e. 11 engines in total.

With regards to inside cylinder casings locomotive numbers 4073–5012 and ex 'Star' class rebuilds had curved side pattern covers whilst locomotives No 5013 onwards and later BR rebuilds had 'Box' or straight pattern sides (later some also had a raised step added). Also from the building of 'Castle' number 5013 onwards oil cups feeding the outside valve spindles were fitted to the footplate angle framing and the inside cylinder valve spindle cups were fitted onto the front of the inside cylinder casing (with variations to some BR engines).

Between 1946 and 1948 oil burning equipment was fitted to locomotives number 100A1, 5039, 5079, 5083 and 5091, the visible evidence of this, still evident after those engines were reconverted to coal, being the sliding shutters in the cab roof. Very noticeably from circa 1947, and for no apparent reason, all of the class up to and including No 5012 had the brass beading removed from the front edge of the cab. A post war minor change was that the cab window handrail was continued upwards forward of the window frame, from engine No 5098 onwards. In general the original GWR taper barrel type buffers were replaced by BR parallel types on many of the engines. Hand operated window wipers can be seen fitted onto some of cab front windows, but that modification did not seem to have been universally adopted by depots. Given that the class was in service for some 41 years it is possible that other detailed changes/modifications were tried on selected engines of the class but not necessarily adopted.

Preserved GWR built 'Castle' class locomotive No 4073 CAERPHILLY CASTLE has an example of the original small (low sided) 3,500 gallon/7 ton coal capacity tender to which the early 'Castles' were coupled until the Collett 4,000 gallon/6ton coal capacity type was put into service from 1927 onwards. The locomotive is seen at STEAM, Museum of the Great Western Railway, Swindon. *Keith Langston Collection*

Tender types

Both Churchward 3,500g/7t and Collett Intermediate 3,500g tenders were used. They were superseded by the Collett 4,000g/6t tender which became very much standard to the class until the Hawksworth straight sided 4000g/6t tender was introduced, and first appeared in service with locomotive numbers 7008–7037. A welded tank version of the Collett 4,000g/6t tender was also introduced and first appeared coupled with locomotive numbers 5098–5099 and 7000–7002.

In keeping with general practice a great deal of type and individual tender changing took place, often following an engine's visit to the works.

Other types of tenders used included the modified Churchward 3,500g 'Oil', and the Collett 4,000g 'Oil' also the Dean 4,000g design. Additionally Collett '8 wheeled' 4,000g (No 2586 coupled to engine numbers 4091, 5001, 5017, 5032, 5049, 5068 and 5071 at various times between September 1931 and April 1948). Also used was a Hawksworth 'Self Weighing' 3,800g tender (No 4127 coupled to engine numbers 4084, 5077, 5080 and 5081 at various times between August 1952 and July 1953). Individual locomotive listings show details of the tender types coupled by date (but not the number of individual tenders of a given type), that information will hopefully assist the reader in the dating of archive images.

Self weighing tenders allowed the more accurate measurement of coal consumption. The actual coal bunker was a separate unit suspended on pivots and connected to the weighing equipment. The bunker could be 'set' in a fixed position during travel and then 'released' when the measurement of coal was needed. The Hawksworth unit No 4127 is seen coupled to GWR ''Castle' class No 5080 DEFIANT at Hereford in August 1953. The tender was later converted back to normal configuration. *Norman Preedy Collection/Rail Photoprints*

Preserved GWR 'Castle' 4-6-0 No 5051 EARL BATHURST is reflected in the waters of the Huntspill River as it heads across the Somerset Levels with the southbound 'Torbay Express', on 1st August 2004. *John Chalcraft/Rail Photoprints Collection*

Fresh from overhaul, preserved GWR 'Castle' class No 5051 EARL BATHURST IS SEEN PASSING passes Dundas Viaduct in the Limpley Stoke Valley as it heads the 15.50 Bristol–Crewe Pathfinder Excursion On 20 October 2001. *John Chalcraft/Rail Photoprints Collection*

Double heading preserved Collett locomotives, GWR 'Castle' No 5051 EARL BATHURST and 'Hall' class No 4930 HAGLEY HALL are seen leaving Newton Abbot with the Bristol - Plymouth 'Great Western Limited', on 7th July 1985. *Brian Robbins/Rail Photoprints Collection*

Chapter 2

LOCOMOTIVES 100A1, 111, 4000, 4016, 4032, 4037, 4073–4099

100 A1 LLOYD'S

Former GWR 'Star' class No 4009 SHOOTING STAR was re-built as a 'Castle' class 4-6-0 in April 1925, initially retaining its 'Star' class number and name. Renumbered 100 (100 A1) and renamed LLOYD'S in January 1936.

GWR 'Castle' class 4-6-0 No 4009 SHOOTING STAR was rebuilt from a 'Star' class engine of the same name and number. No 4009 is thought to be on shed at Laira in this 1930s study. *J. J. Cunningham/Transport Treasury*

GWR 'Castle' class No A1 seen in Swindon's 'A' shop during an overhaul in January 1936. It looks likely that the picture was taken just after the 'A1' plate had been affixed, the LLOYD'S nameplate was absent from the supporting bracket at that time. Note the locomotive's original 4009 number written on the dragbox. The locomotive was made serviceable and put back into traffic. However, shortly afterwards a GWR official realised that 'A1' simply didn't fit the scheme of things, as it was not a number. Accordingly the decision was taken to bring 'A1' back to Swindon and additionally affix the number '100', on the cab sides, above the 'A1'. *Mike Morant Collection*

Introduced into service as a 'Castle' class locomotive 9th April 1925. Diagram HA boiler fitted. Locomotive No 100 A1 was converted to oil-burning in 1948 with a cab roof vent fitted, and then later converted back to coal burning. This locomotive had a cut out section in the bottom cab step support.

The locomotive's last 'Heavy General' overhaul including boiler (HB 6600) and tender change took place at Swindon Works between 12th June and 4th August 1945. In January 1947 a further boiler change took place (HA 4611). The engine was the first of the class to be withdrawn in March 1950, from Swindon depot (82C). Recorded 'Castle' mileage 1,164,297, (total 1,974,651) service life 42 years, 10 months and 13 days. Disposal Swindon Works, May 1950.

Tender type principal fitted dates as 'Castle', Churchward 3500g April 1925, Collett Intermediate 3500g January 1926, Churchward 3500g December 1926, Collett 4000g July 1929, Collett 4000g Oil 9th January 1947, Collett 4000g 13th August 1949.

Allocated Depots from 1925

PDN Old Oak Common	09/04/25	LA Laira	06/12/30	CDF Cardiff Canton	05/33
LA Laira	25/06/26	EXE Exeter	03/09/31	PDN Old Oak Common	20/04/34
NA Newton Abbot	16/06/27	BRD Bristol Bath Road	28/01/32	82C Swindon	01/03/50

Shooting Star is another name for a meteor that burns up as it passes through the Earth's atmosphere.
A1 at Lloyd's was a category of ship in Lloyd's Register of Shipping, which used an alphanumeric code to classify ships for insurance purposes.

111 VISCOUNT CHURCHILL

Designed by C.J. Churchward No 111 was originally built as a Pacific and named THE GREAT BEAR, it was introduced by the GWR in 1908.

GWR No 111 THE GREAT BEAR was the first Pacific (4-6-2) locomotive built in Great Britain, and the only one built by the GWR. The locomotive is seen 'on shed' at Old Oak Common (PDN) circa 1915. The locomotive had by that time been fitted with a boiler top feed. The footplateman is thought to be Thomas Blackhall, an Oxfordshire man and regular driver of the 4-6-2. *Mike Bentley Collection*

The Churchward Pacific No 111 was rebuilt as a 'Castle' class 4-6-0 in September 1924 (boiler HA 4608) and renamed VISCOUNT CHURCHILL. The locomotive's last 'Heavy Intermediate' overhaul with boiler (HB 6634) and tender change took place at Swindon Works between 7th November and 11th December 1951. The engine was withdrawn in July 1953 from Laira MPD (83D). Recorded 'Castle' mileage 1,462,356 (total 1,989,628), service life 45 years 5 months and 12 days. Disposal Swindon Works, October 1953.

Tender type principal fitted dates as 'Castle', Churchward 3500g 17th November 1928, Collett 4000g 19th August 1929.

Allocated Depots

| PDN Old Oak Common | September 1924 | 83D Laira | May 1950 |

GWR 'Castle' class 4-6-0 No 111 VISCOUNT CHURCHILL, seen at Old Oak Common depot (PDN) in 1934. The locomotive has a tall single chimney of a style which was gradually replaced from 1936 onwards. The engine is coupled with a Collett 4000 gallon/6 ton capacity tender. Note the tapered barrel buffers, original style inside valve spindle covers and curved side inside cylinder casing, plus the stencilled front buffer beam number. The original style brass beading embellishments to the cab front edge, number and nameplates and wheel splashers can also be seen. *Mike Morant Collection*

The Great Bear the name refers to Ursa Major, the star constellation.
Viscount Churchill, Major Victor Albert Francis Charles Spencer, 1st Viscount Churchill GCVO JP (23 October 1864–3 January 1934), known as The Lord Churchill between 1886 and 1902, he was a peer and courtier. Attended Sandhurst and later became a Lieutenant in the Coldstream Guards. He was created the first Viscount Churchill in July 1902 and joined the Great Western Board in 1905, he was elected chairman in 1908 and served longer in that post than anyone else.

4000 NORTH STAR

Formerly GWR No 40 a 4-4-2 (Atlantic) which was re-built by Churchward in 1909 as a 'Star' class 4-6-0 retaining its original No 40 until renumbered 4000 in 1912. That locomotive was then re-built as a 'Castle' class 4-6-0 in November 1929. Diagram HA boiler number 4647 fitted during an 'Intermediate' overhaul between 29th April and 1st August 1931. The locomotive retained its original 'Atlantic' frames therefore the footplating was 2½ inches higher than all other 'Star' and 'Castle' class engines.

GWR No 40 NORTH STAR seen as outshopped from Swindon Works as a 'Star' class 4-6-0 in September 1909, re-built as a 'Castle' in November 1929. *Authors Collection*

The locomotive's last heavy overhaul took place at Swindon Works between 10th August and 3rd October 1955, and included the fitting of a replacement boiler (HA 4629) and tender.

The engine was withdrawn in May 1957 from Landore depot (87E). Recorded 'Castle' mileage 1,191,592 (total 2,110,396), service life 51 years, 1 month and 19 days. Disposal Swindon Works, July 1957.

Tender type principal fitted dates as 'Castle', Collett 4000g November 1929, Hawksworth 4000g 1st April 1954, Collett 4000g 27th May 1954, Hawksworth 4000g 3rd October 1955.

Allocated Depots post 1929

SDN Swindon	21/11/29	SRD Stafford Road	11/05/37	84K Chester West	05/01/55
NA Newton Abbot	16/12/30	TYS Tyseley	03/38	84A Stafford Road	31/01/55
PDN Old Oak Common	01/08/31	SALOP Shrewsbury	04/38	87G Carmarthen	09/56
SALOP Shrewsbury	22/06/34	SRD Stafford Road	04/05/39	87E Landore	10/56

GWR 'Castle' class 4-6-0 No 4000 NORTH STAR, with a post 1936 shorter style chimney, is seen outside the works at Swindon in May 1954, at that time light repairs were carried out and a replacement Collett tender fitted. Note the delivery pipe to the rear driving wheel sanders, which was fed by a sandbox located below the footplate. *Rail Photoprints Collection*

North Star also known as the Northern Pole Star, is a bright star which always appears due north in the sky.

4016 THE SOMERSET LIGHT INFANTRY (PRINCE ALBERT'S)

Formerly GWR 'Star' class No 4016 KNIGHT OF THE GOLDEN FLEECE, it was rebuilt as a 'Castle' class 4-6-0 in October 1925, initially retaining its 'Star' class number and name. Diagram HA boiler fitted. The locomotive was renamed in January 1938.

Re-built from a 'Star' 4-6-0 'Castle' class No 4016 KNIGHT OF THE GOLDEN FLEECE, is seen at Bristol Bath Road, circa 1933. Note the distinctive brass beading on the cab front edges, cab side windows, number/name plates and wheel splashers. This locomotive also had a cut out section in the bottom cab step support. *Ray Hinton Collection/Rail Photoprints*

The locomotive's last 'Heavy General' overhaul including boiler (HA 4628) and tender change took place at Swindon Works between 19th January and the 1st March 1950. The engine was withdrawn in September 1951, from Swindon depot (82C). Recorded 'Castle' mileage 1,186,663, (total 1,972,559) service life 43 years, 5 months and 24 days. Disposal Swindon Works, October 1951.

Tender type principal fitted dates as 'Castle', Collett Intermediate 3500g October 1925, Collett 4000g 2nd April 1929.

Allocated Depots

PDN Old Oak Common	27/02/26	OXY Oxley	03/10/28	BRD Bristol Bath Road	17/06/39
SRD Stafford Road	01/04/26	SRD Stafford Road	17/04/29	NA Newton Abbot	18/07/40
PDN Old Oak Common	25/05/26	BRD Bristol Bath Road	02/33	81A Old Oak Common	07/50
SRD Stafford Road	16/08/26	SDN Swindon	14/04/39	82C Swindon	27/09/51

THE SOMERSET LIGHT INFANTRY (PRINCE ALBERT'S) is seen at Old Oak Common depot in April 1950. The locomotive was re-named in a ceremony at Paddington station on 18 February 1938. Note the regimental crest below the nameplate on the centre wheel splasher. *Ray Hinton Collection/Rail Photoprints*

Knight Of The Golden Fleece, the order of the Golden Fleece was founded in Burgundy in 1430 and claimed pride of place amongst all Christian orders.

The Somerset Light Infantry (Prince Albert's), was an infantry regiment of the British Army active from 1685 to 1959.

4032 QUEEN ALEXANDRA

Formerly a GWR 'Star' class built in 1910 and then re-built as a 'Castle' class 4-6-0 in October 1925, retaining its 'Star' class number and name. Diagram HA boiler fitted.

GWR 'Castle' Class No 4032 QUEEN ALEXANDRA at Oxford depot circa 1946. Note the Collett 3500 gallon/5 ton 10 cwt tender. Ex 'Star' class rebuilds and 'Castles' 4073–4092 were built with 'joggled' frames i.e. set inward at the front end in order to clear the leading bogie wheels. Norman Preedy Collection/Rail Photoprints

The locomotive's last 'Heavy General' overhaul including boiler (HB 6607) and tender change took place at Swindon Works between 28th September and 2nd November 1949. The engine was withdrawn in September 1951 from Swindon depot (82C). Recorded 'Castle' mileage 1,225,908, (total 1,981,335) service life 41 years 27 days. Disposal Swindon Works,1951/2.

Tender type principal fitted dates as 'Castle', Collett Intermediate 3500g April 1926, Collett 4000g November 1928, Collett 3500g 10th August 1946, Collett 4000g 25th January 1947.

Allocated Depots from 1926

LA Laira	16/04/26	NA Newton Abbot	05/43	LA Laira	11/46
NA Newton Abbot	27/03/29	EXE Exeter	06/43	PZ Penzance	12/05/49
PDN Old Oak Common	19/03/32	LA Laira	06/09/43	LA Laira	02/11/49
LA Laira	01/04/33	NA Newton Abbot	08/06/44	82C Swindon	27/06/50
TR Truro	07/38	LA Laira	18/07/44	83B Taunton	10/50
LA Laira	10/38	NA Newton Abbot	08/10/46	82C	19/09/51

GWR 'Castle' Class 4-6-0 NO 4032 QUEEN ALEXANDRA seen at Newton Abbot in the summer of 1928. This loco was rebuilt from Star Class 4-6-0 No 4032. Note the Collett 'Intermediate' 3500g tender. Rail Photoprints Collection

Queen Alexandra was a princess of Danish extraction (Alexandra of Denmark) who married Albert Edward, Prince of Wales (1863), and thereafter became the longest serving Princess of Wales. She became Queen Consort to King Edward VII after the 1902 coronation.

4037 THE SOUTH WALES BORDERERS

Formerly GWR 'Star' class No 4037 QUEEN PHILIPPA, rebuilt as a 'Castle' class 4-6-0 in June 1926 and renamed on 14th April 1937. Diagram HA boiler fitted.

This member of the class is credited with having the greatest mileage 2,429,722 of any GWR engine. Of that total 776, 764 miles in service were run as a 'Star' class engine. The combined 'Star'/'Castle' mileages exceed any 'Castle' proper mileage, with 7 of the re-builds topping the 2 million mile mark. The locomotive's last 'Heavy Intermediate' overhaul including boiler (HB 6684) and tender change took place at Swindon Works between 21st May September and 12th August 1960. The engine was withdrawn in September 1962 from Exeter depot (83C). Recorded Castle mileage 1,652,958, service life 51 years, 8 months and 18 days.

Disposal Cashmores, Newport December 1962.

Tender type principal fitted dates as 'Castle', Churchward 3500g June 1926, Collett Intermediate 3500g December 1926, Churchward 3500g June 1928, Collett 4000g 20th May 1930, Churchward 3500g September 1930, Collett 4000g 19th August 1931, Hawksworth 4000g March 1954, Collett 4000g 10th September 1955, Hawksworth 4000g 12th August 1960.

No 4037 QUEEN PHILIPPA seen as a GWR 'Star' class 4-6-0 circa 1930. *Mike Bentley Collection*

Allocated Depots

SRD Stafford Road	02/07/26	PDN Old Oak Common	27/01/30	83G Penzance	16/06/56
PDN Old Oak Common	27/08/26	CARM Carmarthen	03/33	83A Newton Abbot	28/09/56
SRD Stafford Road	12/11/26	SDN Swindon	28/11/33	87E Landore	23/02/57
TYS Tyseley	27/07/29	CARM Carmarthen	19/12/33	83A Newton Abbot	06/57
SRD Stafford Road	09/08/29	PDN Old Oak Common	18/05/34	83C Exeter	14/07/62

GWR Castle Class 4-6-0 No 4037 THE SOUTH WALES BORDERERS approaches Bristol Temple Meads in August 1960. Note the newer BR style 'Box' pattern inside cylinder cover with central step, Hawksworth 4000 gallon/6 ton tender, BR style parallel buffers and the regimental crest on the centre wheel splasher. Circa 1947 the brass beading was removed from the front end of the cabs on all engines up to and including No 5012. *Rail Photoprints Collection*

Queen Philippa, Philippa of Hainault, daughter to Count William of Hainault, married Edward, Prince of Wales, later King Edward III of England, (Queen Consort). The Queen's College Oxford was founded in her honour.

The South Wales Borderers, was an infantry regiment of the British Army which was the successor of the 24th Regiment of Foot (formed 1689). The Borderers were so named in 1881 and absorbed into the Royal Regiment of Wales in 1969.

4073 CAERPHILLY CASTLE Preserved

Prior to entering revenue earning service No 4073 was displayed at the British Empire Exhibition, Wembley. The exhibition, which should have opened in 1923 was postponed until 1924 and also re-opened for an 6 additional months in 1925. The GWR publicity team had introduced the first actually 'new' 'Castle' class 4-6-0 as 'Britain's most powerful express passenger locomotive'. Diagram HA boiler fitted.

GWR 'Castle' Class No 4073 CAERPHILLY CASTLE is seen at Starcross station with a down local train, on 25 July 1956. This image clearly shows the original style GWR curved sided inside cylinder casing. The steam leak indicates that the engine was only one month away from a heavy overhaul. *David Anderson*

Allocated Depots

PDN Old Oak Common	11/08/23	PDN Old Oak Common	06/04/35	82A Bristol Bath Road	15/07/50
Display Wembley	08/24	OXF Oxford	02/39	82B St Philips Marsh	10/52
PDN Old Oak Common	06/11/24	PDN Old Oak Common	03/39	82C Swindon	27/01/53
CDF Cardiff Canton	04/03/34	SDN Swindon	21/04/43	82A Bristol Bath Road	27/03/53
LDR Landore	02/10/34	PDN Old Oak Common	07/43	86C Cardiff Canton	23/01/57

The locomotive's last 'Heavy General' overhaul including boiler (HB 6638) and tender change took place at Swindon Works between 25th August 1956 and 23rd January 1957. The locomotive was withdrawn by BR in May 1960 from Cardiff Canton depot (86C) and after cosmetic restoration the engine was initially put on display at the Science Museum, London. The National Collection locomotive was later moved and placed on static display at Steam: Museum of the Great Western Railway, Swindon. Recorded mileage 1,910,730, service life 36 years, 8 months and 29 days.

Tender type principal fitted dates, Churchward 3500g August 1923, Collett 4000g October 1930.

The first true production 'Castle' Class 4-6-0 No 4073 'Caerphilly Castle', with original tall chimney is seen in all its splendour at Old Oak Common circa 1933. *Rail Photoprints Collection*

Caerphilly Castle, in South Wales is one of the world's greatest surviving medieval castles. Its building was instigated in 1268 by Anglo-Norman Marcher Lord, Gilbert de Clare. The remains of the magnificent historic fortress stand on a 30 acre site and are a major tourist attraction, the castle is listed as being the second largest in the Britain.

4074 CALDICOT CASTLE (Converted to double chimney)

Introduced into service in December 1923. Diagram HA boiler fitted. During March 1924 this engine was tested with the dynamometer car between Swindon and Plymouth. The locomotive was fitted with a double chimney and 4-row superheater in April 1959 (boiler HD 7648). The locomotive's last 'Heavy General' overhaul including boiler (HD 7663) and tender change took place at Swindon Works between 8th February and 19th April 1961. The engine was withdrawn in May 1963 from Old Oak Common depot (81A). Recorded mileage 1,844,072, service life 39 years, 5 months and 3 days. Disposal Swindon Works, October 1963.

Tender type principal fitted dates, Churchward 3500g December 1923, Collett Intermediate 3500g March 1925, Churchward 3500g August 1927, Collett 4000g 11th February 1929, Hawksworth 15th February 1952, Collett 4000g 20th August 1952, Hawksworth 4000g 27th November 1952, Collett 4000g 27th March 1954, Hawksworth 15th April 1959, Collett 4000g 30th October 1959.

GWR 'Castle' class 4-6-0 No 4074 CALDICOT CASTLE is seen passing Didcot at speed on the Oxford line with a Paddington-Worcester/Hereford service in August 1962, note the double chimney. In 1929 this engine (then with single chimney) was one of two 'Castles' trialled on the Cornish Riviera route against the LNER 'A1' Pacific No 4474 VICTOR WILD (later 'A3' class). The 'A1' was proved unsuitable for the many curves on the chosen route with the better suited 'Castle' engine burning less fuel whilst keeping better time. *David Anderson*

Allocated Depots

PDN Old Oak Common	12/23	CDF Cardiff Canton	29/08/37	87E Landore	12/08/59
NA Newton Abbot	04/24	LDR Landore	08/04/40	81D Reading WR	03/05/60
BRD Bristol Bath Road	27/05/32	PDN Old Oak Common	26/04/41	82C Swindon	31/10/60
NA Newton Abbot	24/06/32	LDR Landore	01/11/41	82B St Philips Marsh	17/01/62
LDR Landore	07/33	87G Carmarthen	09/56	81E Didcot	19/05/62
EXE Exeter	16/09/34	87E Landore	06/57	81A Old Oak Common	17/12/62
PDN Old Oak Common	28/03/37	81A Old Oak Common	13/07/59		

GWR 'Castle' class 4-6-0 No 4074 CALDICOT CASTLE (BR 'Box' style un-stepped inside cylinder cover) is seen at Patney & Chirton station on the Berks and Hants line with a local service in July 1958. It appears that 3 maroon coaches are being removed from the rear of the train. *Alan Sainty Collection*

Caldicot Castle was a once extensive stone medieval castle in Monmouthshire, south east Wales. The castle ruins, which stand in a delightful country park, are open to visitors between April and October of each year.

4075 CARDIFF CASTLE

Introduced into service in January 1924. Diagram HA boiler fitted.

The locomotive's last 'Heavy Intermediate' overhaul including boiler (HB 6642) and tender change took place at Swindon Works between 24th October and 19th December 1960. The locomotive was fitted with a nearside housing for short fire irons by BR. The engine was withdrawn in November 1961 from Old Oak Common depot (81A). Recorded mileage 1,807,802, service life 37 years, 10 months and 3 days. Disposal Swindon Works, March 1962.

Tender type principal fitted dates, Churchward 3500g January 1924, Collett 3500g February 1930, Collett 4000g 4 November 1931, Hawksworth 4000g 4th March 1957, Collett 4000g 26 December 1959.

Smartly turned out GWR 'Castle' class 4-6-0 No 4075 CARDIFF CASTLE comes off Bristol Bath Road depot (82A) prior to working the up 'Merchant Venturer' to London Paddington, in 1956. 'The Merchant Venturer' was one of two BR/WR expresses named specifically for the Festival of Britain (1951). The title was bestowed on the then 11.15am Paddington–Weston-super-Mare via Bristol and the return 4.35 working from Weston. *Rail Photoprints Collection*

Allocated Depots

PDN Old Oak Common	04/02/24	NA Newton Abbot	12/01/29	82B St Philips Marsh	10/52
LA Laira	15/04/26	CDF Cardiff Canton	20/11/31	82A Bristol Bath Road	26/02/53
NA Newton Abbot	18/08/27	PDN Old Oak Common	19/09/32	81A Old Oak Common	04/11/59
EXE Exeter	18/08/28	82A Bristol Bath Road	06/11/50		

Recently outshopped from Swindon Works following a 'Heavy General' overhaul GWR 'Castle' 4-6-0 No 4075 CARDIFF CASTLE (original style inside cylinder covers) arrives at a snowy Bath Spa station on 11th January 1959, with the 09.05 (Sun) Paddington–Weston-super-Mare service. *Hugh Ballantyne/Rail Photoprints*

Cardiff Castle, situated in the heart of the Welsh capital city, was transformed in Victorian times and rejoices in over 2000 years of Welsh history. The fascinating site is open throughout the whole year.

4076 CARMARTHEN CASTLE

Introduced into service in February 1924. Diagram HA boiler fitted. Modifications to this locomotive included new front section frames (straight replacing 'joggled'). The locomotive's last 'Heavy Intermediate' overhaul including boiler (HB 6683) and tender change took place at Swindon Works between 5th June and 15th August 1961. The engine was withdrawn in February 1963 from Llanelly depot (87F). Recorded mileage 1,697,895, service life 39 years and 2 days. Disposal Hayes Bridgend, October 1963.

Tender type principal fitted dates, Churchward 3500g February 1924, Dean 4000g October 1927, Collett 4000g 30th January 1929, Dean 4000g 8th June 1935, Collett 4000g 26th August 1935, Hawksworth 4th February 1957, Collett 23rd October 1959.

GWR 'Castle' class 4-6-0 No 4076 CARMARTHEN CASTLE is seen approaching Teignmouth with an up 'Torquay Pullman' service, circa 1931. The delightfully period image begs the question was the photographer more interested in the young lady or the express train?
Mike Morant Collection

Allocated depots

Depot	Date	Depot	Date	Depot	Date
PDN Old Oak Common	07/02/24	SDN Swindon	28/08/38	CHR Chester West	03/49
82A Bristol Bath Road	30/11/32	NA Newton Abbot	10/38	83A Newton Abbot	27/10/54
PDN Old Oak Common	04/01/33	4A Shrewsbury	17/06/40	84K Chester West	01/1955
BRD Bristol Bath Road	20/01/33	PDN Old Oak Common	24/07/42	87E Landore	30/11/57
CARM Carmarthen	20/05/34	SRD Stafford Road	08/48	87F Llanelly	15/08/61
LDR Landore	11/34	CHR Chester West	25/12/48	87A Neath Court Sart	28/05/62
EXE Exeter	30/08/35	TYS Tyseley	04/02/49	87F Llanelly	16/07/62

GWR 'Castle' class 4-6-0 No 4076 CARMARTHEN CASTLE is seen at Plymouth in original condition, circa 1926.
Keith Langston Collection

Carmarthen Castle, in 1094 there was a Norman castle built in the town. The site of the current ruins date from 1105 and that fortification was extended in the 13th century. The castle was sacked by Owain Glyndwr in 1405, when later rebuilt it became a prison during the late 18th century.

4077 CHEPSTOW CASTLE

Introduced into service in February 1924. Diagram HA boiler fitted.

The locomotive's last 'Heavy Intermediate' overhaul including boiler (HB 6678) and tender change took place at Swindon Works between 12th September and 10th November 1960. The engine was withdrawn in August 1962 from St Philips Marsh depot (82B). Recorded mileage 1,823,488, service life 38 years, 6 months and 3 days. Disposal Cashmores, Newport, December 1962.

Tender type principal fitted dates, Churchward 3500g February 1924, Dean 4000g July 1928, Collett Intermediate 3500g 30th April 1929, Collett 4000g 14th November 1930, Hawksworth 4000g 28 March 1950, Collett 4000g 16th May 1952, Hawksworth 28th June 1955, Collett 4000g 19th March 1957, Hawksworth 4000g 18th January 1959, Collett 4000g 10 November 1960.

Allocated Depots

PDN Old Oak Common	07/02/24	NA Newton Abbot	01/03/39	NA Newton Abbot	01/47
CDF Cardiff Canton	08/10/29	PZ Penzance	04/39	83D Laira	11/09/54
CARM Carmarthen	10/07/32	LA Laira	14/01/40	83A Newton Abbot	05/05/59
LA Laira	10/33	PZ Penzance	03/41	82A Bristol Bath Road	10/02/60
NA Newton Abbot	14/03/35	NA Newton Abbot	30/11/41	88A Cardiff Canton	10/11/60
EXE Exeter	01/39	LA Laira	11/46	82B St Philips Marsh	30/11/60

Chepstow Castle, in Monmouthshire, Wales is the oldest surviving post-Roman stone fortification in the UK. The castle ruins were used during the 'Doctor Who 50th Anniversary' TV broadcast. The site is open to the public.

GWR 'Castle' class 4-6-0 No 4077 CHEPSTOW CASTLE, with Hawksworth tender, is seen at Bristol Temple Meads on 12th August 1960. *Norman Preedy Collection/Rail Photoprints*

4078 PEMBROKE CASTLE

Introduced into service in February 1924. Diagram HA boiler fitted. Modifications to this locomotive included new front section frames (straight replacing 'joggled'). The locomotive's last 'Heavy Intermediate' overhaul including boiler (HC 7623) change took place at Swindon Works between 17th May and 29th July 1960. The engine was withdrawn in July 1962 from Llanelly depot (87F). Recorded mileage 1,823,488, service life 38 years 6 months and 3 days. Disposal Hayes Bridgend, December 1962.

Tender type principal fitted dates, Churchward 3500g 24th February 1924, Collett 4000g 12th November 1929, Dean 4000g 5th July 1935, Collett 4000g 1st September 1936, Hawksworth 4000g 28th March 1950, Collett 4000g 4th December 1950, Hawksworth 4000g 23rd December 1955.

Allocated depots

PDN Old Oak Common	24/02/24	LDR Landore	01/11/35	84A Stafford Road	11/07/59
CDF Cardiff Canton	23/04/31	84K Chester West	27/01/58	84C Banbury	04/11/59
PDN Old Oak Common	17/12/32	81D Reading WR	15/06/58	81A Old Oak Common	04/04/60
4A Shrewsbury	10/07/35	82A Bristol Bath Road	08/11/58	87F Llanelly	13/06/61

Pembroke Castle, in Wales stands on a site which was fortified as early as 1093 by Arnulf de Montgomery and the medieval fortification was expanded up to the late 12th century, and beyond. In the 15th and 16th centuries the castle was a place of peace. But at the outbreak of the English Civil War, although most of South Wales sided with the King, Pembroke declared for Parliament. It was besieged by Royalist troops but was saved after Parliamentary reinforcements arrived by sea from nearby Milford Haven.

In 1648, when the war was at its close, Pembroke's leaders changed sides and led a Royalist uprising. Oliver Cromwell came to Pembroke and took the castle after a seven-week siege. Its three leaders were found guilty of treason and Cromwell ordered the castle to be destroyed. Townspeople were even encouraged to disassemble the fortress and re-use its stone for their own purposes.

World War I veteran Major-General Sir Ivor Philipps acquired the castle in 1928 and started extensive restoration work. After his death a trust was set up for the castle, jointly managed by the Philipps family and Pembroke Town council.

GWR 'Castle' class 4-6-0 No 4078 PEMBROKE CASTLE is seen at Landore depot in 1954. Note the mechanical lubricator mounted forward of the steam pipe in this instance. *Rail Photoprints Collection*

4079 PENDENNIS CASTLE Preserved

Introduced into service in March 1924. Diagram HA boiler fitted.

The locomotive's last 'Heavy Intermediate' overhaul including boiler (HB 6672) and tender change took place at Swindon Works between 25th August and 20th October 1961. BR fitted the locomotive with a nearside housing for the storage of short fire irons. The engine was withdrawn in May 1964 from St Philips Marsh (82B), and sold for preservation. Recorded mileage 1,758,398, service life 40 years 1 month and 26 days.

Tender type principal fitted dates, Churchward 3500g February 1924, Dean 4000g November 1926, Collett 4000g 20th March 1929, Hawksworth 4000g 30th November 1950, Collett 4000g 31st March 1951.

In 1925 the GWR loaned the locomotive to the London & North Eastern Railway for trials against Gresley's then new Pacifics. Working 16-coach trains on the East Coast main line from Kings Cross, the Collett designed 'Castle' 4-6-0 earned a lasting place in railway folklore, by comprehensively out-performing the larger LNER 4-6-2 engines!

Thereafter the GWR sent **PENDENNIS CASTLE** to stand alongside **FLYING SCOTSMAN** at the re-opened 1925 British Empire Exhibition at Wembley, with a notice cheekily proclaiming it to be 'the most powerful passenger express locomotive in Britain'.

The preservation of the engine was not a straightforward affair, but it does thankfully have a happy ending. **PENDENNIS CASTLE** was purchased for preservation by Mike Higson and appeared at one of the Great Western Society's first open days in 1965. The engine was later sold again and moved on first to Didcot, and then in the early 1970s to Steamtown Carnforth. In May 1977 the engine was sold to Hamersley Iron (later a Rio Tinto company), one of the largest iron ore producers in Australia, where it was used by the company hauling excursion trains in the care of the Pilbara Railways Historical Society.

No 4079 steamed in Australia for the last time in October 1994 and after being stored out of use for several years the iconic locomotive was offered to the Great Western Society (GWS). Repatriated to the UK the engine arrived back in 2000. Restoration at the Didcot base of the GWS was still underway as this book went to press. Restoring steam locomotives is a costly business and in this instance can only be achieved by the addition of public donations.

For the full PENDENNIS CASTLE story visit www.didcotrailwaycentre.org.uk/guide/

GWR 'Castle' class 4-6-0 No 4079 PENDENNIS CASTLE is seen just prior to being shipped to Australia where the engine resided for 23 years before bring repatriated to the UK. *Keith Langston Collection*

Allocated Depots

PDN Old Oak Common	04/03/24	NPT Ebbw Junction	05/37	82A Bristol Bath Road	13/06/57
Exhibition Wembley	17/05/25	CDF Cardiff Canton	06/37	83B Taunton	13/09/60
LA Laira	13/04/26	85 Gloucester Horton Rd	01/11/39	82B St Philips Marsh	18/01/61
PDN Old Oak Common	25/06/26	HFD Hereford	06/44	Stored	14/03/62
BRD Bristol Bath Road	11/09/31	85 Gloucester Horton Rd	03/11/48	82C Swindon (Reinstated)	11/08/62
SRD Stafford Road	01/12/32	84A Stafford Road	29/06/53	82B St Philips Marsh	05/64
CDF Cardiff Canton	14/12/35				

Pendennis Castle, (Device Fort or Henrician Castle) near Falmouth was an important artillery installation from 1539 until modern times in 1956. It was originally built for defending the naval and mercantile anchorages adjacent to the port of Falmouth in the time of Henry VIII. Pendennis Castle was built as one of a chain of forts running along the coast of the southern half of Britain from Hull to Milford Haven, this was in response to the threat of invasion from the French and Spanish.

Smartly turned out GWR 'Castle' class 4-6-0 No 4079 PENDENNIS CASTLE storms through Badminton station with the 11.45 Bristol - Paddington service, on 22nd November 1959. *Hugh Ballantyne/Rail Photoprints*

GWR 'Castle' class 4-6-0 No 4079 PENDENNIS CASTLE looked to be well off its home base cleaning roster, when seen at Oxford in May 1961, it was then a St Philips Marsh allocated locomotive. *David Anderson*

4080 POWDERHAM CASTLE (Converted to double chimney)

Introduced into service in March 1924. Diagram HA boiler fitted. Modifications to this locomotive included new front section frames (straight replacing 'joggled'). The locomotive was fitted with a double chimney and 4-row superheater in August 1958 (boiler HD 7676 fitted). The locomotive's last 'Heavy General' overhaul including boiler (HD 7647) and tender change took place at Swindon Works between 21st November 1961 and 19th January 1962. The engine was withdrawn in August 1964 from Southall depot (81C). Recorded mileage 1,974,461, service life 40 years, 4 months and 18 days. Disposal Cashmores, Newport, December 1964.

Tender type principal fitted dates, Churchward 3500g 23rd March 1924, Collett 4000g 23rd March 1929, Hawksworth 4000g 10th February 1956, Collett 4000g 15th August 1956, Hawksworth 4000g 13th August 1958, Collett 4000g 14th April 1960, Hawksworth 4000g 19th January 1962.

GWR 'Castle' class 4-6-0 No 4080 POWDERHAM CASTLE is seen climbing past Stoneycombe whilst assaulting Dainton Bank with a down express, in May 1957 some 15 months before being fitted with a double chimney. The engine achieved the highest recorded mileage of any 'Castle' proper (excluding re-built 'Star' class engines) and was allocated/re-allocated on 28 separate occasions. *Rail Photoprints Collection*

Allocated Depots

PDN Old Oak Common	23/03/24	LDR Landore	23/12/41	82D Westbury	04/11/50
LA Laira	02/09/26	BRD Bristol Bath Road	09/11/42	83A Newton Abbot	19/05/53
NA Newton Abbot	03/08/28	Brd Weston-super-Mare	10/43	82A Bristol Bath Road	17/07/54
LA Laira	27/03/29	BRD Bristol Bath Road	06/01/44	83A Newton Abbot	13/05/59
NA Newton Abbot	26/04/30	Brd Weston-super-Mare	08/46	84G Shrewsbury	22/04/60
LA Laira	29/12/32	BRD Bristol Bath Road	09/46	86C Cardiff Canton	02/08/60
NA Newton Abbot	12/33	NA Newton Abbot	07/01/49	88L Cardiff East Dock	07/09/62
PZ Penzance	01/35	LA Laira	06/49	81A Old Oak Common	13/04/64
LDR Landore	26/05/35	82F Weymouth GWR	02/06/50	81C Southall	22/06/64
LA Laira	09/01/41				

GWR 'Castle' class 4-6-0 No 4080 POWDERHAM CASTLE seen at Newport with the down 'Capitals United Express' in 1962, note the double chimney, Hawksworth tender, mechanical lubricator forward of the steam pipe and BR Box pattern stepped inside cylinder casing. The blade of the non-standard hand operated front cab window wiper can also be seen. Cardiff became the official capital of Wales on 20th December 1955, the 8am Paddington–Cardiff/Swansea departure and 3.55 pm return service were titled in recognition of that event. *Rail Photoprints Collection*

Powderham Castle is located in Exeter, Devon and stands beside the river Exe. It is one of England's oldest family homes which Sir Philip Courtenay commenced building it in 1391, and it has remained in the same family to the current day. The grounds and part of the castle are open to visitors on a limited basis.

4081 WARWICK CASTLE

Introduced into service in March 1924. Diagram HA boiler fitted.

The locomotive's last 'Heavy Intermediate' overhaul including boiler (HB 6674) and tender change took place at Swindon Works between 22nd August and 18th October 1959. The engine was withdrawn in February 1963 from Carmarthen depot (87G). Recorded mileage 1,894,998, service life 38 years, 11 months and 11 days. Disposal Hayes, Bridgend, October 1963.

Tender type principal fitted dates, Churchward 3500g March 1924, Collett 4000g March 1929, Churchward 3500g 19th December 1929, Collett 4000g 18th June 1931, Hawksworth 3rd September 1952, Collett 4000g 28th August 1953, Hawksworth 4000g 3rd October 1959, Collett 4000g 22nd January 1960.

GWR 'Castle' Class 4-6-0 No 4081 WARWICK CASTLE is seen heading a Newcastle–Cardiff train west between Over Junction and Oakle Street, in September 1955. Note the BR/ER coaching stock. *Hugh Ballantyne/Rail Photoprints*

Allocated Depots

PDN Old Oak Common	06/04/24	BRD Bristol Bath Road	12/05/34	86C Cardiff Canton	20/03/58
RDG Reading W.R.	05/03/29	Brd Weston-super-Mare	21/04/40	83C Exeter	16/05/58
PDN Old Oak Common	15/03/29	BRD Bristol Bath Road	05/40	82A Bristol Bath Road	02/12/58
CDF Cardiff Canton	09/01/31	Brd Weston-super-Mare	03/41	84G Shrewsbury	18/06/59
LA Laira	08/01/32	BRD Bristol Bath Road	12/07/41	82A Bristol Bath Road	15/07/59
EXE Exeter	08/32	LDR Landore	26/11/46	87G Carmarthen	16/09/60
LA Laira	05/11/32	SDN Swindon	10/07/48	87F Llanelly	18/10/61
CDF Cardiff Canton	04/33	87E Landore	04/11/50	87G Carmarthen	14/07/62

GWR 'Castle' Class 4-6-0 No 4081 WARWICK CASTLE is seen at the buffer stops with a train at Swansea High Street station in 1955. Note the advertising hoardings and in particular the Wymans book stall. The station is a terminus, at the end of a short branch off the South Wales Main Line and the West Wales Line. *S. Rickard/ J&J Collection*

Warwick Castle, has history dating back over 11 centuries. It is in modern times an entertainment centre operated by a private company, and thus a 'pay to visit' venue.

4082 WINDSOR CASTLE

Introduced into service in April 1924. Diagram HA boiler fitted. Modifications to this locomotive included new front section frames (straight replacing 'joggled'). Re-numbered as engine No 7013 and re-named BRISTOL CASTLE in February 1952 (No 7013 was introduced in July 1948 by BR). When rostered for King George VI's funeral train from Paddington to Windsor on 15th February 1952 locomotive No 4082 was in Swindon Works undergoing repair. To overcome the problem BR swopped the plates with those of No 7013*, and they were never changed back. The 'new' WINDSOR CASTLE then hauled the aforementioned funeral train.

The locomotive's last 'Heavy General' overhaul including boiler (HC 7640) and tender change took place at Swindon Works between 28th October and 22nd December 1961.The engine was withdrawn in September 1964 from Tyseley depot (2A). Recorded mileage 1,898,571, service life 40 years, 4 months and 19 days. Disposal Cashmores, Newport, January 1965.

Tender type principal fitted dates, Churchward 3500g 12th April 1924, Collett 4000g May 1929, Hawksworth 9th November 1948, Collett 4000g 14th June 1949, Hawksworth 4000g 24th January 1950, Collett 4000g 21st December 1951, Hawksworth 5th January 1954, Collett 4000g 16th March 1955.

*See also No 7013 BRISTOL CASTLE/WINDSOR CASTLE

The first GWR 'Castle' class No 4082 WINDSOR CASTLE, seen at Reading in 1934. Note the extra plate above the cabside numberplate, commemorating the occasion of the engine being driven from Swindon Works to Swindon Station by King George VI on April 28th 1924. Note GWR original style curved sided inside cylinder casing. *Rail Photoprints Collection*

Allocated Depots

PDN Old Oak Common	12/04/24	PDN Old Oak Common	13/03/38	WOS Worcester	02/49
NA Newton Abbot	25/05/28	85 Gloucester Horton Road	02/41	82C Swindon	08/02/52
LA Laira	13/05/29	SDN Swindon	08/10/46	81A Old Oak Common	05/01/54
PDN Old Oak Common	23/08/31	85 Gloucester Horton Road	08/02/47	81A Stored	22/10/62
SRD Stafford Road	16/12/32	STJ Severn Tunnel Junction	13/01/48	81A Reinstated	13/04/64
PDN Old Oak Common	22/02/33	85 Gloucester Horton Road	09/03/48	2A Tyseley	20/06/64
BRD Bath Bristol Road	25/08/35				

GWR 'Castle' class 4-6-0 No 4082 WINDSOR CASTLE (BR style stepped inside cylinder cover) climbs away from the Severn Tunnel towards Pilning with a South Wales-Paddington service, in August 1961. This engine was originally No 7013 BRISTOL CASTLE. *A.E.Durrant/ Rail Photoprints*

Windsor Castle is notably the oldest and largest occupied castle in the world and it is an Official Residence of the British Monarch. Public access is allowed to the imposing castle, which covers an area of approximately 13 acres and spans over 1000 years of history.

4083 ABBOTSBURY CASTLE

Introduced into service in May 1925. Diagram HA boiler fitted. The locomotive's last 'Heavy Intermediate' overhaul including boiler (HB 6658) change took place at Swindon Works between 30th July and 9th October 1959. The engine was withdrawn in December 1961 from Cardiff Canton depot (88A). Recorded mileage 1,677,060, service life 36 years, 7 months and 10 days. Disposal Swindon Works, January 1962.

Tender type principal fitted dates, Churchward 3500g May 1925, Dean 4000g 1st June 1926, Collett 4000g 9th September 1929, Hawksworth 4000g 26th October 1946, Collett 4000g 16th January 1948, Hawksworth 4000g 10th November 1949, Collett 4000g 29th August 1951, Hawksworth 4000g 6th November 1953, Collett 4000g 2nd February 1954, Hawksworth 4000g 29th March 1955, Collett 4000g 17th April 1957, Hawksworth 4000g 21st October 1958.

GWR 'Castle' class 4-6-0 No 4083 ABBOTSBURY CASTLE is seen at Newton Abbot (83A) in May 1958. *Keith Langston Collection*

Allocated Depots

PDN Old Oak Common	09/05/25	CDF Stored	06/09/41	84A Stafford Road	16/11/50
CDF Cardiff Canton	05/06/32	CDF Reinstated	09/09/41	83A Newton Abbot	24/03/58
PDN Old Oak Common	07/33	CDF Stored	21/02/50	83C Exeter	13/09/60
LA Laira	28/12/34	84G Shrewsbury. Reinstated	15/07/50	88A Cardiff Canton	13/09/61
CDF Cardiff Canton	08/02/36				

GWR 'Castle' class 4-6-0 No 4083 ABBOTSBURY CASTLE seen to the west of Brent station, with a summer Saturday working. Brent Hill, Devon is the backdrop. *Transport Treasury*

Abbotsbury Castle is in fact the site of an Iron Age Fort in South West Dorset, the earthworks, which cover an area of approximately 10 acres, are situated on a rise called Wears Hill above the village of Abbotsbury located to the west of Dorchester.

4084 ABERYSTWYTH CASTLE

Introduced into service in May 1925. Diagram HA boiler fitted.

The locomotive's last 'Heavy General' overhaul including boiler (HB 6642) and tender change took place at Swindon Works between 25th June and 24th September 1958. The engine was withdrawn in October 1960 from Cardiff Canton depot (88A). Recorded mileage 1,674,812, service life 35 years, 4 months and 11 days. Disposal Swindon Works, December 1960.

Tender type principal fitted dates, Churchward 3500g May 1925, Collett Intermediate 3500g March 1927, Collett 4000g 23rd October 1930, Hawksworth 'Self Weighing' 3800g 11th August 1952, Collett 4000g 6th September 1952, Hawksworth 4000g 4th February 1955, Collett 4000g 24th September 1958.

GWR 'Castle' class 4-6-0 No 4084 ABERYSTWYTH CASTLE seen at Newton Abbot in 1926. Note the Churchward 3500g tender. *Mike Morant Collection*

Allocated Depots

LA Laira	30/05/25	PDN Old Oak Common	03/07/35	Brd Weston-super-Mare	09/46
NA Newton Abbot	02/12/29	BRD Bristol Bath Road	21/03/38	BRD Bristol Bath Road	11/46
LA Laira	07/02/31	Brd Weston-super-Mare	09/42	Brd Weston-super-Mare	03/48
NA Newton Abbot	13/08/31	BRD Bristol Bath Road	10/42	BRD Bristol Bath Road	04/48
CDF Cardiff Canton	03/33	Brd Weston-super-Mare	05/43	81D Reading	04/11/59
CARM Carmarthen	19/04/34	BRD Bristol Bath Road	27/08/43	86C Cardiff Canton	22/12/59
LDR Landore	10/34				

Aberystwyth Castle is an Edwardian fortress in Mid Wales which was built circa 1277, on the site of an earlier bailey castle. The ruins are open to the public.

4085 BERKELEY CASTLE

Introduced into service in June 1925. Diagram HA boiler fitted.

The locomotive's last 'Heavy Intermediate' overhaul including boiler (HB 6643) and tender change took place at Swindon Works between 26th May and 18th August 1958. The engine was withdrawn in May 1962 from Old Oak Common depot (81A).Recorded mileage 1,651,000, service life 36 years, 10 months and 22 days. Disposal Cashmores, Newport, December 1962.

Tender type principal fitted dates, Churchward 3500g May 1925, Collett Intermediate 3500g July 1927, Collett 4000g 12th June 1929, Hawksworth 4000g 12th December 1946, Collett 4000g 13th October 1950, Hawksworth 4000g 25th March 1955, Collett 4000g 25th August 1955, Hawksworth 4000g 18th August 1960.

GWR 'Castle' class 4-6-0 No 4085 BERKELEY CASTLE is seen at Oxford (81F) in May 1961. Note the BR style parallel barrel buffers, stepped inside cylinder casing, but the original design sandboxes. *David Anderson*

Allocated Depots

LA Laira	10/06/25	CARM Carmarthen	07/32	85A Worcester	15/04/58
PDN Old Oak Common	01/04/30	EXE Exeter	17/07/34	85D Gloucester Horton Road	20/05/58
CARM Carmarthen	12/02/32	PDN Old Oak Common	02/05/37	85A Worcester	18/02/60
LDR Landore	06/32	RDG Reading WR	01/39	81A Old Oak Common	02/05/62

Berkeley Castle (historically often spelt Berkley) is located in the town of Berkeley, Gloucestershire and its origins date back to the 11th century. It is thought to be the site of the murder of King Edward II in 1327. The ghost of King Edward II is said to walk the castle remains annually on the anniversary of his murder in October 1327. So horrific was the reported manner of his killing that his screams of pain were said to have been heard throughout, and far beyond the castle. Edward was later interred at Gloucester Cathedral. The castle has been the home of the Berkeley family from late 12th century to the present day and the grounds are opened to visitors from April to October each year.

4086 BUILTH CASTLE

Introduced into service in June 1925. Diagram HA boiler fitted.

The locomotive's last 'Heavy Intermediate' overhaul including boiler (HB 6650) and tender change took place at Swindon Works between 27th July and 21st September 1960. The loco achieved fame as the first GWR engine to reach 100mph since the earlier success of CITY OF TRURO.

The engine was withdrawn in April 1962 from Reading WR depot (81D). Recorded mileage 1,791,633, service life 36 years, 9 months and 14 days. Disposal Cashmores, Newport, November 1962.

Tender type principal fitted dates, Churchward 3500g June 1925, Collett 4000g 17th December 1929, Collett 3500g 25th August 1931, Collett 4000g 31st August 1932, Hawksworth 4000g 22nd January 1950, Collett 4000g 29th March 1950, Hawksworth 4000g 20th August 1951, Collett 4000g 15th May 1952, Hawksworth 4000g 17th January 1957, Collett 4000g 10th February 1958, Hawksworth 4000g 19th April 1958, Collett 4000g 21st November 1958.

It was blisteringly hot, hence no exhaust as 'Castle' Class 4-6-0 4086 BUILTH CASTLE' and 2-6-2T No 5148 climb to Dainton tunnel with the 08.35 Liverpool - Penzance service, on 8th August 1959. *Hugh Ballantyne/Rail Photoprints*

Allocated Depots

LA Laira	20/06/25	BRD Bristol Bath Road	11/34	87G Carmarthen	10/52
EXE Exeter	09/29	CDF Cardiff Canton	26/03/35	83D Laira	09/02/53
LA Laira	19/12/29	WOS Worcester	02/06/36	81D Reading WR	28/09/59
CARM Carmarthen	07/09/31	GLO Gloucester Horton Road	01/12/37	86C Cardiff Canton	09/12/59
BRD Bristol Bath Road	07/09/32	WOS Worcester	22/06/39	81D Reading WR	10/05/61
BRD Stored	01/01/34	WOS Stored	22/08/50	84A Stafford Road	11/12/61
PDN Old Oak Common	20/10/34	WOS/85A Reinstated	20/08/51	81D Reading WR	19/01/62

GWR 'Castle' class No 4086 BUILTH CASTLE is seen on the approach to Teignmouth with 'The Cornishman', up train circa 1957. Note the Hawksworth straight sided tender. 'The Cornishman' Wolverhampton Low Level–Penzance (30/6/52) Sheffield Midland–Penzance (10/9/62) Bradford Forster Square–Penzance (14/6/65), Bradford Exchange–Penzance (1/5/67). *Rail Photoprints Collection*

Builth Castle was a castle built under King Edward I, today only the mound and ditches remain, the site is just outside Builth Wells, Powys, Wales. The castle was besieged in 1294 during the revolt of Madog ap Llywelyn, and attacked by Owain Glyndŵr's forces during his revolt in the early 15th century. Repairs in 1409 reportedly cost £400 however, the castle was then destroyed by fire in the 17th century.

4087 CARDIGAN CASTLE (Converted to double chimney)

Introduced into service in June 1925. Diagram HA boiler fitted. Modifications to this locomotive included new front section frames (straight replacing 'joggled') and a Davies & Metcalf patent valveless lubricator. Double chimney and 4-row superheater fitted February 1958 (boiler HD 7665). The locomotive's last 'Heavy General' overhaul including boiler (HD 7645) and tender change took place at Swindon Works between 19th August and 10th October 1961. The engine was withdrawn in April 1962 from Laira depot (84A). Recorded mileage 1,812,341, service life 38 years, 3 months and 10 days. Disposal Coopers Metals, Sharpness, May 1964.

Tender type principal fitted dates, Churchward 3500g June 1925, Collett 4000g 22nd June 1929, Churchward 3500g 20th December 1929, Collett 4000g 13th August 1931, Churchward 3500g 15th June 1946, Collett 4000g 2nd November 1946, Hawksworth 4000g 31st March 1950, Collett 4000g 6th November 1951, Hawksworth 4000g 30th April 1953, Collett 4000g 5th July 1956, Hawksworth 10th October 1961.

Laira based 'Castle' class 4-6-0 No 4087 CARDIGAN CASTLE freshly out of Swindon Works (General overhaul outshopped 13th August) and coupled to a Collett 4000 gallon tender is seen with a 'running in turn' at Reading General in August 1959. Note the double chimney, Davies & Metcalf valveless lubricator with additional oil reservoir attached to the smokebox, BR pattern parallel barrel buffers and stepped inside cylinder cover. *Alan Sainty Collection*

Allocated Depots

LA Laira	27/06/25	EXE Exeter	21/02/36	PZ Penzance	12/49
NA Newton Abbot	16/04/27	SRD Stafford Road	07/05/37	83D Laira	23/04/52
LA Laira	24/05/27	TR Truro	08/07/37	83G Penzance	10/52
NA Newton Abbot	08/28	PZ Penzance	15/10/37	83D Laira	08/54
LA Laira	18/08/31	NA Newton Abbot	04/02/39	83D Stored	13/08/62
CDF Cardiff Canton	29/07/32	TR Truro	28/06/39	82B St Phillips Marsh Reinstated	06/04/63
PDN Old Oak Common	07/33	LA Laira	03/01/41	82B Stored	09/09/63

GWR 'Castle' class 4-6-0 No 4087 CARDIGAN CASTLE is seen passing Langley with a down fitted mixed freight and milk train in April 1951. Note by that time the locomotive had modified frames and 'Box' pattern inside cylinder casing, but was still to receive a double chimney, also the blade of the nearside hand operated window wiper can be seen. *Dave Cobbe Collection-C.R.L. Coles/Rail Photoprints*

Cardigan Castle has its beginnings in the 12th century and represents over 900 years of Ceredigion history. Decades of neglect left the Cardigan town centre site in ruins but, after years of local campaigning the castle is being brought back to life and was reportedly on course to open its doors to the public in 2014.

4088 DARTMOUTH CASTLE (Converted to double chimney)

Introduced into service in July 1925. Diagram HA boiler fitted. Modifications to this locomotive included new front section frames (straight replacing 'joggled'), new cylinders and a Davies & Metcalf patent valveless lubricator. Double chimney and 4-row superheater fitted May 1958 (boiler HD 7674). The locomotive's last 'Heavy Intermediate' overhaul including boiler(HD 7649) tender change and double chimney fitting took place at Swindon Works between 19th May and 8th July 1961. The engine was withdrawn in May 1964 from St Philips Marsh depot (82B). Recorded mileage 1,848,430 (to 28/12/63), service life 38 years, 9 months and 5 days. Disposal Cohens, Morriston, September 1964.

Tender type principal fitted dates, Collett Intermediate 3500g 25th July 1925, Collett 4000g 9th January 1929, Churchward 3500g 30th October 1929, Collett 3500g 21st December 1929, Collett 4000g 18th March 1931, Dean 4000g 22nd September 1942, Collett 4000g 14th April 1943, Hawksworth 4000g 27th March 1953, Collett 4000g 28th October 1953.

GWR 'Castle' class 4-6-0 No 4088 DARTMOUTH CASTLE seen tenderless, and with others of the class and a Mogul, at Swindon Works in January 1950. Note that the engine at that time was still un-modified. *Rail Photoprints Collection*

Allocated Depots

LA Laira	25/07/25	LA Laira	03/08/35	83D Laira	09/54
NA Newton Abbot	14/01/29	PDN Old Oak Common	03/03/37	85A Worcester	28/01/58
SRD Stafford Road	30/12/29	LA Laira	02/39	82C Swindon	07/02/61
NA Newton Abbot	01/33	PZ Penzance	02/49	82C Stored	24/09/62
LA Laira	25/06/34	LA Laira	25/05/49	82B St Philips Marsh. Reinstated	02/11/63
PZ Penzance	05/35	83A Newton Abbot	28/10/53		

Dartmouth Castle is one of a pair of forts, the other being Kingswear Castle, sited to guard the mouth of the Dart Estuary in Devon. Built circa 1388 the English Heritage owned castle is open to the public.

4089 DONNINGTON CASTLE

Introduced into service in July 1925. Diagram HA boiler fitted. Modifications to this locomotive included new front section frames (straight replacing 'joggled'). The locomotive's last 'Heavy General' overhaul including boiler (HC 6697) change took place at Swindon Works between 8th August and 5th October 1961. The engine was withdrawn in September 1964 from Reading WR depot (81D). Recorded mileage 1,876,807, service life 39 years, 1 month and 30 days. Disposal Hayes, Bridgend, January 1965.

Tender type principal fitted dates, Churchward 3500g July 1925, Collett 4000g 14th August 1929, Hawksworth 4000g 18th January 1952, Collett 4000g 1st May 1953, Hawksworth 4000g 27th November 1959, Collett 4000g August 1963.

Allocated Depots

PDN Old Oak Common	08/07/25	CDF Cardiff Canton	07/01/37	81A Old Oak Common	20/07/51
CDF Cardiff Canton	15/06/28	LDR Landore	17/02/37	83A Newton Abbot	18/01/52
PDN Old Oak Common	17/09/29	SDN Swindon	09/02/38	83D Laira	02/52
SRD Stafford Road	20/12/32	BRD Bristol Bath Road	02/42	85A Worcester	02/12/58
LDR Landore	02/11/35	Brd Weston-super-Mare	08/47	81A Old Oak Common	05/07/60
PDN Old Oak Common	04/04/36	BRD Bristol Bath Road	30/20/47	81A Stored	22/10/62
LDR Landore	30/04/36	LA Laira	07/48	81D Reading WR. Reinstated	31/12/63

Donnington Castle is a ruined medieval castle just north of the town of Newbury in Berkshire. It was built by Richard Abberbury and the castle was besieged several times during the English Civil War. All that remains of the castle in modern times is the substantial four towered gatehouse, and the surrounding earthworks. The castle ruins are reportedly haunted by several different ghosts. In 1990 several visitors witnessed the apparition of a white dog running down the hill from the castle towards the woods where it mysteriously vanished before reaching the nearby tree line! The 14th century English Heritage owned site is open to the public.

Newton Abbot Shed 18th May 1958, on the left GWR 'Castle' class 4-6-0 No 4089 DONNINGTON CASTLE, note the post modification stepped straight sided, inside cylinder cover. *Hugh Ballantyne/Rail Photoprints*

4090 DORCHESTER CASTLE (Converted to double chimney)

Introduced into service in August 1925. Diagram HA boiler fitted. Modifications to this locomotive included new front section frames (straight replacing 'joggled'). The first engine of the class to be fitted with a double chimney and 4-row superheater (which included an extended smokebox) March 1957 (boiler HD 7671). The locomotive's last 'Heavy Intermediate' overhaul including boiler (HB 6688) and tender change took place at Swindon Works between 15th September and 7th November 1960. The engine was withdrawn in June 1963 from Cardiff East Dock depot (88L). Recorded mileage 1,848,646, service life 37 years, 9 months and 23 days. Disposal Cashmores Newport, June 1964.

Tender type principal fitted dates, Churchward 3500g July 1925, Collett 4000g 21st June 1929, Churchward 3500g 21st December 1929, Collett 4000g 10th April 1930, Hawksworth 4000g 4th April 1957, Collett 4000g 1st January 1959.

Double chimney GWR 'Castle' class 4-6-0 No 4090 DORCHESTER CASTLE takes water at Cardiff as it heads the last up steam hauled 'South Wales Pullman' on 8th September 1961. The duty fitter appears to be examining the off side brake gear. Note the extended smokebox, modified steam pipes, double chimney, external sandboxes, stepped inside cylinder cover and burnished buffers. *Hugh Ballantyne/Rail Photoprints*

Allocated Depots

Depot	Date	Depot	Date	Depot	Date
PDN Old Oak Common	15/08/25	NA Newton Abbot	30/12/38	87E Landore	16/06/60
LA Laira	20/06/31	LA Laira	10/01/39	87A Neath Court Sart	28/08/61
NA Newton Abbot	18/01/34	PZ Penzance	02/50	87A Stored	17/04/62
PZ Penzance	04/35	81A Old Oak Common	11/52	89A Shrewsbury. Reinstated	14/07/62
PDN Old Oak Common	30/11/35	84A Stafford Road	03/07/53	89A Stored	07/09/62
LA Laira	22/03/37	81A Old Oak Common	12/55	88L Cardiff East Dock. Reinstated	24/09/62
EXE Exeter	04/38	87E Landore	11/08/59		
LA Laira	05/38	87G Carmarthen	22/09/59		

The last up steam hauled 'South Wales Pullman' prepares to leave Swansea High Street for London Paddington behind GWR 'Castle' class 4-6-0 No 4090 DORCHESTER CASTLE. The mechanical lubricator can clearly be seen on the platform side running board. 'South Wales Pullman' from Paddington- Swansea High Street introduced 27th June 1955, last titled run 8th September 1961. *Hugh Ballantyne/Rail Photoprints Collection*

Dorchester Castle was in the town of Dorchester, Dorset and dated from between 1154 and 1175, becoming disused circa 1290. There are no remains to be seen and in modern times a prison building stands on the site.

4091 DUDLEY CASTLE

Introduced into service in August 1925. Diagram HA boiler fitted.

The locomotive's last 'Heavy Intermediate' overhaul including boiler (HB 6625) and tender change took place at Swindon Works between 15th December 1956 and 12th March 1957 and it was the first original built 'Castle' to be withdrawn. The engine was withdrawn in January 1959 from Old Oak Common depot (81A). Recorded mileage 1,691,856, service life 33 years, 5 months and 18 days. Disposal Swindon Works, March 1959.

Tender type principal fitting dates, Dean 4000g August 1925, Churchward 3500g August 1927, Collett 4000 23rd March 1929, Collett (8 wheeled) 4000g 1st September 1931, Collett 4000g 11th September 1931, Hawksworth 4000g 2nd December 1952, Collett 4000g 15th December 1952.

Allocated Depots

PDN Old Oak Common	01/08/25	CDF Cardiff Canton	03/10/34	PDN Old Oak Common	01/11/41
CDF Cardiff Canton	30/06/30	LDR Landore	07/38	WOS Worcester	21/03/46
BRD Bristol Bath Road	16/09/31	CDF Cardiff Canton	10/38	PDN Old Oak Common	03/10/46
NA Newton Abbot	03/33	PDN Old Oak Common	10/09/39	82A Bristol Bath Road	11/06/50
LA Laira	19/06/34	SDN Swindon	04/08/41	81A Old Oak Common	19/01/59

Dudley Castle is a ruined castle dated circa 1066 and located in the town of Dudley, West Midlands, there is a privately run zoo in the castle's extensive grounds. Dudley Castle is regarded as one of the most haunted castles in England. The sighting of many spirits have been reported over hundreds of years. Perhaps the most famous of all being that of the 'so called' Grey Lady, believed to be the spirit of Dorothy Beaumont. She lived in the castle for a time, and gave birth to a daughter there. Unfortunately the daughter died during birth and after that lady died her restless spirit is said to wander aimlessly around the castle and its grounds, whilst looking for her daughter. There is a public house on the site which is called the Grey Lady Tavern where there have been reports of 'things going bump in the night', without explanation.

GWR 'Castle' class 4-6-0 No 4091 DUDLEY CASTLE is seen approaching Bristol Temple Meads station, circa 1938. *Dave Cobbe Collection – C. R. L. Coles/Rail Photoprints*

4092 DUNRAVEN CASTLE

Introduced into service in August 1925. Diagram HA boiler fitted.

The locomotive's last 'Heavy General' overhaul including boiler (HB 6604) and change took place at Swindon Works between 3rd May and 30th October 1956. The engine was withdrawn in December 1961 from Oxford depot (81F). Recorded mileage 1,718,879, service life 36 years, 4 months and 13 days. Disposal Swindon Works, January 1962.

Tender type principal fitted dates, Churchward 3500g August 1925, Collett Intermediate 3500g 5th January 1926, 4500 type 22nd May 1929, Collett 4000g 11th April 1930, Hawksworth 4000g 5th December 1946, Collett 4000g 11th April 1947, Hawksworth 4000g 16 July 1955, Collett 4000g 3 December 1955.

Allocated Depots

PDN Old Oak Common	06/08/25	CDF Cardiff Canton	28/04/31	84A Stafford Road	07/11/50
SRD Stafford Road	26/05/26	LA Laira	15/01/34	81D Reading WR	20/03/58
PDN Old Oak Common	05/09/26	WOS Worcester	21/02/39	81F Oxford	31/10/60

Dunraven Castle was a mansion on the South Wales coast near Southerndown. It was built in 1803 and demolished in 1963. The castle's walled garden survived and can still be visited. The castle and surrounding parkland have been the subject of myth, rumor and tragic stories, mainly about the Vaughan family who lived there for many years. A ghostly figured called the Blue Lady is also said to have haunted the castle. During both World Wars the building was reportedly used as a hospital (Glamorgan Red Cross County Hospital), and later as a Workers Tourist Authority guest house. The beach and spectacular cliffs at both Southerndown and Dunraven Bay have been used as locations whilst filming several TV programs, including Doctor Who.

GWR 'Castle' Class 4-6-0 No 4092 DUNRAVEN CASTLE is seen at an unknown location, circa 1957. *Rail Photoprints Collection*

4093 DUNSTER CASTLE (Converted to double chimney)

Introduced into service in May 1926. Diagram HA boiler fitted. This was the first of the class to be built with straight pattern frames. Double chimney (included an extended smokebox) and 4-row superheater, fitted December 1957 (boiler HB 6688). The locomotive's last 'Heavy Intermediate' overhaul including boiler (HD 7686) and tender change took place at Swindon Works between 29th December 1961 and 9th March 1962. The engine was withdrawn in September 1964 from St Philips Marsh depot (82B). Recorded mileage 1,842,985, to end of January 1963, service life 38 years, 3 months and 5 days. Disposal Cashmores Newport, January 1965.

Tender type principal fitting dates, Churchward 3500g 26 May 1926, Collett 4000g 14th March 1929, Hawksworth 4000g 15th March 1956, Collett 4000g 29th December 1956, Hawksworth 4000g 28th March 1960. This locomotive reportedly also ran for a short period with Collett's '8 wheeled' tender but those details were not recorded on the official record card.

GWR 'Castle' class 4-6-0 No 4093 DUNSTER CASTLE backs out of Weymouth having arrived with a service from Bristol, 22nd July 1963. Note the Hawksworth 4000 gallon, 6 ton tender attached 28/03/60 and the stepped inside cylinder cover. *Rail Photoprints Collection*

Allocated Depots

PDN Old Oak Common	26/05/26	LA Laira	08/07/37	87E Landore	10/52
TYS Tyseley	15/10/32	PZ Penzance	03/38	87A Neath Court Sart	13/06/61
PDN Old Oak Common	24/10/32	LA Laira	13/05/39	87F Llanelly	11/02/63
CDF Cardiff Canton	12/33	BRD Bristol Bath Road	06/43	82B St Philips Marsh	09/64
NA Newton Abbot	02/03/36	84A Worcester	07/11/50		

Dunster Castle is a former motte and bailey castle, now a country house, in Somerset. The Tor top castle has been fortified since the late Anglo-Saxon period. It is now a National Trust property and is open to the public.

4094 DYNEVOR CASTLE

Introduced into service in May 1926. Diagram HA boiler fitted.

The locomotive's last 'Heavy Intermediate' overhaul including boiler (HB type) and tender change took place at Swindon Works between 11th January and 29th March 1960. The engine was withdrawn in March 1962 from Carmarthen depot (87G). Recorded mileage 1,881,886, service life 35 years, 9 months and 18 days. Disposal Swindon Works, April 1962.

Tender type principal fitted dates, Churchward 3500g May 1926, Collett 4000g 19th December 1929, Hawksworth 4000g 9th December 1952, Collett 4000g 28 June 1954, Hawksworth 4000g 29 March 1960.

Allocated Depots

PDN Old Oak Common	05/06/26	LA Laira	10/10/34	82A Bristol Bath Road	09/12/52
LA Laira	22/12/29	CDF Cardiff Canton	07/11/37	84A Stafford Road	07/54
NA Newton Abbot	26/03/31	CDF Stored	12/01/42	87E Landore	06/57
LA Laira	07/07/32	CDF Reinstated	07/11/42	87G Carmarthen	11/09/61
NA Newton Abbot	25/06/34				

Dynevor Castle (Dinefwr) in Wales overlooks the River Tywi near the town of Llandeilo, Carmarthenshire. Often described as a magical land of power and influence for more than 2,000 years, Dinefwr Park and Castle is an iconic place in the history of Wales. There are the signs of two forts which are thought to be evidence of a dominant Roman presence. The castle ruins and grounds are owned by the 'Wildlife Trust of South and West Wales' and lie within Dinefwr Park a designated National Trust area, accordingly the site is open to the public.

GWR 'Castle' class 4-6-0 No 4094 DYNEVOR CASTLE is seen with a train of fitted vans at Oxford station in July 1954. *David Anderson*

4095 HARLECH CASTLE

Introduced into service in June 1926. Diagram HA boiler fitted.

The locomotive's last 'Heavy Intermediate' overhaul including boiler (HB 6663) and tender change took place at Swindon Works between 14th December 1959 and 19th February 1960. The engine was withdrawn in December 1962 from Reading WR depot (81D). Recorded mileage 1,695,899, service life 36 years, 5 months and 26 days. Disposal R. A. Kings, Norwich, April 1964.

Tender type principal fitted dates, Churchward 3500g 16 June 1926, Collett 4000g 17th April 1929, Hawksworth 4th November 1950, Collett 4000g 4th February 1952, Hawksworth 4000g 21st August 1953, Collett 4000g 6th December 1955.

Allocated Depots

LA Laira	16/06/26	NA Newton Abbot	19/05/35	83B Taunton	22/04/60
NA Newton Abbot	16/05/28	LDR Landore	22/08/36	83D Laira	16/06/60
LA Laira	26/05/31	84C Banbury	07/06/52	83D Stored	14/03/62
NA Newton Abbot	09/31	87E Landore	17/06/52	83D Reinstated	06/10/62
LA Laira	18/01/34	83G Penzance	12/12/57	81D Reading WR	06/10/62

Harlech Castle in Gwynedd, Wales, is a medieval fortification, constructed on a spur of rock close to the Irish Sea. It was built by Edward I during his invasion of Wales between 1282 and 1289. Described as one of the finest examples of late 13th century/14th century military architecture in Europe. The sea originally came much closer to Harlech than it does in modern times, accordingly a water-gate and a long flight of steps leads down from the castle to the former shore, that walkway allowed the castle to be resupplied by sea during sieges. In keeping with Edward's other castles in North Wales, the architecture of Harlech has close to links to that found in the Kingdom of Savoy during the same period, an influence probably derived from the Savoy origins of the main architect, James of Saint George. The castle is a World Heritage Site, and it is open to the public.

GWR 'Castle' class 4-6-0 No 4095 HARLECH CASTLE is seen leaving Swindon in April 1956. *A.E. Bennett/Transport Treasury*

4096 HIGHCLERE CASTLE

Introduced into service in June 1926. Diagram HA boiler fitted.

The locomotive's last 'Heavy Intermediate' overhaul including boiler (HB 6660) and tender change took place at Swindon Works between 21st September and 17th November 1961. The engine was withdrawn in February 1963 from Old Oak Common depot (81A). Recorded mileage 1,958,378, service life 36 years, 7 months and 17 days. Disposal Hayes, Bridgend October 1963.

Tender type principal fitted dates, Churchward 3500g 23rd June 1926, Collett 4000g 9th March 1929, Hawksworth 4000g 26th November 1959, Collett 4000g 7th October 1961, Hawksworth 4000g 17th November 1961.

Allocated Depots

LA Laira	23/06/26	BRD Bristol Bath Road	18/11/35	Brd Weston-super-Mare	10/48
NA Newton Abbot	02/04/28	Brd Weston-super-Mare	03/41	BRD Bristol Bath Road	11/48
LA Laira	15/03/30	BRD Bristol Bath Road	25/07/41	81A Old Oak Common	20/03/58
NA Newton Abbot	04/04/31	Brd Weston-super-Mare	09/48	81D Reading WR	14/07/62
SRD Stafford Road	02/33	BRD Bristol Bath Road	10/48	81A Old Oak Common	12/12/62
LDR Landore	03/06/34				

Highclere Castle is a Victorian country house which stands in a magnificent park designed by Capability Brown. The 1,000-acre estate is in Hampshire, about 5 miles south of Newbury, Berkshire. Admittance to the castle is seasonal and by pre ordered ticket. This building became the main location during the filming of the television series Downton Abbey.

GWR 'Castle' class 4-6-0 No 4096 HIGHCLERE CASTLE is seen at Newton Abbot on 16th August 1957. Note GWR 'King' class No 6022 KING EDWARD III with the up 'Mayflower' working, standing in the adjacent platform. *Willy Hermiston/Transport Treasury*

4097 KENILWORTH CASTLE (Converted to double chimney)

Introduced into service in June 1926. Diagram HA boiler fitted. Double chimney and 4-row superheater fitted during the locomotive's last 'Heavy General' overhaul which included boiler (HD 7657) and tender change, and took place at Swindon Works between 16th April and 4th June 1958. The engine was withdrawn in May 1960 from Swindon depot (82C). Recorded mileage 1,713,966, service life 33 years, 10 months and 6 days. Disposal Swindon Works June 1960.

Tender type principal fitted dates, Churchward 3500g 30th June 1926, Dean 4000g 3rd May 1928, Collett 4000g 31st July 1929, Hawksworth 4000g 5th December 1956, Collett 4000g 4th June 1958.

GWR 'Castle' class 4-6-0 No 4097 KENILWORTH CASTLE is examined by the rostered driver before moving off shed at Taunton on 8th June 1955. Note the shorter single chimney which contrasts well with the taller chimney on the tank locomotive to the left, BR re-build style un-stepped inside cylinder cover and (81A) Old Oak Common shed plate. The 'Castle' is in the company of GWR Modified '4500' class 2-6-2T No 5503 which was at that time a Taunton (83B) engine. *David Anderson*

Allocated Depots

PDN Old Oak Common	30/06/26	BRD Bristol Bath Road	24/07/34	EXE Exeter	10/48
WOS Worcester	02/08/29	LA Laira	06/01/36	83D Laira	03/50
CARM Carmarthen	11/09/29	TR Truro	08/39	81A Old Oak Common	02/10/51
PDN Old Oak Common	23/12/30	NA Newton Abbot	31/12/39	87E Landore	06/57
CDF Cardiff Canton	06/01/31	LA Laira	24/05/45	82C Swindon	04/04/60
SRD Stafford Road	07/33	PZ Penzance	17/12/46		

Kenilworth Castle is located in the town of the same name in Warwickshire. Constructed from Norman through to Tudor times, the castle has been described by architectural historian Anthony Emery as "the finest surviving example of a semi-royal palace of the later middle ages, significant for its scale, form and quality of workmanship". The castle ruins and grounds are maintained by English Heritage and are open to the public.

4098 KIDWELLY CASTLE

Introduced into service in July 1926. Diagram HA boiler fitted.

The locomotive's last 'Heavy Intermediate' overhaul including boiler (HB 6664) and tender change took place at Swindon Works between 11th November 1960 and 27th January 1961. The engine was withdrawn in December 1963 from Old Oak Common depot (81A). Recorded mileage 1,723,879, service life 37 years, 4 months and 29 days. Disposal Cashmores, Great Bridge June 1964.

Tender type principal fitted dates, Churchward 3500g July 1926, Collett 4000g 26th November 1929, Hawksworth 22nd January 1953, Collett 4000g 2nd February 1955, Hawksworth 4000g 15th March 1957, Collett 4000g 28th November 1959.

GWR 'Castle' class 4-6-0 No 4098 KIDWELLY CASTLE is seen arriving at Paddington Station. Note the Hawksworth straight sided tender with which the engine was paired between 15/03/1957 and 28/11/1959.
Mike Morant Collection

Allocated Depots

PDN Old Oak Common	29/07/26	EXE Exeter	10/34	LA Laira	05/05/39
NA Newton Abbot	02/12/29	NA Newton Abbot	27/01/36	NA Newton Abbot	25/04/47
BRD Bristol Bath Road	25/10/30	TR Truro	06/03/37	83A NA Stored	14/03/62
NA Newton Abbot	12/11/30	EXE Exeter	18/08/37	81A OOC Reinstated	14/07/62
PDN Old Oak Common	06/33	LA Laira	24/09/38	81A Stored	28/12/63
TN Taunton	29/04/34	NA Newton Abbot	18/04/39		

Looks like a 'Big job broke out'! Three enginemen on top of the tender as Newton Abbot (83A) allocated GWR 'Castle' class 4-6-0 No 4098 KIDWELLY CASTLE takes water at Bristol Temple Meads station in this 1961 study. Note also Swindon built 'Warship' class No D820, possibly steam enthusiasts would say that the enemy is looking on!
Rail Photoprints Collection

Kidwelly Castle is a Norman castle overlooking the River Gwendraeth and the town of Kidwelly, in Carmarthenshire. The present remains of the castle include work dating from circa 1200 to circa 1476. The castle fell to the Welsh several times in the twelfth century and later in its history it was unsuccessfully besieged by forces of Owain Glyndŵr in 1403. The magnificent castle ruins are open to the public.

4099 KILGERRAN CASTLE

Introduced into service in August 1926. Diagram HA boiler fitted.

The locomotive's last 'Heavy Intermediate' overhaul including boiler (HB 6616) and tender change took place at Swindon Works between 13th February and 14th April 1961. The engine was withdrawn in September 1962 from Llanelly depot (87F). Recorded mileage 1,873,985, service life 36 years, 1 month and 18 days. Disposal Hayes, Bridgend September 1962.

Tender type principal fitted dates, Churchward 3500g August 1926, Collett 3500g 5th December 1929, Hawksworth 4000g 26th June 1959.

GWR 'Castle' 4-6-0 No 4099 KILGERRAN CASTLE is seen ex works at Swindon, in October 1957 after a 'Heavy Intermediate' overhaul. Note also No 7923 SPEKE HALL and Collett 'Pannier' tank No 6730. *Rail Photoprints Collection*

Allocated Depots

PDN Old Oak Common	03/08/26	PDN Old Oak Common	16/06/34	87E Landore	02/11/57
CDF Cardiff Canton	02/03/31	EXE Exeter	17/10/36	87A Neath Court Sart	13/05/61
NA Newton Abbot	18/04/32	NA Newton Abbot	18/12/43	87F Llanelly	14/07/62
CDF Cardiff Canton	07/33	83G Penzance	26/03/55		

Kilgerran Castle (Cilgerran Castle) is a 13th-century ruined castle located in Cilgerran, Pembrokeshire, the ruins stand on a rocky promontory above the River Teifi. The castle site is National Trust property, in the guardianship of Cadw: Welsh Historic Monuments Executive Agency, and it is open to the public.

GWR 'Castle' class 4-cylinder locomotives, Swindon Works 'Lot Numbers'

No 111 Originally built as Pacific THE GREAT BEAR Lot 171

No 4000 Originally built as 'Star' class 4-4-2 and then 4-6-0, Lot 161

No 100A1 Originally built as 'Star' class 4-6-0 Lot 168

No 4016 Originally built as 'Star' class 4-6-0 Lot 173

No 4032 Originally built as 'Star' class 4-6-0 Lot 180

No 4037 Originally built as 'Star' class 4-6-0 Lot 180

Nos 4073–4082 Lot 224 built 1923/24 (Average cost per engine £6835)

Nos 4083–4092 Lot 232 built 1925 (Average cost per engine £6644)

Nos 4093–4099 Lot 234 built 1926 (Average cost per engine £6719)

GWR Coat of Arms incorporating the shields of London (left) and Bristol (right)

On the Works

No 5003 LULWORTH CASTLE after withdrawal at Swindon, in August 1962. *John Chalcroft/Rail Photoprints*

No 5011 TINTAGEL CASTLE at Swindon following a 'Heavy Intermediate' overhaul, June 1955. Note the parallel barrel buffers and original design curved inside cylinder casing. *Rail Photoprints Collection*

No 5014 GOODRICH CASTLE at Swindon following a 'Heavy Intermediate' overhaul in 1957. Note tapered barrel buffers and box pattern inside cylinder casing, sandboxes under cab floor. The 'Castle' is in the company 'Hall' class No 5951 CLYFFE HALL. *Mike Morant Collection*

No 5035 COITY CASTLE at Swindon following a 'Heavy Intermediate' overhaul in 1954. The 'Castle' is in the company of BR 'Standard Britannia' class No 70016 ARIEL. *Rail Photoprints Collection*

Chapter 3

LOCOMOTIVES 5000–5042

5000 LAUNCESTON CASTLE
Introduced into service in August 1926. Diagram HA boiler fitted.

The locomotive's last 'Heavy General' overhaul including boiler (HC 7616) and tender change took place at Swindon Works between 22nd June and 18th September 1961. The engine was withdrawn in October 1964 from Oxley depot (2B). Recorded mileage 1,870,200 to the end of 1963, service life 38 years, 1 month and 2 days. Disposal Birds, Morriston, October 1965.

Tender types principal fitted dates, Churchward 3500g August 1926, Collett 4000g June 1928, Churchward 3500g 1929, Collett 4000g 20th June 1929, Hawksworth 4000g 17th October 1946, Collett 4000g 13th November 1946, Hawksworth 4000g 19th August 1952, Collett 4000g 23rd September 1953, Hawksworth 7th August 1958.

In 1926 the Great Western Railway loaned 'Castle' class 4-6-0 No 5000 LAUNCESTON CASTLE to the London, Midland and Scottish Railway where in the care of LMS engine crews the locomotive ran a series of trials between London and Carlisle, on the West Coast Main Line. The 'Castle' easily met the stringent trial criteria set by the LMS and the engine's performance statistics greatly impressed the LMS engineers and footplate crews. At the conclusion of the trials the LMS asked the GWR to accept from them an order for 50 of the Collett 4-6-0s, but those in charge of policy at Swindon Works declined acceptance of the order. The GWR then reportedly further upset the LMS by also refusing to lend them a set of 'Castle' class drawings. However, you could say that the LMS eventually got their Swindon technology when in 1932 they 'head hunted' and successfully recruited a new Chief Mechanical Engineer, in the person of Swindon Works trained locomotive engineer William A. Stanier.

On 15th September 1931 LAUNCESTON CASTLE created the first GWR World Record for a daily start to stop service, covering 77.25 miles at an average speed of 79.5mph in 58 minutes 28 seconds, with a top speed of 90mph. See also details for No 5006 TREGENA CASTLE.

Allocated Depots

PDN Old Oak Common	28/08/26	PDN Old Oak Common	02/49	85B Gloucester Horton Road	19/05/62
LA Laira	02/33	82A Bristol Bath Road	07/50	86C Hereford	02/11/62
PDN Old Oak Common	19/04/36	82C Swindon	03/11/55	2B Oxley	14/06/64
CARM Carmarthen	10/48				

Launceston Castle is located close to the town of the same name in Cornwall. The castle is a Norman motte and bailey castle raised by Robert, Count of Mortain, half-brother of William the Conqueror shortly after the Norman conquest, possibly as early as 1067. The English Heritage administered castle ruins and grounds are open to the public.

GWR 'Castle' class 4-6-0 No 5000 LAUNCESTON CASTLE, is seen in Swindon shed yard (82C) on 6th May 1956, note the original GWR inside cylinder casing. *Hugh Ballantyne/Rail Photoprints Collection*

GWR 'Castle' class 4-6-0 No 5001 LLANDOVERY CASTLE is seen in ex works condition at Didcot in August 1961. Note the BR style higher central step section of the 'Box' style inside cylinder cover, and also the mechanical lubricator located in front of the offside outside steam pipe. *David Anderson*

5001 LLANDOVERY CASTLE (Converted to double chimney)

Introduced into service in August 1926. Diagram HA boiler fitted.

For a short period during August 1931 this engine was fitted with smaller (6ft 6in diameter) driving wheels to evaluate possible performance gain. Double chimney and 4 row superheater fitted during the locomotive's last 'Heavy General' overhaul which included boiler (HD 9607) and tender change and took place at Swindon Works between 27th May and 28th July 1961. The engine was withdrawn in February 1963 from Old Oak Common depot (81A). Recorded mileage 1,885,495, service life 36 years, 6 months and 4 days. Disposal Cashmores, Great Bridge, May 1964.

Tender types principal fitted dates, Dean 4000g September 1926, Collett 4000g 22nd March 1930, Collett (8 Wheeled) 4000g October 1931, Collett 4000g 14th August 1936, Hawksworth 4000g 27th January 1954, Collett 5th October 1955, Hawksworth 6th January 1960.

Allocated Depots

PDN Old Oak Common	21/08/26	CDF Cardiff Canton	13/12/35	84G Shrewsbury	26/09/58
CDF Cardiff Canton	26/08/31	PDN Old Oak Common	15/12/37	81A Old Oak Common	02/08/60
PDN Old Oak Common	20/09/31	CDF Cardiff Canton	17/08/39	81A Stored	14/09/62
SRD Stafford Road	14/04/35	81A Old Oak Common	22/01/58	81A Reinstated	04/02/63

Llandovery Castle is a Welsh ruin in the town of Llandovery, Carmarthenshire, possibly dating from as early as 1116. The Normans began construction of the castle in 1116. It was attacked and partially destroyed by Welsh forces under Gruffydd ap Rhys. The castle then remained in Norman hands until 1158, when Rhys ap Gruffydd seized the castle from its owner. The castle then changed hands over several years, finally falling to the English under Edward I, in 1277. It was then briefly retaken by Welsh forces under Llywelyn ap Gruffudd in 1282. It was attacked during the Owain Glyndŵr rebellion in 1403 and left as a partial ruin. The castle fell into decline from the 14th century onward, and was never rebuilt. It occupies a hilltop site overlooking the town of the same name and the impressive castle site is open to the public.

GWR 'Castle' class 4-6-0 No 5001 LLANDOVERY CASTLE is seen at Oxford station with a train of fitted vans on 18th July 1959. Note the brass beading embellishments and stepped inside cylinder cover (BR rebuild). *Norman Preedy Collection/Rail Photoprints*

5002 LUDLOW CASTLE

Introduced into service in August 1926. Diagram HA boiler fitted.

The locomotive's last 'Heavy Intermediate' overhaul including boiler(HC 7638) and tender change took place at Swindon Works between 18th September and 6th November 1961.The engine was withdrawn in September 1964 from Southall depot (81C). Recorded mileage 1,817,218, service life 38 years and 4 days. Disposal Hayes, Bridgend, November 1964.

Tender types principal fitted dates Collett 4000g, Hawksworth 4000g 26th October 1951, Collett 4000g 10th September 1953, Hawksworth 4000g 25th February 1956, Collett 4000g 31st October 1959, Hawksworth 4000g 6th November 1961.

Allocated Depots

PDN Old Oak Common	28/08/26	SDN Swindon	12/01/41	82C Swindon	08/02/60
CDF Cardiff Canton	18/06/29	LDR Landore	02/41	82C Stored	24/09/62
LA Laira	29/08/30	CARM Carmarthen	07/49	81D Reading WR. Reinstated	03/63
NA Newton Abbot	23/12/32	87E Landore	10/01/50	82B St Philips Marsh	30/11/63
CDF Cardiff Canton	28/01/34	82C Swindon	03/01/58	81D Reading WR	13/04/64
LDR Landore	13/06/39	85A Worcester	12/11/59	81C Southall	22/06/64

Ludlow Castle is a partly ruined and uninhabited medieval building in the Shropshire town of the same name. It stands on a high point overlooking the River Teme. The castle was in all probability founded by Norman invader Walter de Lacy around 1075. The castle changed hands several times but was always closely associated with the development of the town and its surrounding area.

When the English Civil War broke out in 1642, between the supporters of King Charles and those of Parliament, Ludlow and the surrounding region supported the Royalists. The ruins and grounds are open to the public.

GWR 'Castle' class 4-6-0 No 5002 LUDLOW CASTLE, is seen on a through road at Bristol Temple Meads station, circa 1959. The higher central step on the inside cylinder casing is clearly visible (BR rebuild). *Rail Photoprints Collection*

5003 LULWORTH CASTLE

Introduced into service in May 1927. Diagram HA boiler fitted.

The locomotive's last 'Heavy Intermediate' overhaul including boiler (HB 6653) and tender change took place at Swindon Works between 6th February and 26th April 1960. The engine was withdrawn in August 1962 from Newton Abbot depot (83A). Recorded mileage 1,698,751, service life 35 years, 3 months and 1 day. Disposal Cashmores, Newport, December 1962.

Tender types principal fitted dates, Collett 4000g May 1927, Hawksworth 4000g 26th April 1960.

Allocated Depots

PDN Old Oak Common	28/05/27	EXE Exeter	03/41	83C Exeter	27/02/51
CDF Cardiff Canton	09/06/34	LA Laira	14/07/41	83D Laira	09/02/57
NA Newton Abbot	13/03/36	EXE Exeter	18/09/41	87G Carmarthen	11/12/57
TN Taunton	05/37	SDN Swindon	07/08/42	86C Cardiff Canton	20/03/58
EXE Exeter	17/08/37	TN Taunton	27/08/42	83A Newton Abbot	17/03/59
SDN Swindon	20/01/41				

Lulworth Castle in Dorset is situated south of Wool, and is an early 17th-century mock castle. The stone building has now been re-built as a museum. The castle, which is surrounded by Lulworth Park and estate, is open to the public.

GWR 'Castle' class 4-6-0 No 5003 LULWORTH CASTLE is seen passing Didcot in the summer of 1961 with a train of milk tank empties bound for the West Country. Note that the locomotive's Hawksworth tender is filled with Ovoids*, not conventional coal. *David Anderson* *Anthracite based solid fuel, sometimes called smokeless ovals.*

5004 LLANSTEPHAN CASTLE

Introduced into service in June 1927. Diagram HA boiler fitted.

The locomotive's last 'Heavy Intermediate' overhaul including boiler (HB 6648) and tender change took place at Swindon Works between 5th May and 13th July 1960. The engine was withdrawn in April 1962 from Neath Court Sart depot (87A). Recorded mileage 1,854,704, service life 34 years, 9 months and 18 days. Disposal Swindon Works, June 1962.

Tender types principal fitted dates, Churchward 3500g June 1927, Collett 4000g 15th April 1929, Hawksworth 4000g 3rd July 1952, Collett 4000g 4th May 1954.

Allocated Depots

TN Taunton	16/06/27	CDF Cardiff Canton	04/04/34	86C Cardiff Canton	20/09/57
LA Laira	07/07/27	PDN Old Oak Common	21/12/35	87E Landore	20/03/58
NA Newton Abbot	21/07/30	84G Shrewsbury	06/56	87A Neath Court Sart	03/04/62

Llanstephan Castle (Llansteffan) stands on a headland guarding the mouth of the river Tywi in Carmarthenshire, close to the village of Llansteffan. The Norman invaders of Wales established an earth-and-timber enclosure on the site of an Iron Age fort, whilst the later masonry castle was built between the 12th and 14th centuries. The impressive castle ruins can be visited by the public.

GWR 'Castle' class 4-6-0 No 5004 LLANSTEPHAN CASTLE is seen approaching Abergavenny with a northbound 'North & West' express, in the summer of 1958. *Rail Photoprints Collection*

5005 MANORBIER CASTLE

Introduced into service in June 1927. Diagram HA boiler fitted.

The locomotive's last 'Heavy General' overhaul including boiler (HB 6631) and tender change took place at Swindon Works between 27th February and 27th May 1956, also 'Heavy Intermediate' only took place between 28th January to 6th March 1958. The engine was withdrawn in February 1960 from Old Oak Common depot (81A). Recorded mileage 1,731,868, service life 32 years, 7 months and 20 days.

Disposal Swindon Works, March 1960.

Tender types principal fitted dates, Collett 4000g 4th June 1927, Hawksworth 4000g 9th February 1953, Collett 4000g 11th July 1953.

In order not to be completely outdone by the other railway companies, and in line with the 1930s fascination with steam locomotive streamlining the Great Western board of directors instructed Collett to design suitable embellishments for 'Castle' and 'King' class locomotives. Streamlining had first been introduced by the GWR in the form of the streamlined diesel powered 'Railcar' No 1, which first ran on 1st December 1933. However, the resultant 1935 steam locomotive design could at best only be described as being semi-streamlined, and perchance not overly imaginative. The chosen 'Castle' class locomotive was No 5005 MANORBIER CASTLE, which entered Swindon works for a 'General' overhaul between 16th January and 15th April 1935 and the streamlining was applied during that 90 day period.

The most striking (some may say incongruous) feature of the Swindon streamlined design was the bullet nose fitted to the smokebox. Other modifications included fairings behind the chimney and safety valve casings. Curved spectacle plates were added to the front of the cabs and additionally an extension piece fabricated which aligned the top of the tender with a cab roof extension. To complete the effect 'V' fronted cabs and plating added in order to aid air smoothing.

The casings at the front end of No 5005 caused problems in service, namely with overheating and restricted accessibility. Importantly the 'Castle' class engines utilised a system of condensing steam and oil in order to provide lubrication for the inside cylinder valve guides. The fairings had the effect of reducing the amount of oil condensed to such a low level that it became ineffective as a lubricant. Simply put, the deposit of oil on the slide bars was so small that it effectively dried out. Measures subsequently taken to rectify this problem included replacing the usual two-feed oil boxes with repositioned four-feed units.

However the streamlining was not destined to be long lasting in service and by the end of 1935 the front end air smoothing and cab roof extensions had been removed from the engine. There was piecemeal removal of embellishments between 1939 and 1945 and by 1947 the streamlining was gone, No 5005 MANORBIER CASTLE also received a new normal square front end cab in that year.

Streamlined GWR 'Castle' class 4-6-0 No 5005 MANORBIER CASTLE seen at Leamington Spa with the full casing and cab roof extension in May 1935. Note the straight nameplate on the splasher. *Mike Bentley Collection*

Allocated Depots

PDN Old Oak Common	11/06/27	LA Laira	01/31	81A Old Oak Common	20/03/58
TN Taunton	09/07/30	PDN Old Oak Common	21/05/32	82C Swindon	26/09/58
LA Laira	09/30	CDF Cardiff Canton	21/12/45		
TN Taunton	23/12/30	83A Newton Abbot	12/56		

Manorbier Castle is a Norman castle located in the village of Manorbier, five miles south-west of Tenby in Pembrokeshire. It was the original seat of the Anglo-Norman de Barry family. The stunning castle remains were featured in the television adaption of 'The Lion, The Witch, and The Wardrobe', and they are open to the public.

Fully streamlined GWR 'Castle' class 4-6-0 No 5005 MANORBIER CASTLE, is seen at speed in this superb 1935 image. *Great Western Society*

Streamlined GWR 'Castle' class 4-6-0 No 5005 MANORBIER CASTLE seen in 1935. The shedmaster is pointing out the location of the front inspection cover. Note the fireman on top of the tender, trimming the coal was not a straightforward job when the tender plating was fitted. *Great Western Society*

GWR 'Castle' class 4-6-0 No 5005 MANORBIER CASTLE seen at Old Oak Common (PDN) in September 1935. Note that the front end air smoothing and cab roof extensions had already been removed. *Rail Photoprints Collection*

GWR 'Castle' class 4-6-0 No 5005 MANORBIER CASTLE without streamlining and with original GWR style inside cylinder casing is seen at Old Oak Common depot (81A) in May 1958. The modified design of curved steam pipe which over time replaced the original straight pattern in order to eliminate occasional incidences of fractures can clearly be seen. Note also the special type of snifting valve on the centre cylinder cover which is a survivor from the locomotives streamlined days. *Keith Langston Collection*

5006 TREGENNA CASTLE

Introduced into service in June 1927. Diagram HA boiler fitted.

On 6 June 1932 the 'Cheltenham Flyer' train hauled by No 5006 covered the 77.25 miles from Swindon to Paddington at an average speed of 81.68 mph start-to-stop, breaking the previous GWR record and setting a new world record for steam traction. See also details for No 5000 LAUNCESTON CASTLE.

The locomotive's last 'Heavy General' overhaul including boiler (HB 6656) and tender change took place at Swindon Works between 9th May and 13th July 1960. The engine was withdrawn in April 1962 from Carmarthen depot (87G). Recorded mileage 1,812,966, service life 34 years, 9 months and 23 days. Disposal Cashmores, Newport, April 1963.

Tender types principal fitted dates, Churchward 3500g June 1927, Collett 4000g 20th June 1929, Hawksworth 4000g 11th July 1953, Collett 4000g 8th September 1954, Hawksworth 4000g 1st August 1958, Collett 4000g 4th October 1958.

Allocated Depots

PDN Old Oak Common	11/06/27	WEY Weymouth GWR	05/38	87G Carmarthen	20/03/58
LA Laira	06/33	BRD Bristol Bath Road	06/38	87E Landore	13/07/60
LDR Landore	29/06/34	LDR Landore	12/42	87F Llanelly	06/07/61
PDN Old Oak Common	17/12/35	CDF Cardiff Canton	07/48	87G Carmarthen	11/09/61
BRD Bristol Bath Road	24/04/38	81A Old Oak Common	06/54		

Tregenna Castle in St Ives, Cornwall, was built by John Stephens in the 18th century. The estate was sold in 1871 and became a hotel, which was for a time leased and then owned by the GWR. It is still in use as a hotel today.

GWR 'Castle' class 4-6-0 No 5006 TREGENNA CASTLE (stepped inside cylinder casing) is seen on 'South Wales Pullman' duty, entering Newport in August 1961. Note the burnished front buffers. *Hugh Ballantyne/Rail Photoprints Collection*

5007 ROUGEMONT CASTLE

Introduced into service in June 1927. Diagram HA boiler fitted. .

The locomotive's last 'Heavy Intermediate' overhaul including boiler (HC 7605) and tender change took place at Swindon Works between 9th May and 5th August 1960. The engine was withdrawn in September 1962 from Gloucester Horton Road depot (85B). Recorded mileage 1,854,951, service life 35 years, 2 months and 1 day. Disposal Cashmores, Newport, December 1962.

Tender types principal fitted dates, Churchward 3500g, Collett 4000g 23rd March 1929, Hawksworth 4000g 26th July 1950, Collett 4000g 29th March 1955, Hawksworth 4000g 5th August 1960.

Allocated Depots

LA Laira	30/06/27	LDR Landore	05/05/38	81A Old Oak Common	18/02/57
PDN Old Oak Common	15/10/32	SDN Swindon	15/03/40	82C Swindon	02/02/59
LA Laira	08/03/35	CDF Cardiff Canton	30/03/40	85B Gloucester Horton Rd	09/03/61
SRD Stafford Road	27/06/35				

Rougemont Castle, (Exeter Castle) is in Devon, England. It was built into the northern corner of the Roman city walls circa 1068, following Exeter's rebellion against William the Conqueror. In 1136 it was besieged for three months by King Stephen. An outer bailey, of which little now remains, was added later in the 12th century. The castle is mentioned in Shakespeare's play 'Richard III'. Devon's county court was located there from at least 1607, and the four Devon Witches, the last people in England to be executed for witchcraft, were tried there in the 1680s. In 2014 the 'listed status' castle/court buildings were in private ownership, with the development of them reportedly planned.

GWR 'Castle' class 4-6-0 No 5007 ROUGEMONT CASTLE seen at Exeter St David's on 17th August 1957, still with original GWR inside cylinder casing. *Norman Preedy Collection/Rail Photoprints .co.uk*

5008 RAGLAN CASTLE (Converted to double chimney)

Introduced into service in June 1927. Diagram HA boiler fitted.

Double chimney and 4-row superheater fitted during the locomotive's last 'Heavy Intermediate' overhaul which included boiler (HD 9601) and tender change, and took place at Swindon Works between 27th January and 27th March 1961. The engine was withdrawn in September 1962 from Old Oak Common depot (81A). Recorded mileage 1,798,646, service life 35 years, 2 months and 8 days. Disposal Cashmores, Great Bridge, December 1962.

Tender types principal fitted dates, Churchward 3500g June 1927, Collett 4000g 22nd July 1929, Hawksworth 4000g 16th January 1956, Collett 4000g 23rd March 1957, Hawksworth 18th June 1960.

Allocated Depots

LA Laira	30/06/27	WOS Worcester	06/12/38	84A Stafford Road	07/50
PDN Old Oak Common	30/12/30	PDN Old Oak Common	01/39	81A Old Oak Common	11/56
CARM Carmarthen	23/12/30	SDN Swindon	21/10/49	87G Carmarthen	30/12/56
CDF Cardiff Canton	09/03/32	81F Oxford	04/02/50	81A Old Oak Common	30/01/57
PDN Old Oak Common	06/33				

Raglan Castle is a late medieval castle located just north of the village of the same name in Monmouthshire. The ruins date from between the 15th and early 17th-centuries. During the English Civil War the castle was taken by Parliamentary forces in 1646. The occupying forces deliberately put the fortress beyond military use, but it was later partly rebuilt. The site is open to the public.

GWR 'Castle' class 4-6-0 No 5008 RAGLAN CASTLE (original GWR inside cylinder casing) is seen approaching Chippenham with a Paddington–Bristol service, circa 1955. *Rail Photoprints Collection*

5009 SHREWSBURY CASTLE

Introduced into service in July 1927. Diagram HA boiler fitted.

    The locomotive's last 'Heavy General' overhaul including boiler (HB 6664) and tender change took place at Swindon Works between 17th May and 7th November 1957. The engine was withdrawn in October 1960 from Swindon depot (82C). Recorded mileage 1,708,246, service life 33 years, 3 months and 18 days. Disposal Swindon Works, December 1960. Tender types principal fitted dates, Churchward 3500g June 1927, Collett 4000g 14th August 1929, Hawksworth 4000g 7th February 1957, Collett 4000g 7th November 1957.

Allocated Depots

LA Laira	06/07/27	LA Laira	07/12/35	NA Newton Abbot	12/06/37
NA Newton Abbot	09/27	EXE Exeter	01/36	LA Laira	03/03/39
PDN Old Oak Common	19/09/29	RDG Reading WR	06/03/36	NA Newton Abbot	19/11/43
LDR Landore	08/07/32	PDN Old Oak Common	05/04/36	LA Laira	10/12/43
LA Laira	20/12/34	EXE Exeter	05/36	SDN Swindon	10/48
RDG Reading WR	04/12/35				

Shrewsbury Castle is a red sandstone castle in the Shropshire town of the same name, which was founded circa 1070. In 1138, King Stephen successfully besieged the castle, held by William FitzAlan for the Empress Maud during the period known as 'The Anarchy'. Since 1985, the castle has housed the Shropshire Regimental Museum, with artifacts from the King's Shropshire Light Infantry. The museum was attacked by the IRA on 25 August 1992 and extensive damage was caused and the museum closed but after restoration re-opened in 1995. Little of this original physical structure remains but the castle site is situated on a hill directly above the modern day Shrewsbury railway station, and it is open to the public.

GWR 'Castle' class 4-6-0 5009 SHREWSBURY CASTLE (original GWR inside cylinder casing) is seen passing Thingley Junction with a Swindon–Bristol service, in 1959. *Rail Photoprints Collection*

5010 RESTORMEL CASTLE

Introduced into service in July 1927. Diagram HA boiler fitted.

The locomotive's last 'Heavy Intermediate' overhaul including boiler (HB 6605) and tender change took place at Swindon Works between 6th May and 17th June 1958. The engine was withdrawn in October 1959 from Reading WR depot (81D). Recorded mileage 1,684,146, service life 32 years, 2 months and 9 days. Disposal Swindon Works, November 1959.

Tender types principal fitted dates, Churchward 3500g July 1927, Collett 4000g 22nd March 1929, Hawksworth 11th June 1948, Collett 4000g 8th May 1950, Hawksworth 4000g 25th January 1952, Collett 4000g 17th May 1956, Hawksworth 4000g June 1958.

Allocate Depots

PDN Old Oak Common	26/07/27	LDR Landore	08/38	84A Stafford Road	08/05/50
CDF Cardiff Canton	26/07/30	CDF Cardiff Canton	10/38	84A Stored	23/05/50
LA Laira	15/06/31	SRD Stafford Road	26/04/40	84A Reinstated	26/07/50
NA Newton Abbot	19/12/33	CDF Cardiff Canton	12/40	83A Laira	04/03/53
CDF Cardiff Canton	24/04/34	SDN Swindon	20/01/43	84A Stafford Road	14/05/53
PDN Old Oak Common	14/12/35	CDF Cardiff Canton	04/43	81A Old Oak Common	20/03/58
CDF Cardiff Canton	31/12/35	LDR Landore	11/06/48	81D Reading WR	10/01/59

Restormel Castle is a 13th century circular fortress sited on high ground overlooking the river Fowey near Lostwithiel, Cornwall. The 13th century circular shell-keep still enclose the principal rooms of the castle which are in remarkably good condition. It stands on an earlier Norman defensive mound and is surrounded by a deep dry ditch, situated on a high spur it is beside the river Fowey. Twice visited by the Black Prince Restormel saw its final action during the English Civil War, in 1644. It commands fantastic views and is a popular picnic spot. The ruins of the Norman castle are in the care of English Heritage and open to the public.

GWR 'Castle' class 4-6-0 No 5010 RESTORMEL CASTLE is seen being serviced at Old Oak Common (81A) on 20th July 1958. Note the Hawksworth tender, also the oil can at the front end of the running plate, brass embellishments and original GWR inside cylinder casing. *A.E Bennett/Transport Treasury*

5011 TINTAGEL CASTLE

Introduced into service in July 1927. Diagram HA boiler fitted.

The locomotive's last 'Heavy General' overhaul including boiler (HB 6679) and tender change took place at Swindon Works between 8th October and 9th December 1960. The engine was withdrawn in September 1962 from Old Oak Common depot (81A). Recorded mileage 1,732,565, service life 35 years, 1 month and 13 days. Disposal Cashmores, Great Bridge, December 1962.

Tender types principal fitted dates, Collett 4000g 4th April 1929, Churchward 3500g 4th January 1930, Collett 4000g 1st July 1930, Hawksworth 4000g 15th September 1953, Collett 4000g 14th June 1954, Hawksworth 4000g 21st December 1960.

Allocated depots

NA Newton Abbot	22/07/27	LA Laira	10/34	PZ Penzance	11/03/41
CDF Cardiff Canton	29/07/30	NA Newton Abbot	13/12/36	NA Newton Abbot	30/07/41
NA Newton Abbot	01/33	EXE Exeter	04/39	81D Reading WR	03/05/60
EXE Exeter	03/03/34	LA Laira	19/12/39	81A Old Oak Common	04/09/60
NA Newton Abbot	04/34				

Tintagel Castle is a medieval fortification sited on the peninsula of Tintagel Island, adjacent to the Cornish village of the same name, the castle has a long association with Arthurian legends. The ruins are set high on the rugged North Cornwall coast, accordingly visitors can enjoy dramatic sea views. Steeped in myths and mystery, this is a spectacular place which has inspired artists and writers throughout history and it has long been associated with the legend of King Arthur. It has been a tourist attraction since the mid-19th century and is now managed by English Heritage and open to the public.

GWR 'Castle' class 4-6-0 No 5011 TINTAGEL CASTLE is seen at Oxford (81F) circa 1961 coupled with a Hawksworth 4000g tender. The ash clearing operation appears to have 'stopped for tea', note the discarded shovel and pile of smokebox ash on the buffer beam and the BR pattern inside cylinder cover, without valve spindle oil cup in this image. *David Anderson*

5012 BERRY POMEROY CASTLE

Introduced into service in July 1927. Diagram HA boiler fitted.

The locomotive's last 'Heavy General' overhaul including boiler (HB 6633) and tender change took place at Swindon Works between 26th October 1959 and 1st January 1960. Circa 1947 the brass beading was removed from the front end of the cabs on all engines up to and including No 5012. The engine was withdrawn in April 1962 from Oxford depot (81F). Recorded mileage 1,625,965, service life 34 years, 8 months and 28 days. Disposal Cashmores, Newport, December 1962.

Tender types principal fitted dates, Churchward 3500g 1929, Collett 4000g 4th September 1929, Hawksworth 14th October 1949, Collett 4000g 19th May 1951.

Allocated Depots

NA Newton Abbot	27/07/27	PDN Old Oak Common	04/07/32	83D Laira	03/50
Carmarthen	13/09/29	CDF Cardiff Canton	01/33	86C Cardiff Canton	11/52
PDN Old Oak Common	10/10/31	EXE Exeter	25/08/39	81F Oxford	12/52
NA Newton Abbot	15/06/32				

Berry Pomeroy Castle is situated near to Totnes in Devon. The ruins have their origins in the 15th century and when originally designed the mansion was intended to be 'the most spectacular house in the county'. However it was abandoned circa 1700 without ever being completed. The English Heritage administered site is open to the public.

GWR 'Castle' class 4-6-0 No 5012 BERRY POMEROY CASTLE is seen preparing to leave Oxford with a Paddington-Hereford/Worcester service in July 1961. The cab side window, number plate and wheel splasher copper embellishments are clearly seen in this image. *David Anderson*

5013 ABERGAVENNY CASTLE

Introduced into service in July 1932. Diagram HB boiler fitted. The first of the class to be built with a larger inside cylinder box with associated valve cylinder lubricator. Front of cab edge brass beading retained. The outside cylinder valve spindle lubrication oil reservoir on the framing became standard on all further members of the class. The locomotive's last 'Heavy General' overhaul took place at Swindon Works between August and October 1958, last tender change 14/07/62 and boiler (HB 6615) modification October 1960. The engine was withdrawn in July 1962 from Llanelly depot (87F). Recorded mileage 1,525,662, service life 30 years, 3 days. Disposal Hayes Bridgend, August 1962.

Tender types principal fitted dates, Collett 4000g June 1932, Hawksworth 4000g 27th November 1951, Collett 4000g 17th June 1955, Hawksworth 4000g 3rd November 1955, Collett 4000g 1st February 1957, Hawksworth 4000g 21st October 1960, Collett 4000g 14th July 1962.

Allocated Depots

NA Newton Abbot	27/06/32	PZ Penzance	07/39	87G Carmarthen	08/51
LA Laira	07/33	NA Newton Abbot	30/08/39	87E Landore	01/52
EXE Exeter	03/07/34	PZ Penzance	19/09/39	87A Neath Court Sart	17/06/61
NA Newton Abbot	31/12/35	LDR Landore	11/03/40	87F Llanelly	06/62
LA Laira	02/36				

Abergavenny Castle is a ruined castle in the market town of Abergavenny, Monmouthshire it was established by the Norman lord Hamelin de Ballon circa 1087. It was the site of a massacre of Welsh noblemen in 1175, and was attacked during the early 15th century Glyndŵr Rising. William Camden, the 16th century antiquary, said that the castle "has been oftner stain'd with the infamy of treachery, than any other castle in Wales." It has been a Grade I listed building since 1952. The town's museum is adjacent to the castle site and both are open to the public.

GWR 'Castle' class No 5013 ABERGAVENNY CASTLE (stepped inside cylinder cover) passes Patchway with the 'South Wales Pullman' during November 1960, no headboard carried. Locomotive No 5013 was the first of the class to be built with a compartment for housing short fire irons which was accessible from the cab, the housing was situated between the left hand (nearside) centre and trailing driving splasher. *Rail Photoprints Collection*

5014 GOODRICH CASTLE

Introduced into service in July 1932. Diagram HB boiler fitted.

The locomotive's last 'Heavy Intermediate' overhaul including boiler (HB 6681) and tender change took place at Swindon Works between 11th December 1961 and 1st March 1962. The engine was withdrawn in February 1965 from Tyseley depot (2A). Recorded mileage (up to end 1963) 1,615,297, service life 32 years, 6 months and 24 days. Disposal Cashmores, Great Bridge, May 1965.

Tender types principal fitted dates, Collett 4000g June 1932, Hawksworth 4000g 15th August 1952, Collett 4000g 4th June 1954, Hawksworth 4000g 26th January 1959, Collett 4000g 1st March 1962, Hawksworth 4000g 8th September 1962.

Changing times, GWR 'Castle' class 4-6-0 No 5014 GOODRICH CASTLE is seen being serviced at Chester in the summer of 1962. The brass beading on the cab front edges and centre cylinder cover step can be seen, as can the short fire iron compartment. Note the BP oil tankers and the Diesel Multiple Units outside the new depot buildings. The embankment in the background carried the Cheshire Lines route, Manchester Central via Northwich to Chester Northgate Station. *Jim Carter/Rail Photoprints*

Allocated Depots

LA Laira	07/07/32	PDN Old Oak Common	19/12/35	Brd Weston-super-Mare	10/42
NA Newton Abbot	12/33	BRD Bristol Bath Road	16/07/38	PDN Old Oak Common	12/42
EXE Exeter	03/34	Brd Weston-super-Mare	08/42	2A Tyseley	16/06/64
NA Newton Abbot	04/34	BRD Bristol Bath Road	09/42		

GWR 'Castle' class 4-6-0 No 5014 GOODRICH CASTLE is seen at Platform 8 Paddington station on 6th July 1963. Note the new BR/WR units standing at an adjacent platform. The larger stepped inside cylinder cover with associated valve cylinder lubricator is clearly visible. *Rail Photoprints Collection*

Goodrich Castle is a Norman medieval castle situated to the north of the village of Goodrich in Herefordshire. It was praised by William Wordsworth who described it as the 'noblest ruin in Herefordshire'. The English Heritage owned site is open to the public.

5015 KINGSWEAR CASTLE

Introduced into service in July 1932. Diagram HB boiler fitted.

The locomotive's last 'Heavy General' overhaul including boiler (HC 7631) and tender change took place at Swindon Works between 12th May and 25th July1961. The engine was withdrawn in April 1963 from Cardiff East Dock depot (88L). Recorded mileage 1,554,288, service life 30 years, 9 months and 16 days. Disposal T.W. Ward, Sheffield, January 1964.

Tender types principal fitted dates, Collett 4000g July 1932, Hawksworth 4000g 2nd May 1950, Collett 4000g 12th October 1951, Hawksworth 4000g 13th October 1959, Collett 4000g 25th July 1961.

Allocated Depots

CDF Cardiff Canton	09/07/32	4A Shrewsbury	23/05/42	82A Bristol Bath Road	20/03/58
EXE Exeter	05/07/34	SRD Stafford Road	16/10/45	87E Landore	16/06/60
LA Laira	26/12/35	SDN Swindon	27/01/47	81A Old Oak Common	25/01/61
4A Shrewsbury	11/12/38	SRD Stafford Road	03/04/47	88L Cardiff East Dock	04/10/63
PDN Old Oak Common	28/06/40				

Kingswear Castle in Devon was built between 1491 and 1502 for use as a coastal artillery tower, incorporating heavy cannon. Owing to the limited range of cannon at the time, the fort at Kingswear was designed to work alongside Dartmouth Castle on the opposite bank of the river Dart, so that between them they could provide complete cover of the narrow entrance into Dartmouth Harbour. In the present day the structure is owned by the Landmark Trust and is available to rent as a holiday let, otherwise there is no public access.

GWR 'Castle' class 4-6-0 No 5015 KINGSWEAR CASTLE is seen passing Lapworth with an up express, on 14th April 1957. *Norman Preedy Collection/Rail Photoprints*

5016 MONTGOMERY CASTLE (Converted to double chimney)

Introduced into service in July 1932. Diagram HB boiler fitted. Double chimney and 4-row superheater fitted during the locomotive's last 'Heavy General' overhaul which also included boiler (HD 7659), tender change, and took place at Swindon Works between 22nd December 1960 and 16th February 1961. The engine was withdrawn in September 1962 from Llanelly depot (87F). Recorded mileage 1,480,896, service life 30 years, 1 month and 26 days.

Disposal Hayes, Bridgend, December 1962.

Tender types principal fitted dates, Collett 4000g July 1932, Hawksworth 4000g 29th October 1946, Collett 4000g 27th July 1948, Hawksworth 4000g 11th October 1954, Collett 4000g 5th May 1955, Hawksworth 4000g 16th February 1961.

Allocated Depots

PDN Old Oak Common	09/07/32	LA Laira	19/01/37	83D Laira	11/10/54
NA Newton Abbot	12/33	PZ Penzance	01/38	87E Landore	12/54
PZ Penzance	04/36	LDR Landore	03/05/38	87E Llanelly	13/06/61

Montgomery Castle is a ruined stone and masonry castle overlooking the town of Montgomery in Powys. It is one of several Norman castles which were built on the border between Wales and England. The walled town of Montgomery was attacked, sacked and burned by the Welsh forces of Owain Glyndŵr in 1402, however, the stone fortress held out against the attack. The castle site is open to the public.

GWR 'Castle' class 4-6-0 No 5016 MONTGOMERY CASTLE (stepped inside cylinder cover) is seen passing Swindon Works at the head of a down South Wales express, in 1959. Rail Photoprints Collection

5017 ST. DONAT'S CASTLE renamed **THE GLOUCESTERSHIRE REGIMENT 28th 61st** on 26th April 1954

Introduced into service in July 1932. Diagram HB boiler fitted.

The locomotive's last 'Heavy General' overhaul, including boiler (HB 6665) change took place at Swindon Works between 27th June and 7th September 1960. The engine was withdrawn in September 1962 from Gloucester Horton Road depot (85B). Recorded mileage 1,598,851, service life 30 years, 2 months and 10 days.

Disposal Cashmores, Newport, December 1962.

Tender types principal fitted dates, Collett 4000g July 1932, Collett (8 Wheeled) 4000g 23rd June 1944, Collett 4000g 17th December 1945, Hawksworth 4000g 28th January 1950, Collett 4000g 29th January 1952, Hawksworth 4000g 5th January 1954, Collett 4000g 12th January 1959.

GWR 'Castle' class 4-6-0 No 5017 is seen at Bristol Temple Meads station as St DONAT'S CASTLE in this 1946 image. Note the number stencilled on the right hand front of the buffer beam and the solid looking GWR tapered barrel buffers and 'Box' style inside cylinder cover with round topped front edge.
Cresselley Photos

Allocated Depots

TN Taunton	11/07/32	NA Newton Abbot	01/35	SDN Swindon	14/02/47
CDF Cardiff Canton	09/11/32	LA Laira	05/03/36	WOS Worcester	04/47
PDN Old Oak Common	11/33	NA Newton Abbot	08/07/37	85B Gloucester Horton Road	10/51
LA Laira	29/12/34	WOS Worcester	01/04/39		

GWR 'Castle' class 4-6-0 No 5017 THE GLOUCESTERSHIRE REGIMENT 28TH 61ST is seen at Paddington station in 1958 after arriving with an express from Gloucester. Note the regimental badge on the centre wheel splasher and the Hawksworth tender. In this instance the loco now shows the later un-stepped design of inside cylinder cover.
Cresselley Photos

St. Donat's Castle is a medieval castle in the Vale of Glamorgan, overlooking the Bristol Channel in the village of St Donat's near Llantwit Major, to the west of Cardiff. Since 1962 the castle has housed the international 'Sixth form Atlantic College'. **The Gloucestershire Regiment** was an infantry regiment of the British Army, they reportedly carried more battle honours on their regimental colours than any other British Army regiment of the line. The regiment was formed in Portsmouth in 1694 by Colonel John Gibson and named the 28th Regiment of Foot in 1751, it was renamed the 28th (North Gloucestershire) Regiment of Foot in 1782. On 1st July 1881 the regiment amalgamated with the 61st (South Gloucestershire) Regiment of Foot to form the two-battalion Gloucestershire Regiment.

5018 ST. MAWES CASTLE

Introduced into service in July 1932. Diagram HB boiler fitted.

The locomotive's last 'Heavy General' overhaul including boiler (HC 7632) and tender change took place at Swindon Works between 2nd September and 1st November 1961. The engine was withdrawn in March 1964 from Reading WR depot (81D). Recorded mileage 1,503,642, service life 31 years, 7 months and 11 days. Disposal Cohens, Kettering November 1964.

Tender types principal fitted dates, Collett 4000g July 1932, Hawksworth 4000g 9th March 1955, Collett 4000g 1st July 1956, Hawksworth 4000g 1st November 1961, Collett 4000g March 1964.

Allocated Depots

PDN Old Oak Common	28/07/32	82A Bristol Bath Road	07/07/50	86C Cardiff Canton	10/52
NA Newton Abbot	23/01/36	82C Swindon	23/09/50	85B Gloucester Horton Road	10/52
PDN Old Oak Common	07/04/36	85B Gloucester Horton Road	01/51	81D Reading WR	03/58
SRD Stafford Road	02/45				

St. Mawes Castle (Henrician Castle or Device Fort) is a sister castle to the larger Pendennis Castle; they were both built as part of a defensive chain by King Henry VIII to protect the south coast of Cornwall, circa 1540-1545. The English Heritage owned building is open to the public.

GWR 'Castle' class 4-6-0 No 5018 ST.MAWES CASTLE is seen without a safety valve cover. Note also the higher central step section of the inside cylinder cover. No 5018 approaches Westbury with a service from Reading, during May 1963. The Hawksworth tender looks to be filled with anthracite ovoids. *Rail Photoprints Collection*

5019 TREAGO CASTLE (Converted to double chimney)

Introduced into service in July 1932. Diagram HB boiler fitted. Double chimney and 4-row superheater fitted during the locomotive's last 'Heavy General' overhaul which also included boiler (HD 9600) and tender change, and took place at Swindon Works between 4th January and 3rd March 1961. The engine was withdrawn in September 1962 from Stafford Road depot (84A). Recorded mileage 1,521,335, service life 30 years, 1 month and 28 days. Disposal Swindon Works, September 1962.

Tender types principal fitted dates, Collett 4000g July 1932, Hawksworth 4000g 8th June 1951, Collett 4000g 10th March 1953, Hawksworth 4000g 29th September 1956, Collett 4000g 8th May 1958.

Allocated Depots

SDN Swindon	24/07/32	LA Laira	13/12/37	Brd Weston-super-Mare	04/48
LA Laira	19/08/32	PDN Old Oad Common	05/02/39	BRD Bristol Bath Road	05/48
NA Newton Abbot	11/33	BRD Bristol Bath Road	17/06/40	84A Stafford Road	08/05/58

Treago Castle is a fortified manor house in the Parish of St. Weonards, Herefordshire. Built circa 1500, it was recorded as a Grade I listed building on 30th April 1986, the house is an occupied privately owned family home.

GWR 'Castle' class 4-6-0 No 5019 TREAGO CASTLE (stepped inside cylinder cover) is seen near Birmingham Snow Hill, during April 1959. *Rail Photoprints Collection*

5020 TREMATON CASTLE

Introduced into service in August 1932. Diagram HB boiler fitted.

The locomotive's last 'Heavy General' overhaul took place at Swindon Works between 1st November and 30th November 1957 also 5th April 1960 Diagram HC boiler 6693 fitted. The engine was withdrawn in November 1962 from Llanelly depot (87F). Recorded mileage 1,636,749, service life 30 years, 3 months and 15 days. Disposal Swindon Works, March 1963.

Tender types principal fitted dates, Collett 4000g July 1932, Hawksworth 4000g 14th December 1950, Collett 4000g 23rd November 1955, Hawksworth 4000g 18th March 1961.

Allocated Depots

LA Laira	05/08/32	83D Laira	26/01/57	83B Taunton	22/05/60
CDF Cardiff Canton	18/02/34	86C Cardiff Canton	20/04/57	83C Exeter	18/06/60
LDR Landore	27/03/35	83D Laira	30/11/57	88A Cardiff Canton	07/10/61
CDF Cardiff Canton	26/06/39	83G Penzance	27/12/58	87F Llanelly	14/07/62

Tremation Castle is situated to the south east of Tremation village near Saltash, Cornwall; it has a round keep and therefore is similar in style to Restormel Castle. The fortress was built soon after the Norman Conquest and overlooks Plymouth Sound. When Sir Francis Drake returned from his circumnavigation voyage in 1580, he came into harbour in Plymouth, then slipped out to anchor behind St Nicholas Island until word came from Queen Elizabeth's Court for the treasures he had gathered to be stored in Tremation Castle. Guided tours of the privately owned ruin and extensive grounds are available.

GWR 'Castle' class 4-6-0 No 5020 TREMATON CASTLE (un-stepped inside cylinder cover) is seen at Shrewsbury, circa 1957. *Rail Photoprints Collection*

5021 WHITTINGTON CASTLE

Introduced into service in August 1932. Diagram HB boiler fitted.

The locomotive's last 'Heavy General' overhaul including tender change took place at Swindon Works between 1st November and 30th November 1957, also 19th September 1962 Diagram HC boiler 6695 fitted. The engine was withdrawn in September 1962 from Cardiff Canton depot (88A). Recorded mileage 1,446,936, service life 30 years, 1 month and 4 days. Disposal Cashmores, Newport, June 1963.

Tender types principal fitted dates, Collett 4000g August 1932, Hawksworth 4000g 3rd May 1950, Collett 4000g 6th September 1962, Hawksworth 4th October 1952, Collett 4000g 17th August 1953, Hawksworth 4000g 17th December 1958.

Allocated Depots

LA Laira	17/08/32	LA Laira	29/08/37	LA Laira	29/06/48
SDN Swindon	10/03/33	4A Shrewsbury	17/12/38	83C Exeter	10/1952
LA Laira	31/03/33	SRD Stafford Road	25/11/40	83D Laira	03/57
NA Newton Abbott	09/01/35	4A Shrewsbury	05/04/41	86C Cardiff Canton	22/09/59
LA Laira	01/02/35	SRD Stafford Road	20/05/42	82B ST Phillips Marsh	15/09/60
NA Newton Abbott	17/03/36	4A Shrewsbury	08/09/45	86C Cardiff Canton	03/10/60

Whittington Castle is in Shropshire near to the historic town of Oswestry and the Welsh Marches ruins date from the 13th century. Whittington Castle is unique in that it is the only castle in the UK which is owned and managed by a community of local residents. There is public access to the castle grounds.

GWR 'Castle' class 4-6-0 No 5021 WHITTINGTON CASTLE is seen on the sea front at Dawlish with an up express, during August 1953. *Rail Photoprints Collection*

5022 WIGMORE CASTLE (Converted to double chimney)

Introduced into service in August 1932. Diagram HB boiler fitted. Double chimney and 4-row superheater fitted during the locomotive's last 'Heavy General' overhaul which included boiler (HD 7651) and tender change, and took place at Swindon Works between 30th December 1958 and 18th February 1959. The engine was withdrawn in June 1963 from Stafford Road depot (84A). Recorded mileage 1,546,104, service life 30 years, 8 months and 18 days. Disposal Cashmores, Great Bridge, June 1964.

Tender types principal fitted dates, Collett 4000g August 1932, Hawksworth 2nd October 1946, Collett 4000g 2nd March 1948, Hawksworth 4000g 7th May 1953, Collett 4000g 17th January 1955.

Allocated Depots

PDN Old Oak Common	30/08/32	PDN Old Oak Common	02/03/48	SRD Stafford Road	09/48
NA Newton Abbot	16/10/47				

Wigmore Castle is a ruined structure which is barely visible from the northwest Herefordshire village of the same name. The castle was founded in 1067 by the Norman invaders. It was the stronghold of the turbulent Mortimer family (1075–1425), later during the English Civil War it was dismantled to prevent its use. The site is English Heritage owned and open to the public.

GWR 'Castle' class 4-6-0 No 5022 WIGMORE CASTLE is seen at Stafford Road (84A) in 1959. Note the stepped inside cylinder cover and the mechanical lubricator located in front of the outside steam pipe. *Keith Langston Collection*

5023 BRECON CASTLE

Introduced into service in May 1934. Diagram HB boiler fitted.

The locomotive's last 'Heavy Intermediate' overhaul including boiler (HC 7644) and tender change took place at Swindon Works between 13th December 1960 and 24th September 1962 (651 days). The engine was withdrawn in February 1963 from Swindon depot (82C). Recorded mileage 1,479,168, service life 28 years, 9 months and 7 days. Disposal Swindon Works, June 1963.

Tender types principal fitted dates, Collett 4000g April 1934, Hawksworth 4000g 24th December 1946, Collett 4000g 22nd June 1948, Hawksworth 4000g 1st January 1952, Collett 4000g 8th February 1961.

Allocated Depots

PDN Old Oak Common	02/05/34	83D Laira Reinstated	07/07/50	85A Worcester	27/01/58
CDF Cardiff Canton	22/04/36	83G Penzance	10/52	82C Swindon	20/03/58
PDN Old Oak Common	18/11/37	83A Laira	08/54	Swindon. Stored	24/09/62
Swindon. Stored	28/02/50				

Brecon Castle, located in the town of the same name was created by the Norman warrior Bernard de Neufmarche who took his surname from a village near Rouen in Normandy. Parts of the old castle were incorporated into a hotel built in the early 19th century and the historic Brecon Castle Hotel still trades in modern times with its restaurant having a reputation for fine foods.

GWR 'Castle' Class 4-6-0 5023 BRECON CASTLE passes Box Mill Lane as it heads for Box Tunnel with the morning 'running in turn' returning to Swindon, the amount of steam suggests all might not be well, dateline 18th March 1961. Records show that this engine was sidelined in Swindon works for a protracted period of 651 days from 13th September 1960, and after being eventually outshopped was later placed into store and scrapped without being reallocated.
Hugh Ballantyne/Rail Photoprints

5024 CAREW CASTLE

Introduced into service in April 1934. Diagram HB boiler fitted.

The locomotive's last 'Heavy Intermediate' overhaul including boiler (HB 6639) and tender change took place at Swindon Works between 7th December 1959 and 14th February 1960. The engine was withdrawn in May 1962 from Newton Abbot depot (83A). Recorded mileage 1,351,161, service life 28 years and 23 days. Disposal Cashmores, Newport, December 1962.

Tender types principal fitted dates, Collett 4000g April 1934, Hawksworth 6th September 1952, Collett 4000g 11th June 1963.

GWR 'Castle' class 4-6-0 No 5024 CAREW CASTLE is seen at Newton Abbot (83A) in April 1956. Note the rounded front edge of the centre cylinder cover. *Roy Vincent Collection/Transport Treasury*

Allocated Depots

LA Laira	28/04/34	PZ Penzance	22/10/36	NA Newton Abbot	12/48
NA Newton Abbot	01/06/34	LA Laira	20/04/37	BRD Bristol Bath Road	07/49
PZ Penzance	25/02/36	BRD Bristol Bath Road	05/43	NA Newton Abbot	18/11/49
NA Newton Abbot	05/36	Brd Weston-super-Mare	11/48		

GWR 'Castle, Class 4-6-0 No 5024 CAREW CASTLE is seen preparing to back onto the down 'Torbay Express' at Paddington circa 1959. Note the stepped inside cylinder cover and the storage compartment for short fire irons between the nearside centre and trailing wheel splashers. The Swindon BR/WR cast headboard carried in this instance is the third and final design incorporating the Devon county crest. *Rail Photoprints Collection*

Carew Castle is in the parish of Carew in Pembrokeshire. The famous Carew family take their name from the place, and still own the castle, the site is leased to the Pembrokeshire Coast National Park and open to the public. The castle grounds incorporate an impressive 11th century Celtic cross and also the only restored tidal mill in Wales.

5025 CHIRK CASTLE

Introduced into service in May 1934. Diagram HB boiler fitted.

The locomotive's last 'Heavy General' overhaul including boiler (HC 6696) and tender change took place at Swindon Works between 15th February and 20th April 1961. The engine was withdrawn in November 1963 from Hereford depot (86C). Recorded mileage 1,401,530 service life 29 years, 6 months and 12 days. Disposal Cashmores, Newport, June 1964.

Tender types principal fitted dates, Collett 4000g April 1934, Hawksworth 4000g 10th October 1951, Collett 4000g 8th January 1953, Hawksworth 4000g 20th April 1961.

Allocated Depots

PDN Old Oak Common	01/05/34	BRD Bristol Bath Road	10/11/45	82A Bristol Bath Road	24/04/51
EXE Exeter	07/03/36	Brd Weston-super-Mare	06/47	82C Swindon	05/56
TN Taunton	17/09/36	BRD Bristol Bath Road	07/47	81F Oxford	20/03/58
EXE Exeter	10/36	Brd Weston-super-Mare	09/47	81F Stored Oxford	12/12/62
BRD Bristol Bath Road	17/09/37	BRD Bristol Bath Road	08/10/47	86C Reinstated Hereford	29/10/63
Brd Weston-super-Mare	11/45	82D Westbury	02/51		

Chirk Castle was built circa 1295 as one of a chain of fortresses across North Wales and its specific purpose was to guard the entrance to the Ceiriog Valley. The castle and grounds are National Trust owned and open to the public.

GWR 'Castle' class 4-6-0 No 5025 CHIRK CASTLE is seen passing its Swindon birthplace with a westbound service circa 1954. *Rail Photoprints Collection*

5026 CRICCIETH CASTLE (Converted to double chimney)

Introduced into service in April 1934. Diagram HB boiler fitted. Double chimney and 4-row superheater fitted during the locomotive's last 'Heavy Intermediate' overhaul which included boiler (HD 7688) and tender change, and took place at Swindon Works between 18th August and 21st October 1959. The engine was withdrawn in November 1964 from Oxley depot (2B). Recorded mileage to December 1963 1,209,457 service life 29 years, 6 months and 12 days. Disposal Cashmores, Great Bridge, February 1965.

Tender type principal fitted dates, Collett 4000g April 1934.

Allocated Depots

NA Newton Abbot	30/04/34	LA Laira	17/05/47	84A Stafford Road	20/03/58
PZ Penzance	12/36	PZ Penzance	08/10/49	84E Tyseley	19/12/60
EXE Exeter	03/05/37	LA Laira	12/49	84A Stafford Road	19/05/61
TN Taunton	10/39	81A Old Oak Common	07/11/50	2B Oxley	09/09/63
EXE Exeter	11/39	81F Oxford	02/12/50		

Cricceith Castle is a native Welsh castle situated on a headland between two beaches in the Gwynedd town of the same name. Built circa 1230, by Llywelyn the Great, a Welsh prince of note. Edward I's forces took the castle some 50 years later, and undertook their own improvements including the addition of a tower for stone-throwing engines. Owain Glyn Dŵr sealed Criccieth's fate when his troops captured and burnt the castle in the early years of the 15th century, scorch marks can still be seen on a section of stonework. Criccieth was also one of several locations used by the artist Joseph Mallord William Turner during the creation of his famous series of paintings depicting shipwrecked mariners. The impressively sited ruins are administered by Cadw and open to the public.

GWR 'Castle' Class 4-6-0 No 5026 CRICCIETH CASTLE seen ex works at Swindon following double chimney fitting in October 1959. Note, the externally accessed rear sandbox, between the cab steps and rear driving wheel and also the mechanical lubricator behind the outside steam pipe. *Rail Photoprints Collection*

5027 FARLEIGH CASTLE (Converted to double chimney)

Introduced into service in May 1934. Diagram HB boiler fitted. Double chimney and 4-row superheater fitted during the locomotive's last 'Heavy General' overhaul which included boiler (HD 9602) and tender change, and took place at Swindon Works between 30th January and 17th April 1961. The engine was withdrawn in November 1962 from Llanelly depot (87F). Recorded mileage 1,465,365 service life 28 years, 6 months and 8 days. Disposal Cashmores, Great Bridge, September 1963.

Tender type principal fitted dates, Collett 4000g April 1934, Hawksworth 4000g 17th January 1956, Collett 4000g 3rd June 1957.

Allocated Depots

PDN Old Oak Common	12/05/34	82A Bristol Bath Road	06/54	87G Carmarthen	05/07/61
84K Chester West	04/11/50	81A Old Oak Common	20/03/58	87F Llanelly	14/07/62
84A Stafford Road	06/11/51				

Farleigh Castle (also known as Farley Castle and Hungerford Castle) is a medieval structure located in Somerset. The castle, which is adjacent to the river Frome was built in two phases between 1377 and 1383. The site, which is approximately 9 miles to the south east of Bath is administered by English Heritage and is open to the public.

GWR 'Castle' class 4-6-0 No 5027 FARLEIGH CASTLE is seen with a westbound service near Corsham, circa 1959. *Norman Preedy Collection/Rail Photoprints*

5028 LLANTILIO CASTLE

Introduced into service in May 1934. Diagram HB boiler fitted.

The locomotive's last 'Heavy General' overhaul including boiler (HB 6643) and tender change took place at Swindon Works between 28th November 1958 and 13th January 1959. The engine was withdrawn in May 1960 from Laira depot (83D). Recorded mileage 1,345,291 service life 25 years 11 months and 24 days. Disposal Swindon Works, June 1960.

Tender type principal fitted dates, Collett 4000g April 1934, Hawksworth 4000g 19th May 1951, Collett 4000g 26th January 1955, Hawksworth 4000g 13th January 1959.

Allocated Depots

LA Laira	26/05/34	TR Truro	06/38	83D Laira	06/56
NA Newton Abbot	03/01/38	NA Newton Abbot	10/38		

Llantilio Castle (also known as White Castle) is a medieval ruin in the Llantilio Crossenny district of Monmouthshire. The name White Castle is derived from the whitewash originally applied to the outer walls of the structure and which is partially visible to the present day. It was built as one of a three castle defensive structure in Norman times, the other two being Grosmont and Skenfrith. The castle site is administered by Cadw and open to the public.

GWR 'Castle' class 4-6-0 No 5028 LLANTILIO CASTLE is seen approaching Exeter St David's with an up mail train on 2nd August 1956. *David Anderson*

GWR 'Castle' class 4-6-0 No 5028 LLANTILIO CASTLE class climbs away from Greenway Tunnel towards Churston with the up 'Torbay Express' service on 16th August 1952. No 5028 spent the period from October 1938 until June 1956 at Newton Abbot depot, which was coded GWR 'NA' and then BR '83A'. The 'Torbay Express' was a originally a GWR service operating between London Paddington and Kingswear, Devon. The service was introduced on 9th July 1923 and was withdrawn during the period 9th September 1939 to 6th May 1946, when it was reintroduced. BR discontinued use of the title after a final diesel hauled run 13th September 1968. Note the BR pattern inside valve cover with valve spindle oil cup. *Rail Photoprints Collection*

5029 NUNNEY CASTLE Preserved

Introduced into service in May 1934. Diagram HB boiler fitted.

The locomotive's last 'Heavy General' overhaul including boiler (HB 6668) and tender change took place at Swindon Works between 23rd February and 22nd March 1961. The engine was withdrawn on 28th December 1963 from Cardiff East Dock depot (88L). Recorded mileage 1,523,415 service life 29 years and 7 months. The engine was sold for scrap and then later rescued for preservation.

Tender type principal fitted dates, Collett 4000g May 1934, Hawksworth 4000g 25th July 1952, Collett 4000g 20th August 1952, Hawksworth 4000g 19th June 1954, Collett 4000g 24th April 1959, Hawksworth 4000g 22nd March 1961.

Nunney Castle had the dubious distinction of being the last steam locomotive to be delivered by rail to the scrapyard of Woodham Brothers, Barry. The Collett 4-6-0 languished at the South Wales scrapyard for some 12 years before being rescued in 1976 being the 81st locomotive to be saved from Barry. Originally the locomotive was sold to, and owned by a consortium consisting of 50% private individuals and 50% the Great Western Society. Following a rebuild to mainline standard at Didcot Railway Centre the locomotive was successfully returned to steam in 1990. In the mid 1990s the private consortium took overall control and the engine continued to work on the national network, in addition to visiting several preserved railways.

Nunney Castle was later bought by businessman and heritage locomotive owner Jeremy Hosking and after a further rebuild the 'Castle' class 4-6-0 returned to the mainline in 2008. In preservation the locomotive has been fitted with air braking (in addition to its vacuum system), a larger capacity tender water compartment and TPWS (Train Protective Warning System).

Allocated Depots

PDN Old Oak Common	28/05/34	83A Newton Abbot	05/05/59	Laira Stored	14/03/62
85A Worcester	20/03/58	83D Laira	04/11/59	88L Cardiff East Dock. Reinstated	15/12/62

Nunney Castle, in Somerset is a medieval structure which was built in the late 14th century by Sir John Delamare, the construction of which was reportedly paid for out of profits from Delamare's involvement in the Hundred Years War. The architectural style is said to have been influenced by French castles of the same period, and Nunney has been described as 'aesthetically the most impressive castle in Somerset'. The English Heritage administered scheduled monument is open to the public.

GWR 'Castle' class 4-6-0 No 5029 NUNNEY CASTLE calls at Bath Spa station with the 4.33 Salisbury - Bristol service on 31st May 1962. Note the low ended roof of the brake immediately behind the engine. *Hugh Ballantyne /Rail Photoprints*

Preserved GWR 'Castle' class 4-6-0 No 5029 NUNNEY CASTLE is seen heading a 'Shakespeare Express' charter past Churchill Cottage on the climb out of Stratford on Avon towards Wilmcote on 27th July 2008. The locomotive is coupled to Collett tender No 2690 which was originally a 4000 gallon capacity unit but in preservation that capacity has been increased to 4610 gallons. In GWR/BR service No 5029 was coupled to several different Collett and Hawksworth 4000g tenders, but never to the one now in use. *Mathew Wilson*

Preserved GWR 'Castle' class 4-6-0 No 5029 NUNNEY CASTLE is seen with the 'Pembroke Coast Express' charter passing Ferryside en-route for Carmarthen on a very grey 12th January in 2005. The air brake pump, forward of the nearside steam pipe, can clearly be seen, as can the stepped inside cylinder cover with lubricator. Note also the BR pattern parallel barrel buffers. *Keith Langston*

5030 SHIRBURN CASTLE

Introduced into service in June 1934. Diagram HB boiler fitted.

The locomotive's last 'Heavy Intermediate' overhaul including boiler (HB 6634) and tender change took place at Swindon Works between 29th November 1960 and 27th January 1961. The engine was withdrawn in September 1962 from Carmarthen depot (87G). Recorded mileage 1,413,084 service life 28 years 3 months and 20 days. Disposal Hayes, Bridgend, October 1962.

Tender type principal fitted dates, Collett 4000g June 1934, Hawksworth 4000g 9th February 1948, Collett 4000g 20th September 1949, Hawksworth 4000g 6th September 1952, Collett 4000g 1st April 1953, Hawksworth 4000g 11th July 1953, Collett 4000g 29th March 1957, Hawksworth 4000g 17th December 1958, Collett 4000g 27th January 1961.

Allocated Depots

EXE Exeter	01/06/34	CDF Cardiff Canton	08/42	87E Landore	16/06/60
CDF Cardiff Canton	14/05/36	87G Carmarthen	19/08/58	87G Carmarthen	07/09/60
NPT Newport Ebbw Jct	03/41				

Shirburn Castle is in Oxfordshire and located adjacent to the village of the same name. The first castle was built on the site in the 14th century and the fortification has been the seat of the Parker family (Earls of Macclesfield) from 1716 to the present day. The building and lands are owned by a private company and are not open to the public.

GWR 'Castle' class 4-6-0 No 5030 SHIRBURN CASTLE is seen passing Patchway with an up express, circa 1960. *Rail Photoprints Collection*

5031 TOTNES CASTLE (Converted to double chimney)

Introduced into service in June 1934. Diagram HB boiler fitted. Double chimney and 4-row superheater fitted during the locomotive's last 'Heavy General' overhaul which included boiler (HD 7654) and tender change and took place at Swindon Works between 24th April and 24th June 1959. The engine was withdrawn in October 1963 from Oxley depot (2B). Recorded mileage 1,434,409 service life 29 years 4 months and 13 days. Disposal Cohens, Morriston, May 1964.

Tender type principal fitted dates, Collett 4000g June 1934, Hawksworth 4000g 9th November 1953, Collett 4000g 1st February 1955.

Allocated Depots

| SRD Stafford Road | 02/06/34 | Stafford Road. Reinstated | 07/11/50 | 84A Stafford Road | 03/55 |
| Swindon Works Stored | 14/09/50 | 84K Chester West | 01/02/55 | 2B Oxley | 09/09/63 |

Totnes Castle is one of the best preserved examples of a Norman motte and bailey castle in England. It is situated in the town of Totnes on the River Dart in Devon. The surviving stone keep and curtain wall date from around the 14th century. The English Heritage administered site is open to the public.

GWR 'Castle class 4-6-0 No 5031 TOTNES CASTLE is seen at Bristol Temple Meads station with a West-North service circa 1938. *Rail Photoprints Collection*

GWR 'Castle' class 4-6-0 No 5031 TOTNES CASTLE is seen in the locomotives final BR form at Wolverhampton in June 1960. *Transport Treasury*

GWR 'Castle' class 4-6-0 No 5031 TOTNES CASTLE is seen at Bristol Temple Meads station in an evocative period image. The northbound 'Cornishman' (behind No 5031) and the up 'Bristolian' behind an unidentified 'Warship' diesel Hydraulic await their appropriate departure times. *Rail Photoprints Collection*

5032 USK CASTLE (Converted to double chimney)

Introduced into service in June 1934. Diagram HB boiler fitted. This locomotive hauled the first BR/WR express service, the 00.05 (12.05pm) Paddington – Birkenhead departure at on 1st January 1948. Double chimney and 4-row superheater fitted May 1959 (boiler HD 7653). The locomotive's last 'Heavy General' overhaul including boiler (HB 7646) and tender change took place at Swindon Works between 19th January and 24th February 1961. The engine was withdrawn in September 1962 from Old Oak Common depot (81A). Recorded mileage 1,288,968 service life 28 years 3 months and 2 days. Disposal Cashmores, Great Bridge, November 1962.

Tender type principal fitted dates, Collett 4000g June 1934, Collett (8 Wheeled) 4000g 27th July 1935, Collett 4000g 6th May 1940, Hawksworth 4000g 27th May 1952, Collett 4000g 17th August 1953, Hawksworth 4000g 23rd April 1960, Collett 4000g 24th February 1961.

Allocated Depots

SALOP Shrewsbury	05/06/34	83A Newton Abbot	20/03/58	81A Old Oak Common	04/03/60
84A Stafford Road	11/51				

Usk Castle is adjacent to the town of the same name in Monmouthshire, and the original structure dates from Norman times. The castle and town of Usk are thought to have become a Norman settlement circa 1120, which is a little later than other Norman settlements and castles in the region. Usk had previous historic military importance having been a Roman Legionary fortress. It is a Grade 1 listed private residence, however, events are held there throughout the summer months.

GWR 'Castle' class 4-6-0 No 5032 USK CASTLE is seen in the company of sister engine No 7027 THORNBURY CASTLE at Laira shed (83D) in July 1958. Note the cab window handrail on 7027 which is not simply under the window but instead carries on upwards forward of the window frame, a feature of 'Castle' class engines from No 5098 onwards. *R.E.Vincent/Transport Treasury*

5033 BROUGHTON CASTLE (Converted to double chimney)

Introduced into service in May 1935. Diagram HB boiler fitted. This was the first engine of the class to be fitted with a Speedometer. Double chimney and 4-row superheater fitted during the locomotive's last 'Heavy General' overhaul which included boiler (HD 7668) and tender change, and took place at Swindon Works between 11th August and 25th October 1960. The engine was withdrawn in September 1962 from Oxford depot (81F). Recorded mileage 1,160,197 service life 27 years 3 months and 21 days. Disposal Cashmores, Great Bridge, November 1962.

Tender type principal fitted dates, Collett 4000g 17th May 1935, Hawksworth 4000g 13th February 1948, Collett 4000g 8th August 1951, Hawksworth 4000g 30th September 1953, Collett 4000g 31st August 1955.

Allocated Depots

SRD Stafford Road	17/05/35	SRD Stafford Road	13/02/48	81F Oxford	15/06/58
CHR Chester West	25/07/47	CHR Chester West	07/48		

Broughton Castle is a medieval moated manor house situated adjacent to the village of the same name and located to the south west of Banbury, north Oxfordshire. It is a moated and fortified manor house located near Banbury in North Oxfordshire. The impressive castle (circa 1306) is built of the rich local Hornton ironstone and is set in parkland. However the majority of building which survives dates from the 1550s. It was a centre of opposition to Charles I and was besieged and damaged after the Battle of Edgehill in 1642. It is the home of the Fiennes family (Barons Saye and Sele). The privately owned castle and grounds are opened to the public during the summer months.

GWR 'Castle, class 4-6-0 No 5033 BROUGHTON CASTLE gets away from Oxford with a down Worcester service, in April 1962. *Rail Photoprints Collection*

5034 CORFE CASTLE (Converted to double chimney)

Introduced into service in May 1935. Diagram HB boiler fitted. Double chimney and 4-row superheater during the locomotive's last 'Heavy General' overhaul which included boiler (HD 7699) and tender change, and took place at Swindon Works between 10th December 1960 and 10th February 1961. The engine was withdrawn in September 1962 from Old Oak Common depot (81A). Recorded mileage 1,250,714 service life 27 years and 4 months. Disposal Cashmores, Great Bridge, November 1962.

Tender type principal fitted dates, Collett 4000g 18 May 1934, Hawksworth 4000g 24th December 1952, Collett 4000g 29th April 1954, Hawksworth 4000g 7th August 1957, Collett 4000g 2nd June 1958.

Allocated Depots

NA Newton Abbot	21/05/35	Swindon Stored	09/10/50	81D Reading WR	12/50
PZ Penzance	01/40	81A Old Oak Common. Reinstated	11/11/50	81A Old Oak Common	12/53
NA Newton Abbot	06/40				

Corfe Castle is an 11th century fortification standing on a natural hill above the village of the same name on the Isle of Purbeck in Dorset, it was built by William the Conqueror. The castle underwent major structural changes in the 12th and 13th centuries and later during the English Civil War it was partially demolished by the Parliamentarians. The thousand year old ruins can be seen from the preserved Swanage Railway and the National Trust owned property is open to the public.

GWR 'Castle' Class 4-6-0 No 5034 CORFE CASTLE passes Thingley West Junction with a down express, circa 1955. *Rail Photoprints Collection*

5035 COITY CASTLE

Introduced into service in May 1935. Diagram HB boiler fitted.

The locomotive's last 'Heavy Intermediate' overhaul including boiler (HB 6682) and tender change took place at Swindon Works between 11th May and 28th July 1960. The engine was withdrawn in May 1962 from Swindon depot (82C). Recorded mileage 1,444,261 service life 27 years 11 months and 18 days. Disposal Cashmores, Newport, December 1962.

Tender type principal fitted dates, Collett 4000g May 1935, Hawksworth 4000g 26th March 1955, Collett 4000g 23rd April 1955, Hawksworth 18th August 1958, Collett 4000g 28th July 1960.

Allocated Depots

CDF Cardiff Canton	29/05/35	PDN Old Oak Common	20/04/40	82C Swindon	06/09/60
SRD Stafford Road	14/12/35				

Coity Castle located in Glamorgan, was a Norman structure built by Sir Payn 'the Demon' de Turberville, one of the legendary 'Twelve Knights of Glamorgan'. The castle ruins stand in the Community of Coity Higher, near to the town of Bridgend. The castle began as a late 11th century ringwork. A rectangular stone keep and the main curtain wall were added by the Normans during the 12th century, under the rule of the de Turberville family. The three-storey keep was primarily a defensive structure. Extensive reworking took place in the 14th century. Administered by Cadw, the site is open to the public.

GWR 'Castle' Class 4-6-0 No 5035 COITY CASTLE near High Wycombe with the 2.10pm Paddington - Birkenhead service, circa 1938. *Dave Cobbe Collection – C. R. L. Coles/Rail Photoprints*

5036 LYONSHALL CASTLE (Converted to double chimney)

Introduced into service in June 1935. Diagram HB boiler fitted. Double chimney and 4-row superheater fitted during the locomotive's last 'Heavy General' overhaul which included boiler (HD 7698) and tender, and change took place at Swindon Works between 25th October and 29th December 1960. The engine was withdrawn in September 1962 from Old Oak Common depot (81A). Recorded mileage 1,304,430 service life 27 years and 3 months. Disposal Cashmores, Newport, November 1962.

Tender type principal fitted dates, Collett 4000g June 1935, Hawksworth 4000g 23rd March 1957, Collett 4000g 5th March 1959, Hawksworth 4000g 13th January 1961, Collett 4000g 8th September 1962.

GWR 'Castle' 4-6-0 No 5036 LYONSHALL CASTLE emerges from Sapperton Tunnel with a Paddington–Cheltenham service, on 16th June 1962. Note the other photographer and youngster trackside. *Norman Preedy/Rail Photoprints*

Allocated Depots

CDF Cardiff Canton	04/06/35	PDN Old Oak Common	28/02/37	81A Old Oak Common	29/12/60
SRD Stafford Road	01/36	81D Reading WR	03/50		

GWR 'Castle' 4-6-0 No 5036 LYONSHALL CASTLE at Old Oak Common depot in 1961. The engine is pictured in light steam with a good load of lump coal in the Hawksworth tender. The double chimney is seen to good effect as is the short fire iron storage compartment and the modified design of outside steam pipe. *Norman Preedy Collection/Rail Photoprints*

Lyonshall Castle is adjacent to the village of the same name near to the town of Kington in Herefordshire. The ruins of the circa 1090 built fortification are on private land and not generally open to the public. The castle was originally part of the border strongholds of the 'Marcher Lords', standing as it does at a then strategically important location.

5037 MONMOUTH CASTLE

Introduced into service in June 1935. Diagram HB boiler fitted.

On 31st December 1947 this locomotive hauled the last GWR train, it was the 11.50pm Paddington–Penzance service. The locomotive's last 'Heavy Intermediate' overhaul including boiler (HB 6676) and tender change took place at Swindon Works between 12th March and 3rd May 1962. The engine was withdrawn in March 1964 from St Philips Marsh depot (82B). Recorded mileage 1,500,851 service life 28 years 9 months and 2 days. Disposal Birds, Risca, June 1964.

Tender type principal fitted dates, Collett 4000g 8th June 1935, Hawksworth 4000g 20th February 1952, Collett 4000g 15th December 1953, Hawksworth 4000g 10th December 1956, Collett 4000g 25th May 1960.

Allocated Depots

PDN Old Oak Common	08/06/35	82A Bristol Bath Road	17/02/51	87A Neath Court Sart	03/11/62
TYS Tyseley	04/02/36	85A Worcester	06/54	87F Llanelly	09/02/63
PDN Old Oak Common	03/36	81A Old Oak Common	25/05/60	Stored Llanelly	09/09/63
82A Bristol Bath Road	07/07/50	87A Neath Court Sart	13/06/61	82B St Philips Marsh. Reinstated	05/11/63
82D Westbury	02/51	87F Llanelly	14/07/62		

Monmouth Castle ruins are located close to the centre of Monmouth, in the county of Monmouthshire and they stand on a hill towering over the river Monnow, behind several shops and adjacent to the main square of the town. Once an important border castle, and the birthplace of Henry V of England, it stood until the English Civil War during which it was damaged and changed hands three times before being put out of use to prevent it being fortified again. After a partial collapse in 1647, the site was reused and built over by Great Castle House. The Royal Monmouthshire, Royal Engineers museum is housed in the former stable block.

GWR Castle 'Class' 4-6-0 No 5037 MONMOUTH CASTLE awaits its next duty at Old Oak Common, circa 1960. *Norman Preedy Collection/rail Photoprints*

5038 MORLAIS CASTLE

Introduced into service in June 1935. Diagram HB boiler fitted.

The locomotive's last 'Heavy Intermediate' overhaul including boiler (HB 6646) and tender change took place at Swindon Works between 5th August 1961 and 19th May 1962. The engine was withdrawn in September 1963 from Reading WR depot (81D). Recorded mileage 1,438,862 service life 28 years 2 months and 27 days. Disposal Cashmores, Newport, June 1964.

Tender type principal fitted dates, Collett 4000g June 1935, Hawksworth 4000g 20th December 1946, Collett 4000g 9th November 1948, Hawksworth 4000g 18th August 1950, Collett 4000g 9th April 1952, Hawksworth 4000g 4th October 1961.

Allocated Depots

PDN Old Oak Common	21/06/35	81F Oxford	19/05/62	81D Reading WR	03/11/62
84G Shrewsbury	20/03/58				

Morlais Castle dates from the 13th-century and the ruins are located above the Taff Gorge near the town of Merthyr Tydfil in Glamorganshire. There is public access to the site.

An interesting every day scene at Oxford. GWR 'Castle' class 4-6-0 No 5038 MORLAIS CASTLE is seen being uncoupled from 10:38 arrival from Birmingham in April 1962. Rebuilt 'West Country' class 4-6-2 No 34039 BOSCASTLE waits to back onto the train to take it forward to its southern destination. *Rail Photoprints Collection*

5039 RHUDDLAN CASTLE

Introduced into service in June 1935. Diagram HB boiler fitted. Converted to oil burning between 14th December 1946 to 22nd September 1948, cab roof vent fitted. The locomotive's last 'Heavy General' overhaul including boiler (HC 7613) and tender change took place at Swindon Works between 10th November 1961 and 18th January 1962. The engine was withdrawn in June 1964 from Cardiff East Dock depot (88A). Recorded mileage 1,380,564 service life 28 years 11 months and 21 days. Disposal Cohens, Morriston, December 1964.

Tender type principal fitted dates, Collett 4000g 22 June 1935, Churchward 3500g 14th December 1946, Collett 4000g 24th December 1946, Hawksworth 4000g 10 May 1950, Collett 4000g 12th October 1953, Hawksworth 4000g 10th September 1955, Collett 4000g 24th May 1957.

Allocated Depots

PDN Old Oak Common	25/06/35	87G Carmarthen	03/56	87F Llanelly	09/02/63
87G Carmarthen	06/52	87E Landore	06/57	81A Old Oak Common	04/05/63
86C Cardiff Canton	23/11/55	85A Worcester	30/12/59	87J Fishguard Goodwick	27/07/63
87G Carmarthen	12/55	87E Landore	18/02/60	87J Stored	09/09/63
81A Old Oak Common	02/56	87G Carmarthen	13/09/60	88A Cardiff East Dock. Reinstated	31/12/63

Rhuddlan Castle is a castle located in Rhuddlan, Denbighshire. It was erected by Edward I in 1277 following the First Welsh War. Owned by Cadw, the site is open to the public. The now disused railway serving Rhuddlan was originally operated by the Vale of Clwyd Railway and thereafter LNWR, BR.

GWR 'Castle' Class 4-6-0 No 5039 RHUDDLAN CASTLE is seen at Weymouth shed (then 71G) after arriving with a private charter, on 17th July 1963. *Rail Photoprints Collection*

5040 STOKESAY CASTLE

Introduced into service in July 1935. Diagram HB boiler fitted.

The locomotive's last 'Heavy Intermediate' overhaul including boiler (HB 6655) and tender change took place at Swindon Works between 17th June and 4th September 1961. The engine was withdrawn in October 1963 from St Philips Marsh depot (82B). Recorded mileage 1,414,142 service life 28 years 2 months and 27 days. Disposal Coopers Metals, Sharpness, May 1964.

Tender type principal fitted dates, Collett 4000g 29th June 1935, Hawksworth 4000g 19th September 1950, Collett 4000g 27th February 1952, Hawksworth 4000g 27th August 1953, Collett 4000g 29th February 1956, Hawksworth 4000g 1st April 1960, Collett 4000g 4th September 1961.

Allocated Depots

PDN Old Oak Common	01/07/35	82B St Philips Marsh	19/10/61	St Philips Marsh Stored	13/02/62
82C Swindon	04/09/61				

Stokesay Castle is a 13th century fortified manor house near to the village of the same name in Shropshire (close to Craven Arms). It was built by Laurence of Ludlow who was reportedly at that time the most prominent wool merchant in England. The impressive brick and timber structure was a part of the regional Marcher fortifications. During the English Civil War (1645) the occupiers of Stokesay surrendered to the advancing Parliamentarian forces, accordingly the magnificent building remained undamaged. Architecturally, Stokesay Castle is described as 'one of the best-preserved medieval fortified manor houses in England'. The English Heritage owned site, which can be seen from the adjacent Marches route railway line, is open to the public.

GWR 'Castle' class 4-6-0 No 5040 STOKESAY CASTLE is seen at Swansea High Street station in 1958. *L. Nicholson/Transport Treasury*

5041 TIVERTON CASTLE

Introduced into service in July 1935. Diagram HB boiler fitted.

The locomotive's last 'Heavy Intermediate' overhaul including boiler (HC 7629) and tender change took place at Swindon Works between 31st March and 26th May 1961. The engine was withdrawn in December 1963 from Old Oak Common depot (81A). Recorded mileage 1,383,804 service life 28 years 5 months and 17 days. Disposal Cashmores, Newport, June 1964.

Tender type principal fitted dates, Collett 4000g July 1935.

Allocated Depots

LA Laira	11/07/35	Brd Weston-super Mare	10/48	87A Neath Court Sart	13/06/61
PZ Penzance	03/02/40	BRD Bristol Bath Road. Stored	17/02/50	87A Neath Court Sart Stored	17/04/62
LA Laira	06/40	83A Newton Abbot. Reinstated	06/07/50	81A Old Oak Common. Reinstated	02/07/62
BRD Bristol Bath Road	07/48	87E Landore	27/09/55	Old Oak Common Stored	14/12/62

Tiverton Castle is the remains of a medieval castle dismantled after the Civil War and then converted in the 17th century into a country house. It occupies what was considered to be a defensive position above the banks of the River Exe at Tiverton in Devon. The site is open to the public.

GWR 'Castle class 4-6-0 No 5041 TIVERTON CASTLE is seen at Exeter St David's station on 31st July 1955. *Norman Preedy Collection*

5042 WINCHESTER CASTLE

Introduced into service in July 1935. Diagram HB boiler fitted.

The locomotive's last 'Heavy Intermediate' overhaul including boiler (HC 7618) and tender change took place at Swindon Works between 16th April and 13th June 1962. The engine was withdrawn in June 1965 from Gloucester Horton Road depot (85B). Recorded mileage 1,339,221 service life 29 years 11 months and 14 days. Disposal Hayes, Bridgend, October 1965.

Tender type principal fitted dates, Collett 4000g 11th July 1935, Hawksworth 4000g 7th April 1952, Collett 4000g 17th February 1953, Hawksworth 4000g 23rd March 1956, Collett 4000g 19th February 1957, Hawksworth 4000g 17th December 1958, Collett 4000g 18th June 1960, Hawksworth 4000g 13th June 1962.

Allocated Depots

PDN Old Oak Common	11/07/35	WOS Worcester	17/10/37	87G Carmarthen. Reinstated	12/01/63
BRD Bristol Bath Road	09/09/35	GLO Gloucester Horton Road	27/05/39	87F Llanelly	09/03/63
PDN Old Oak Common	21/03/36	85A Worcester	02/02/59	Llanelly. Stored	09/09/63
BRD Bristol Bath Road	24/05/36	81A Old Oak Common	07/04/60	88A Cardiff East Dock. Reinstated	31/12/63
PDN Old Oak Common	16/10/36	83A Newton Abbot	11/08/62	86C Hereford	13/04/64
BRD Bristol Bath Road	10/11/36	Newton Abbot. Stored	24/09/62	85B Gloucester Horton Road	20/07/64

Winchester Castle is a medieval building in Hampshire, England, which dates from circa 1067. Only the Great Hall still stands; it houses a museum of the history of Winchester. Since 1889 the Great Hall of Winchester Castle has been the seat of Hampshire County Council. Nearby, the excavated remains of the round tower and parts of the medieval city wall can also be seen.

GWR 'Castle' class 4-cylinder locomotives, Swindon Works 'Lot Numbers'

Nos 5000–5012 Lot 234 built 1926/27 (Average cost per engine £6839)
Nos 5013–5022 Lot 280 built 1932 (Average cost per engine £6191)
Nos 5023–5032 Lot 295 built 1934 (Average cost per engine £5942)
Nos 5033–5042 Lot 296 built 1935 (Average cost per engine £5914)

GWR 'Castle' Class 4-6-0 No 5042 WINCHESTER CASTLE is seen approaching Bath with the down 'Merchant Venturer', on 30th April 1960. *Hugh Ballantyne/Rail Photoprints*

Tight fit! GWR 'Castle' class 4-6-0 No 5042 WINCHESTER CASTLE separated from its tender is seen at Worcester depot on 12th July 1964, a month after being withdrawn. *Hugh Ballantyne*

Chapter 4

LOCOMOTIVES 5043–5070

5043 BARBURY CASTLE renamed **EARL OF MOUNT EDGCUMBE** September 1937. Preserved (Converted to double chimney)

Introduced into service in March 1936. Diagram HB boiler fitted. Double chimney and 4-row superheater fitted May 1958 (HD boiler number 7673 previously fitted during September/October 1956). The locomotive's last 'Heavy Intermediate' overhaul including boiler (HD 7655) and tender change took place at Swindon Works between 8th February and 24th April 1962. The engine was withdrawn in December 1963 from Cardiff East Dock depot (88L). Recorded mileage 1,400,817, service life 27 years, 9 months and 3 days.

Tender types principal fitted dates, Collett 4000g 14th March 1936, Hawksworth 4000g 7th February 1951, Collett 4000g 16th May 1958, Hawksworth 4000g 3rd March 1960, Collett 4000g 6th April 1962.

The engine was sold for scrap by British Railways to Woodham Bros of Barry, South Wales. In September 1973 the then Birmingham Railway Museum rescued the locomotive and No 5043 left Barry as the 43rd departure from the well known scrapyard. The original plan was to use the locomotive as a component donor for other rescued 'Castle' class engines.

However, in 1996 the trustees announced an ambitious plan to restore the engine to its late 1950s condition, i.e. with a double chimney and coupled to a Hawksworth 4000g tender. The restoration fund was set up and work on the formidable task of restoring the 'Castle' hulk to working order began. As part of the project a new Hawksworth style tender body was constructed and fitted to restored tender frames, which had been obtained.

In 2000 No 5043 was moved inside Tyseley Locomotive works so that the very exacting work could continue, and because of the truly magnificent efforts of the many hands on helpers and supporters the EARL OF MOUNT EDGCUMBE finally moved under her own steam on 3rd October 2008. In the years that have followed the Tyseley Locomotive Works based engine has been seen steaming with special trains on the mainline, on numerous occasions.

For more information about No 5043 EARL OF MOUNT EDGCUMBE see www.tyseleylocomotiveworks.co.uk

GWR 'Castle' class 4-6-0 No 5043 EARL OF MOUNT EDGCUMBE with Hawksworth 4000g tender is seen leaving Exeter St David's station with a Liverpool–Plymouth service on 23rd July 1956. David Anderson

Allocated Depots

PDN Old Oak Common	13/03/36	PDN Old Oak Common	16/06/47	81A Old Oak Common	02/56
SDN Swindon	12/41	Old Oak Common. Stored	17/02/51	88A Cardiff Canton	21/04/62
PDN Old Oak Common	04/04/42	87G Carmarthen. Reinstated	06/52	88L Cardiff East Dock	07/09/62
SDN Swindon	23/05/47				

Earl of Mount Edgcumbe is a title in the Peerage of Great Britain. It was created in 1789 for George Edgcumbe, 3rd Baron Edgcumbe. The ancestral seat of the Edgcumbe family is Mount Edgcumbe House, near Plymouth. The 5th Earl was a director of the GWR. The present family seat is Empacombe House, also near Plymouth. In January 2013 Robert Charles Edgcumbe, a New Zealand-British peer was recorded as being the 8th Earl.

Preserved 'Castle' class 4-6-0 No 5043 EARL OF MOUNT EDGCUMBE is pictured at speed passing Hatton North Junction ex Stratford-on-Avon, Birmingham bound with 'The Shakespeare Express' on 18th April 2010. *Phil Neale*

Two preserved GWR 'Castle' class 4-6-0 locomotives are seen on the Tyseley Works depot during an October 2008 'Open Day', No 5043 EARL OF MOUNT EDGCUMBE leads No 5029 NUNNEY CASTLE. *Clive Hanley*

The only word to describe this portrait of GWR 'Castle' class 4-6-0 No 5043 EARL OF MOUNT EDGCUMBE is Superb!. *Brian Wilson*

An evocative study of GWR 'Castle' class 4-6-0 No 5043 EARL OF MOUNT EDGCUMBE, seen on 'The Shakespeare Express' in 2009. *Clive Hanley*

5044 BEVERSTON CASTLE renamed EARL OF DUNRAVEN September 1937

Introduced into service in March 1936. Diagram HB boiler fitted. In 1954 this locomotive was fitted with a heavy cadmium whistle chain and was the first of the class to be fitted with a shorter chimney from new. The locomotive's last 'Heavy General' overhaul took place at Swindon Works between 28th April and 29th June 1960. Diagram HC boiler number 7629 fitted during a May 1961 works visit. The engine was withdrawn in April 1962 from Cardiff Canton depot (88A). Recorded mileage 1,377,644, service life 26 years and 5 days. Disposal Swindon Works, June 1962.

Tender types principal fitted dates, Collett 4000g 21st March 1936.

Allocated Depots

PDN Old Oak Common	29/03/36	86C Cardiff Canton	05/07/60	88A Cardiff Canton	05/07/61
82C Swindon	04/07/60	87A Neath Court Sart	13/06/61		

Earl of Dunraven was a title in the Peerage of Ireland associated with County Limerick, it was created in 1922. The title became extinct when the seventh Earl died on 25th March 2011. The family seat until that time was Kilgobbin House in Adare Ireland. The Welsh home of the family, Dunraven House, near Bridgend, no longer exists. Dunraven Castle, as it was often called, was demolished in 1963 after having been used as a guest house for some years. During both World Wars the house was used as a military hospital. A walled garden and some floors and steps survive.

GWR 'Castle' class 4-6-0 No 5044 EARL OF DUNRAVEN is seen at Reading General station on 7th September 1958. *A.E. Bennett/Transport Treasury*

5045 BRIDGWATER CASTLE renamed EARL OF DUDLEY September 1937

Introduced into service in April 1936. Diagram HB boiler fitted. The locomotive's last 'Heavy General' overhaul including boiler (HA 4643) and tender change took place at Swindon Works between 10th December 1957 and 19th February 1958. The engine was withdrawn in September 1962 from Stafford Road depot (84A). Recorded mileage 1,383,737, service life 26 years, 5 months and 18 days. Disposal Cox & Danks, Oldbury, September 1962.

Tender types principal fitted dates, Collett 4000g 28th March 1936, Hawksworth 4000g 11th January 1949, Collett 4000g 22nd September 1950, Hawksworth 4000g 6th June 1952, 2nd April 1954 Collett 4000g, Hawksworth 4000g 7th November 1956, Collett 4000g 19th February 1958.

Allocated Depots

| PDN Old Oak Common | 03/04/36 | 82C Swindon. Stored | 28/09/50 | 84A Stafford Road. Reinstated | 06/11/50 |

Earl of Dudley, of Dudley Castle in Staffordshire, is a title that has been created twice in the Peerage of the United Kingdom, 1827 and 1860 both times for members of the Ward family. In January 2014 the title was held by William Humble David Jeremy Ward, the fifth Earl.

GWR 'Castle' class 4-6-0 No 5045 EARL OF DUDLEY is seen at Seer Green on 28th August 1954. *Rail Photoprints Collection*

5046 CLIFFORD CASTLE renamed EARL CAWDOR August 1937.

Introduced into service in April 1936. Diagram HB boiler fitted. The locomotive's last 'Heavy Intermediate' overhaul including boiler (HB 6644) and tender change took place at Swindon Works between 23rd April and 24th June 1958. The engine was withdrawn in September 1962 from Stafford Road depot (84A). Recorded mileage 1,358,388, service life 26 years, 5 months and 13 days. Disposal Swindon Works, March 1963.

Tender types principal fitted dates, Collett 4000g April 1936, Hawksworth 4000g 19th February 1953, Collett 4000g 30th September 1955, Hawksworth 4000g 24th June 1958, Collett 4000g 15th February 1961.

Allocated Depots

CDF Cardiff Canton	08/04/36	CDF Cardiff Canton	24/10/43	84A Stafford Road	20/03/58
PDN Old Oak Common	09/09/43				

Earl Cawdor of Castlemartin in the County of Pembroke, is a title in the Peerage of the United Kingdom. It was created in 1827 for John Campbell, 2nd Baron Cawdor. In January 2014 the 7th Earl was recorded as being Colin Robert Vaughan Campbell.

GWR 'Castle' class 4-6-0 No 5046 EARL CAWDOR is seen at Stafford Road (84A) on 2nd August 1955. The engine is in the company of GWR 'Hall' class No 4973 SWEENEY HALL and an unidentified Pannier Tank. *Norman Preedy Collection/Rail Photoprints*

5047 COMPTON CASTLE renamed EARL OF DARTMOUTH on 20th August 1937

Introduced into service in April 1936. Diagram HB boiler fitted. The locomotive's last 'Heavy General' overhaul including boiler (HB 6687) and tender change took place at Swindon Works between 17th October and 16th December 1960. The engine was withdrawn in September 1962 from Stafford Road depot (84A). Recorded mileage 1,225,670, service life 26 years and 5 months. Disposal Swindon Works, March 1963.

Tender types principal fitted dates, Collett 4000g 11th April 1936, Hawksworth 4000g 23rd February 1953, Collett 4000g 16th December 1960.

Allocated Depots

LDR Landore	21/04/36	NA Newton Abbot	27/11/43	NA Newton Abbot	27/04/48
NA Newton Abbot	27/04/40	LA Laira	16/03/48	84A Stafford Road	03/11/54
LA Laira	09/43				

Earl Of Dartmouth is a title in the Peerage of Great Britain. It was created in 1711 for William Legge, 2nd Baron Dartmouth. William Legge, in January 2014 the 10th Earl of Dartmouth was recorded as being a 'Member of the European Parliament' (MEP) and reportedly preferred to be known as William Dartmouth.

GWR 'Castle' class 4-6-0 No 5047 EARL OF DARTMOUTH had a privileged young visitor on the footplate when this image was taken at Wolverhampton Low Level station. Note that the Hawksworth tender has a mixed load of coal and ovoids. Note also the BR so called cycling lion (Lion on a Bike) emblem. *Keith Langston Collection*

5048 CRANBROOK CASTLE renamed EARL OF DEVON August 1937

Introduced into service in May 1936. Diagram HB boiler fitted. The locomotive's last 'Heavy General' overhaul and tender change took place at Swindon Works between 31st August and 3rd November June 1960. The engine was withdrawn in August 1962 from Llanelly depot (87F). Recorded mileage 1,327,811, service life 26 years, 3 months and 10 days. Disposal Hayes, Bridgend, August 1962.

Tender types principal fitted dates, Collett 4000g 25th April 1936, Hawksworth 4000g 22nd June 1951, Collett 4000g 26th March 1953.

GWR 'Castle' class 4-6-0 No 5048 EARL OF DEVON is seen with an up Paddington via Bristol service at Exeter St David's station in June 1955. *David Anderson*

Allocated Depots

BRD Bristol Bath Road	04/05/36	Brd Weston-super-Mare	12/40	88A Cardiff Canton	03/11/60
LDR Landore	19/01/38	BRD Bristol Bath Road	01/41	87A Neath Court Sart	05/07/61
SDN Swindon	18/12/39	SDN Swindon	06/02/42	Neath Court Sart. Stored	17/04/62
BRD Bristol Bath Road	02/40	BRD Bristol Bath Road	02/43	87F Llanelly. Reinstated	11/08/62

One of the last steam operated 'South Wales Pullman' services stands at Swansea High Street after arrival behind Castle 4-6-0 5048 EARL OF DEVON, September 1961. Part of 'Castle' class No 7016 CHESTER CASTLE can be also be seen. Note the Mechanical lubricator forward of the steam pipe and the stepped inside cylinder cover. *Hugh Ballantyne/Rail Photoprints*

Earl of Devon, the title was created several times in the English peerage, and was possessed first by the de Redvers family, and later by the Courtenays. In January 2014 the 18th Earl was recorded as being Lord Devon of Powderham Castle.

5049 DENBIGH CASTLE renamed **EARL OF PLYMOUTH** August 1937. (Converted to double chimney) Introduced into service in May 1936. Diagram HB boiler fitted. Double chimney fitted September 1959 (Diagram HD boiler number 7647). This was the first 'Castle' class engine to be fitted with a 4-row superheater. The locomotive's last 'Heavy General' overhaul including boiler (HD 9608) and tender change took place at Swindon Works between 15th June and 1st September 1961. The engine was withdrawn in March 1963 from St Philips Marsh depot (82B). Recorded mileage 1,282,965, service life 26 years, 10 months and 14 days. Disposal, Cashmores, Newport, April 1964.

Tender types principal fitted dates, Collett 4000g 02/05/36, Collett 4000g (8 Wheeled) 21st April 1942, Collett 4000g 23rd June 1944, Hawksworth 4000g 13th June 1952, Collett 4000g 22nd October 1952, Hawksworth 4000g 24th December 1957, Collett 4000g 1st September 1961.

Allocated Depots

| WOS Worcester | 08/05/36 | 83D Laira | 12/56 | 82A Bristol Bath Road | 22/04/60 |
| CDF Cardiff Canton | 13/08/39 | 83A Newton Abbot | 24/07/58 | 82B St Philips Marsh | 16/09/60 |

Earl of Plymouth is a title that has been created three times, twice in the Peerage of England and once in the Peerage of the United Kingdom. In January 2014 the holder of the title was recorded as being Other Robert Windsor-Clive the 3rd Earl of Plymouth. The family seat was Hewell Grange, Worcestershire, and is now Oakly Park, Bromfield near Ludlow, Shropshire. The unusual forename 'Other' is traditional in the family and derives from a legendary Viking ancestor 'Otho' or 'Othere'. The Earls of Plymouth are reportedly amongst the largest landowners in the country.

GWR 'Castle' class 4-6-0 No 5049 EARL OF PLYMOUTH is seen at Taunton Station circa 1958 with 'The Cornishman'. *Keith Langston Collection*

5050 DEVIZES CASTLE renamed EARL OF ST. GERMANS August 1937

Introduced into service in May 1936. Diagram HB boiler fitted. The locomotive's last 'Heavy General' overhaul including boiler (HC 7627) and tender change took place at Swindon Works between 13th March and 4th May 1961. The engine was withdrawn in September 1963 from St Philips Marsh depot (82B). Recorded mileage 1,135,797, service life 27 years, 4 months and 3 days. Disposal Coopers Metals, Sharpness, May 1964.

Tender types principal fitted dates, Collett 4000g May 1936, Hawksworth 4000g 9th September 1949, Collett 4000g 27th June 1950, Hawksworth 4000g 22nd May 1952, Collett 4000g 24th February 1954, Hawksworth 4000g 20th October 1956, Collett 4000g 3rd May 1961.

Allocated Depots

WOS Worcester	05/36	4A* Shrewsbury	09/48	82C Swindon	18/01/62
GLO Gloucester Horton Road	22/07/39	81A Old Oak Common	16/09/60	82B St Philips Marsh	05/04/62
EXE Exeter	13/11/39	82B St Philips Marsh	08/08/61		

*4A LMS 01/01/35 then 84G BR from 01/02/50

Earl of St Germans, in Cornwall is a title in the Peerage of the United Kingdom. It was created in 1815 for John Eliot, 2nd Baron Eliot. Several members of this family have held prominent political positions, in both the United Kingdom and Ireland. The title takes its name from the village of St Germans in Cornwall; however, the family seat is Port Eliot near Saltash, in the same county. In January 2014 Peregrine Nicholas Eliot was recorded as being the 10th Earl.

GWR 'Castle' class 4-6-0 No 5050 EARL OF ST. GERMANS is seen leaving Exeter St David's with a Liverpool–Plymouth service on 23rd July 1956. *David Anderson*

5051 DRYSLLWYN CASTLE renamed EARL BATHURST August 1937. Preserved

Introduced into service in May 1936. Diagram HB boiler fitted. The locomotive's last 'Heavy Intermediate' overhaul including boiler (HB 6661) and tender change took place at Swindon Works between 26th April and 23rd June 1961. The engine was withdrawn in May 1963 from Llanelly depot (87F). Recorded mileage 1,316,659, service life 27 years.

Tender types principal fitted dates, Collett 4000g 9th May 1936, Hawksworth 4000g 21st June 1961.

After being withdrawn former GWR 'Castle' class 4-6-0 No 5051 Earl Bathurst was sold by British Railways for scrap to dealers Woodham Brothers of Barry, South Wales. The iconic Collett locomotive only remained there until November 1970 when it was fortunately purchased by a member of the Great Western Society (GWS). It was the fourth locomotive to leave the Woodham's yard and was actually delivered by rail to the Society's then developing Didcot base and steam centre.

Since that time No 5051 has been lovingly restored to working order and steamed again in 1980, in addition to operating at Didcot the engine was successfully put to work hauling special trains on the mainline. The engine also famously took part in the 'Rocket 150' celebrations at Rainhill, in the May of that year.

The locomotive's mainline certificate expired in 1986 and thereafter No 5051 was restricted to non-mainline steaming duties until 1990. In 1987 the GWS purchased the engine from the Mynors family. A second overhaul, to mainline standard then took place allowing the engine to once more grace the national network and also visit preserved railways. In 2008 the engine's boiler certificate expired and as a result of which the locomotive was placed on static display at Didcot until a further overhaul can take place. For more information see www.didcotrailwaycentre.org.uk/locos/5051/5051.html

Preserved GWR 'Castle' class 4-6-0 No 5051 EARL BATHURST seen leaving Banbury with a Didcot–Stratford special working on 14th April 1984. Hugh Ballantyne/Rail Photoprints

Allocated Depots

| LDR Landore | 24/05/36 | Neath Court Sart | 23/06/61 | Llanelly | 09/02/63 |

Earl Bathurst, of Bathurst in the County of Sussex, is a title in the Peerage of Great Britain. It was created in 1772 for Allen Bathurst, 1st Baron Bathurst. In January 2014 Allen Christopher Bertram Bathurst was recorded as being the 9th Earl.

A nice smile from the footplate as GWR 'Castle' class 4-6-0 No 5051 EARL BATHURST is seen approaching the east end of Swindon station circa 1958. The signal box clock was an interesting railway landmark, well known to enthusiasts of the era. Rail Photoprints Collection

Preserved GWR 'Castle' class 4-6-0 No 5051 EARL BATHURST is seen on Welsh Marches duty in April 1983, operating then as DRYSLLWYN CASTLE. *Keith Langston Collection*

Preserved GWR 1936 built 'Castle' class 4-6-0 No 5051 EARL BATHURST makes a fine sight and the clean powerful looks of Collett's design are seen to good effect in this 1992 study taken at Didcot. *Keith Langston Collection*

5052 EASTNOR CASTLE renamed EARL OF RADNOR July 1937

Introduced into service in May 1936. Diagram HB boiler fitted. The locomotive's last 'Heavy Intermediate' overhaul including boiler (HB 6677) and tender change took place at Swindon Works between 25th June and 26th August 1960. The engine was withdrawn in September 1962 from St Philips Marsh depot (82B). Recorded mileage 1,396,894, service life 26 years, 5 months and 27 days. Disposal Cashmores, Newport, September 1962.

Tender types principal fitted dates, Collett 4000g May 1936, Hawksworth 4000g 17th November 1954, Collett 4000g 5th November 1955, Hawksworth 4000g 26th August 1960.

Allocated Depots

CDF Cardiff Canton	25/05/36	82A Bristol Bath Road	06/09/60	82B St Philips Marsh	16/09/60
81A Old Oak Common	15/01/57				

Earl Of Radnor is a title which was created twice, first in the Peerage of England in 1679 for John Robartes, 2nd Baron Robartes, a notable political figure of the reign of Charles II, and he was made Viscount Bodmin at the same time. Secondly in the Peerage of Great Britain in 1765, on that occasion for William Bouverie, 2nd Viscount Folkestone. In January 2014 William Pleydell-Bouverie was recorded as being the 9th Earl, having succeeded his father in 2008. The family seat is Longford Castle in Wiltshire.

GWR 'Castle' class 4-6-0 No 5052 EARL OF RADNOR is seen approaching Twerton Tunnel with the 2.35 Weston-super-Mare–Paddington, on 30th June 1962. *Hugh Ballantyne/Rail Photoprints*

5053 BISHOP'S CASTLE renamed EARL CAIRNS August 1937

Introduced into service in June 1936. Diagram HB boiler fitted. The locomotive's last 'Heavy Intermediate' overhaul including boiler (HA 4650) and tender change took place at Swindon Works between 11th August and 10th October 1960. The engine was withdrawn in July 1962 from Cardiff Canton depot (88A). Recorded mileage 1,293,786, service life 26 years, 1 month and 7 days. Disposal Cashmores, Newport, September 1962.

Tender types principal fitted dates, Collett 4000g June 1936, Hawksworth 4000g 11th December 1952, Collett 4000g 31st March 1954, Hawksworth 4000g 8th December 1954.

Allocated Depots

4A Shrewsbury	06/06/36	83A Newton Abbot	18/12/54	88A Cardiff Canton	11/09/61
SRD Stafford Road	25/10/37	83D Laira	04/11/59		

Earl Cairns is a title in the Peerage of the United Kingdom. It was created in 1878 for the prominent politician Hugh Cairns, 1st Baron Cairns. He was twice Lord Chancellor of the United Kingdom, first in 1868 and then again from 1874 to 1880. Hugh Cairns had already been created Baron Cairns, of Garmoyle in the County of Antrim, in 1867, and was also made Viscount Garmoyle. Lord Cairns was a great supporter of Dr. Thomas John Barnardo and his Barnado's Homes project. Today a property called Cairns house still stands on the one remaining green at Barkingside. The Right Honourable Earl Cairns was the first president of Dr. Barnado's Homes. In January 2014 Simon Dallas Cairns was recorded as being the 6th Earl.

GWR 'Castle' class 4-6-0 No 5053 EARL CAIRNS and Mogul 2-6-0 No 5331 are seen passing Bentley Heath with a passenger service, on a warm 21st July 1951.
Rail Photoprints Collection

5054 LAMPHEY CASTLE renamed EARL OF DUCIE September 1937

Introduced into service in June 1936. Diagram HB boiler fitted. The locomotive's last 'Heavy General' overhaul including boiler (HB 6686) and tender change took place at Swindon Works between 14th June and 4th September 1962. The engine was withdrawn in October 1964 from Gloucester Horton Road depot (85B). Recorded mileage 1,412,394, service life 28 years, 4 months and 11 days. Disposal Swindon Works, December 1964.

Tender types principal fitted dates, Collett 4000g 6th June 1936, Hawksworth 4000g 22nd April 1953, Collett 4000g 24th March 1954, Hawksworth 4000g 18th June 1960, Collett 4000g 26th November 1960, Hawksworth 4000g 4th September 1963.

GWR 'Castle' class 4-6-0 No 5054 is seen as LAMPHEY CASTLE at Newton Abbot in 1936. Note the original profile outside steam pipe and the tall style chimney.
Rail Photoprints Collection

Allocated Depots

PDN Old Oak Common	13/06/36	87G Carmarthen	31/10/60	86C Hereford. Reinstated	30/11/63
CDR Cardiff Canton	01/04/38	87A Neath Court Sart	03/11/62	85A Worcester	13/04/64
82A Bristol Bath Road	10/04/57	87F Llanelly	09/02/63	85B Gloucester Horton Road	14/09/64
81A Old Oak Common	04/11/59	87F Llanelly Stored	09/09/63		

GWR 'Castle' class 4-6-0 No 5054 EARL OF DUCIE is seen passing Langley with an up South Wales–Paddington express, on 14th August 1954. Note the profile of the modified pattern steam pipe and the shorter style chimney.
C. R. L. Coles (Dave Cobbe Collection)/Rail Photoprints

Earl of Ducie is a title in both the Peerage of Great Britain (1720) and a Peerage of the United Kingdom (1837). In January 2014 David Leslie Moreton, who is a landowner and associated with agriculture in the county of Gloucestershire, was listed as being the 7th Earl.

5055 LYDFORD CASTLE renamed EARL OF ELDON September 1937

Introduced into service in June 1936. Diagram HB boiler fitted. The locomotive's last 'Heavy Intermediate' overhaul including boiler (HC 7635) and tender change took place at Swindon Works between 15th December 1961 and 16th February 1962. The engine was withdrawn in September 1964 from Gloucester Horton Road depot (85B). Recorded mileage 1,439,975, service life 28 years, 3 months and 14 days. Disposal Cashmores, Newport, December 1965.

Tender types principal fitted dates, Collett 4000g 13th June 1937, Hawksworth 4000g 12th January 1951, Collett 4000g 18th September 1952.

Allocated Depots

PDN Old Oak Common	14/06/36	83A Newton Abbot	20/03/58	87J Fishguard.* Reinstated	27/07/63
OXF Oxford	05/39	Newton Abbot. Stored	24/09/62	87J Fishguard.* Stored	09/09/63
PDN Old Oak Common	07/39	87G Carmarthen. Reinstated	21/12/62	86C Hereford. Reinstated	02/11/63
RDG Reading WR	15/06/42	87G Carmarthen. Stored	14/01/63	85B Gloucester Horton Road	20/07/64
PDN Old Oak Common	10/42				

(*Goodwick)

Earl of Eldon is a title in the Peerage of the United Kingdom which was created in 1821 for John Scott, 1st Baron Scott and Lord Chancellor from 1801 to 1806 and 1807 to 1827. In January 2014 John Joseph Nicholas Scott, was listed as being the 5th Earl.

GWR 'Castle' class 4-6-0 No 5055 EARL OF ELDON approaches Reading with the up 'Torbay Express', circa 1957. *Rail Photoprints Collection*

5056 OGMORE CASTLE renamed **EARL OF POWIS** September 1937. (Converted to double chimney)
Introduced into service in June 1936. Diagram HB boiler fitted. Double chimney and 4-row superheater fitted during the locomotive's last 'Heavy General' overhaul which included boiler (HD 7656) and tender change, and took place at Swindon Works between 26th September and 17th November 1960. The engine was withdrawn in November 1964 from Oxley depot (2B). Recorded mileage to December 1963, 1,434,833, service life 28 years, 4 months and 3 days. Disposal Cashmores, Great Bridge, February 1965.

Tender types principal fitted dates, Collett 4000g 20th June 1936, Hawksworth 4000g 26th January 1954, Collett 4000g 11th January 1955.

Allocated Depots

PDN Old Oak Common	28/06/36	Old Oak Common. Reinstated	04/11/50	86C Hereford	13/04/64
Swindon Stored	23/10/50	88L Cardiff East Dock	26/07/63	2B Oxley	20/06/64

Earl of Powis is a title which has been created on three occasions. Firstly in 1674 in the Peerage of England and that title became extinct in 1748, secondly in 1748 in the Peerage of Great Britain and that title became extinct in 1801 and thirdly in 1804 in the Peerage of the United Kingdom when Edward Clive 2nd Baron Clive was made Earl of Powis. In January 2014 John George Herbert (styled Viscount Clive between 1988 and 1993) was listed as the 8th Earl.

GWR 'Castle' class 4-6-0 No 5056 EARL OF POWIS is seen at Shrewsbury in October 1962. Note the mechanical lubricator mounted in front of the 'steam' pipe, also the box cover housing the lubricator pipes to valves, pistons and the regulator valve as they leave the 4 row superheater boiler and enter the smokebox (seen above the handrail and below the double chimney). *Rail Photoprints Collection*

5057 PENRICE CASTLE renamed EARL WALDEGRAVE October 1937. (Converted to double chimney)

Introduced into service in July 1936. Diagram HB boiler fitted. Double chimney and 4-row superheater fitted July 1958 (boiler HD 7675). The locomotive's last 'Heavy General' overhaul including boiler (HD 7672) and tender change took place at Swindon Works between 12th March and 17th May 1962. The engine was withdrawn in March 1964 from Old Oak Common depot (81A). Recorded mileage 1,273,324, service life 27 years, 8 months and 1 day. Disposal Swindon Works, August 1964.

Tender types principal fitted dates, Collett 4000g 27th June 1936, Hawksworth 4000g 17th February 1950, Collett 4000g 31st August 1950, Hawksworth 4000g 30th April 1952, Collett 4000g 9th September 1952, Hawksworth 4000g 8th June 1954, Collett 4000g 9th May 1955, Hawksworth 4000g 24th March 1960, Collett 4000g 17th May 1962.

GWR 'Castle' class 4-6-0 No 5057 EARL WALDEGRAVE draws forward to make a second stop with the 09.45 Paddington–Weston-super-Mare service, on 29th June 1963. Note the banner repeater signal on the up platform is 'off' as that train leaves the station. Hugh Ballantyne/Rail Photoprints

Allocated Depots

NA Newton Abbot	09/07/36	81A Old Oak Common	01/03/51	82A Bristol Bath Road	08/06/54
EXE Exeter	03/38	83A Newton Abbot	02/52	84C Banbury	04/11/59
NA Newton Abbot	04/38	83D Laira	30/04/52	81A Old Oak Common	24/03/60
LA Laira	01/39				

GWR 'Castle' class 4-6-0 No 5057 is seen in the roundhouse at Old Oak Common (81A) in August 1962. This image shows several features to good effect, the cabside 'D' route indicator disc, the exterior mounted rear sandbox behind the trailing driving wheel, the cab edge beading and short handrail below the side window, the elliptical nameplate and the mechanical lubricator (mounted behind the modified outside steam pipe). Rail Photoprints Collection

Earl Waldegrave is a title in the Peerage of Great Britain. It was created in 1729 for James Waldegrave, 2nd Baron Waldegrave. In January 2014 James Sherbrooke Waldegrave (styled Viscount Chewton until 1995) who is associated with agriculture and business in the county of Somerset was listed as the 13th Earl.

5058 NEWPORT CASTLE renamed EARL OF CLANCARTY September 1937

Introduced into service in May 1937. Diagram HB boiler fitted. The locomotive's last 'Heavy Intermediate' overhaul including boiler (HB 6647) took place at Swindon Works between 16th May and 16th July 1962. The engine was withdrawn in March 1964 from Gloucester Horton Road depot (85B). Recorded mileage 1,224,735, service life 25 years, 9 months and 11 days. Disposal Swindon Works, April 1963.

Tender types principal fitted dates, Collett 4000g May 1937.

GWR 'Castle' class 4-6-0 No 5058 EARL OF CLANCARTY is seen at Plymouth Laira on 17th May 1960. Note the 'Ferret and Dartboard' BR emblem on the Collett 4000g tender. This locomotive was only ever coupled to Collett tenders during its service life (17 tender swops, the last on 21st July 1962). *R.E. Vincent/ Transport Treasury*

Allocated Depots

NA Newton Abbot	23/05/37	83D Laira	01/06/57	85B Gloucester Horton Road	11/09/61
83D Laira	03/50	82C Swindon	22/09/59	Gloucester Horton Road. Stored	12/11/62
83A Newton Abbot	29/05/57	83D Laira	30/11/59		

GWR 'Castle' class 4-6-0 No 5058 EARL OF CLANCARTY climbs past Dainton Tunnel signal box with a 10 coach Plymouth–Exeter excursion, on 7th August 1961. Note the down line sign instructing drivers of 'Goods and mineral trains with 35 wagons or less to STOP DEAD' at that point, in order that unfitted trains could pin down brakes. The large post mounted mirror beyond the up line (above 2nd coach) gave the signalman in the downside box a view into the tunnel. *Hugh Ballantyne/Rail Photoprints*

Earl of Clancarty is a title that has been created twice in the Peerage of Ireland. For the first time in 1658 in favour of Donough MacCarty, 2nd Viscount Muskerry. In the second instance it was created in favour of William Trench, 1st Viscount Dunlo in 1801. In January 2014 Nicholas Le Poer Trench, who is also the 8th Marquees of Heusden, was listed as the 9th Earl. He is an Irish peer as well as a member of the Dutch nobility and at the time of writing he was a member of the British House of Lords.

5059 POWIS CASTLE renamed EARL ST. ALDWYN October 1937

Introduced into service in June 1937. Diagram HB boiler fitted. The locomotive's last 'Heavy General' overhaul including boiler (HC 6691) took place at Swindon Works between 3rd March and 24th April 1961. The engine was withdrawn in June 1962 from Shrewsbury depot (89A). Recorded mileage 1,054,602, service life 25 years and 14 days. Disposal Swindon Works, February 1963.

Tender types principal fitted dates, Collett 4000g 29th May 1937, Hawksworth 4000g 24th August 1950, Collett 4000g 20th May 1954, Hawksworth 4000g 27th March 1956, Collett 4000g 2nd April 1958.

Allocated Depots

EXE Exeter	08/06/37	84A Stafford Road	02/04/58	84G Shrewsbury	17/05/60
83A Newton Abbot	05/53				

Earl St. Aldwyn, of Coln St. Aldwyn, Gloucestershire is a title in the Peerage of the United Kingdom. It was created in 1915 for Michael Hicks Beach, 1st Viscount St. Aldwyn, a politician who was Chancellor of the Exchequer 1885–1886 and 1895–1902. In January 2014 Michael Henry Hicks Beach was listed as being the 3rd Earl.

GWR 'Castle' class 4-6-0 No 5059 EARL ST ALDWYN runs along the sea wall at Teignmouth with an up express, on 1st August 1951. The then Exeter allocated Hawksworth tendered engine looked to be in fine fettle. *Norman Preedy Collection/Rail Photoprints*

5060 SARUM CASTLE renamed **EARL OF BERKELEY** October 1937. (Converted to double chimney)
Introduced into service in June 1937. Diagram HB boiler fitted. Double chimney and 4-row superheater fitted during the locomotive's last 'Heavy General' overhaul which included boiler change (HD 9609) and took place at Swindon Works between 30th May and 11th August 1961. The engine was withdrawn in June 1962 from Old Oak Common depot (81A). Recorded mileage 1,316,240, service life 25 years and 12 days. Disposal Cashmores, Newport, March 1964.

Tender types principal fitted dates, Collett 4000g 5th June 1937, Hawksworth 4000g 6th December 1957, Collett 4000g 26th August 1959, Hawksworth 4000g 22nd April 1961, Collett 4000g 11th August 1961.

Allocated Depots

| SRD Stafford Road | 10/06/37 | LA Laira | 04/12/40 | 81A Old Oak Common | 13/01/51 |

Earl Berkeley. The title Baron Berkeley was created twice in the Peerage of England, firstly in 1295 for Sir Thomas de Berkeley and secondly in 1421 for James Berkeley. The title survived into modern times however, Randal Thomas Mowbray Rawdon Berkeley (1865–1942) who was born in Brussels became the 8th Earl of Berkeley and he died without issue. The 8th Earl was educated in France but after coming to England he joined Burney's Naval Academy at Gosport (1878) and thereafter perused a naval career. The historic house, of which he was the head, is one of a very few that could claim a pre-Norman pedigree, and which was able to trace its descent to Saxon times. Three Berkeley tombs can be seen in the church formerly known as St Augustine's Abbey, the present day Bristol Cathedral.

GWR 'Castle' class 4-6-0 No 5059 EARL OF BERKELEY is seen at Plymouth Laira depot (83D) in 1950. *R.E. Vincent/Transport Treasury*

5061 SUDELEY CASTLE renamed EARL OF BIRKENHEAD October 1937. (Converted to double chimney)

Introduced into service in June 1937. Diagram HB boiler fitted. Double chimney and 4-row superheater fitted September 1958 (boiler HD 7677). The locomotive's last 'Heavy Intermediate' took place at Swindon Works between 15th November 1960 and 4th January 1961. However, in September 1962 boiler HD 7654 was reportedly fitted during a subsequent works visit even though the engine had been officially withdrawn on that date, from Cardiff Canton depot (88A). Recorded mileage 1,020,412, service life 25 years, 3 months and 10 days. Disposal Cashmores, Newport December 1962.

Tender types principal fitted dates, Collett 4000g 12th June 1937, Hawksworth 4000g 4th July 1952, Collett 4000g 23rd June 1954, Hawksworth 4000g January 1961.

Allocated Depots

4A Shrewsbury	11/06/37	4A Shrewsbury	22/04/43	84K Chester West	05/51
SRD Stafford Road	10/38	Swindon Stored	07/03/50	81D Reading WR	05/09/58
4A Shrewsbury	11/38	Stafford Road. Reinstated	11/50	86C Cardiff Canton	09/12/59
SRD Stafford Road	16/04/43				

Earl of Birkenhead was a title in the Peerage of the United Kingdom, it was created in 1922 for the noted lawyer and politician Frederick Edwin Smith, 1st Viscount Birkenhead. He was Solicitor-General in 1915, Attorney-General from 1915 to 1919 and Lord High Chancellor from 1919 to 1922. The 1st Earl served on the 1924 Olympic Committee (Paris games) and he was played by the actor Nigel Davenport in the 1981 film 'Chariots of Fire'. The title became extinct after the death of the 3rd Earl in 1985.

GWR 'Castle' class 4-6-0 No 5061 EARL OF BIRKENHEAD is seen departing from Didcot with the 'Capitals United Express', Paddington–South Wales service on 25th March 1961 (headboard not carried). *David Anderson*

5062 TENBY CASTLE renamed EARL OF SHAFTESBURY November 1937

Introduced into service in June 1937. Diagram HB boiler fitted. The locomotive's last 'Heavy Intermediate' overhaul including boiler (HB 6629) took place at Swindon Works between 23rd November 1960 and 12th January 1961. The engine was withdrawn in August 1962 from Llanelly depot (87F). Recorded mileage 1,143,143, service life 25 years, 1 month and 22 days. Disposal Hayes Metals, Bridgend December 1962.

Tender types principal fitted dates, Collett 4000g 19th June 1937, Hawksworth 27th November 1951, Collett 4000g 8th January 1954, Hawksworth 4000g 12th January 1961.

Allocated Depots

SRD Stafford Road	23/06/37	82C Swindon	14/10/52	87A Neath Court Sart	13/06/61
NA Newton Abbot	09/37	82A Bristol Bath Road	23/04/58	Neath Court Sart. Stored	17/04/62
83C Exeter	05/50	87E Landore	16/09/60	87F Llanelly. Reinstated	02/07/62
83B Taunton	02/51				

GWR 'Castle' class 4-6-0 No 5062 EARL OF SHAFTESBURY is seen with an express service passing Sydney Gardens outside Bath, in August 1959. *Keith Langston Collection*

Earl of Shaftesbury is a title in the Peerage of England. It was created in 1672 for Anthony Ashley-Cooper, 1st Baron Ashley, a prominent politician in the Cabal which at that time dominated the policies of King Charles II. In 2004 Anthony Ashley-Cooper, 10th Earl of Shaftesbury was murdered by his third wife, Jamila M'Barek, and her brother. They were convicted of the crime in 2007, two years after the 10th Earl's dismembered body was found in the French Alps. In January 2014 Nicholas Ashley-Cooper was listed as being the 12th Earl.

5063 THORNBURY CASTLE renamed EARL BALDWIN in 1937

Introduced into service in June 1937. Diagram HB boiler fitted. The locomotive's last 'Heavy General' overhaul including boiler (HC 7628) took place at Swindon Works between 1st June and 24th August 1962. The engine was withdrawn in February 1965 from Oxley depot (2B). Recorded mileage (up to September 1963) 1,235,058, service life 27 years, 6 months and 28 days. Disposal Cashmores, Great Bridge, May 1965.

Tender types principal fitted dates, Collett 4000g 26th June 1937, Hawksworth 4000g 1st June 1954, Collett 4000g 12th April 1956, Hawksworth 4000g 16th April 1958, Collett 4000g 7th December 1959.

Allocated Depots

WOS Worcester	03/07/37	84A Stafford Road	16/04/58	2B Oxley	09/09/63
82A Bristol Bath Road	01/06/54				

GWR 'Castle' class 4-6-0 No 5063 EARL BALDWIN approaches Standish Junction and is signalled to cross from BR/WR to BR/MR metals, as it heads the 08.00 Wolverhampton–Minehead service, on 20th July 1963. *Hugh Ballantyne/Rail Photoprints*

Earl Baldwin, of Bewdley is a title in the Peerage of the United Kingdom which was created in 1937 for the prominent politician Stanley Baldwin. He was Prime Minister of the United Kingdom for three terms, 1923 to 1924, 1924 to 1929 and again from 1935 to 1937. During his third term as PM Baldwin faced the 1936 abdication crisis concerning King Edward VIII, his management of which was highly praised. In January 2014 Edward Alfred Alexander Baldwin was listed as being the 4th Earl.

5064 TRETOWER CASTLE renamed **BISHOP'S CASTLE** September 1937. (Converted to double chimney)
Introduced into service in July 1937. Diagram HB boiler fitted. Double chimney and 4-row superheater fitted September 1958 (HD boiler number 7646 previously fitted during November/December 1956). The locomotive's last 'Heavy General' overhaul including boiler (HB 6629) and tender change took place at Swindon Works between 16th September and 18th November 1960. The engine was withdrawn in September 1962 from Gloucester Horton Road depot (85B). Recorded mileage 1,155,986, service life 25 years, 2 months and 13 days. Disposal Cashmores, Newport, December 1962.

Tender types principal fitted dates, Collett 4000g 26th July 1937, Hawksworth 4000g 3rd October 1950, Collett 4000g 17th December 1952, Hawksworth 4000g 9th December 1953, Collett 4000g 17th February 1955, Hawksworth 4000g 24th January 1956, Collett 4000g 26th September 1958, Hawksworth 4000g 18th November 1960.

Allocated Depots

NA Newton Abbot	08/07/37	4A Shrewsbury	10/37	82C Swindon	23/04/58
SRD Stafford Road	09/37	82A Bristol Bath Road	05/10/50	85B Gloucester Horton Road	11/09/61

Bishop's Castle, the first fortification in the Shropshire village of the same name, was built circa 1087 in order to defend the settlement from the Welsh. In the Early Middle Ages the castle and parish were situated partly in Wales and partly in England, so territorial disputes were reportedly 'extremely common'. In 1557 the castle was described as being 'thirteen rooms covered with lead, a tower on the outer wall on the eastern side containing a stable, and two rooms covered with tiles'. In 1618 the castle started to deteriorate and in the 1700s the stone keep and surroundings were flattened to make way for a bowling green. Little remains of the castle, but in modern times a building trading as the Castle Hotel stands in the town.

GWR 'Castle' class 4-6-0 No 5064 BISHOP'S CASTLE is seen at Taunton station with the 2.25pm express to London Paddington on 8th June 1955. *David Anderson*

5065 UPTON CASTLE renamed NEWPORT CASTLE September 1937

Introduced into service in July 1937. Diagram HB boiler fitted. The locomotive's last 'Heavy General' overhaul including boiler (HC 7620) and tender change took place at Swindon Works between 8th December 1960 and 2nd February 1961. The engine was withdrawn in February 1963 from Old Oak Common depot (81A). Recorded mileage 1,222,961, service life 25 years and 7 months. Disposal R.A. Kings, Norwich, December 1963.

Tender types principal fitted dates, Collett 4000g 3rd July 1937, Hawksworth 4000g 2nd May 1952, Collett 4000g 23rd March 1953, Hawksworth 4000g 19th October 1955, Collett 4000g 9th October 1956, Hawksworth 4000g 6th August 1957, Collett 4000g 8th June 1959, Hawksworth 4000g 2nd February 1961, Collett 4000g 22nd April 1961, Hawksworth 4000g 7th October 1961.

Allocated Depots

| EXE Exeter | 09/07/37 | PDN Old Oak Common | 22/12/44 | Swindon. Stored | 14/04/50 |
| CDF Cardiff Canton | 03/08/39 | Old Oak Common. Stored | 26/10/49 | Old Oak Common. Reinstated | 08/50 |

Newport Castle is located in Newport Gwent, it was built in the 14th century in order to control a crossing over the River Usk. It was sacked by Owain Glyndŵr in 1402 and although still in a state of disrepair it was taken by the forces of Oliver Cromwell during the Civil War. The ruins were awarded listed building status in 1951, but have been closed to the public since 2011 due to concerns over structural safety.

GWR 'Castle' class 4-6-0 No 5065 NEWPORT CASTLE is seen complete with 'Royal Duchy' headboard at Laira depot on 17th June 1958. Note the forward position of the mechanical lubricator. *Norman Preedy Collection/Rail Photoprints*

Note: The 'Royal Duchy' (Paddington–Penzance) nameplate incorporates a shield showing the arms of the Duchy of Cornwall and was carried from 28th January 1957 to 12th June 1965. The title was bestowed on the 11am ex Penzance and the 1.30pm from Paddington.

5066 WARDOUR CASTLE renamed **SIR FELIX POLE** April 1956. (Converted to double chimney)

Introduced into service in July 1937. Diagram HB boiler fitted. Double chimney and 4-row superheater fitted September 1958. The locomotive's last 'Heavy Intermediate' overhaul including boiler (HC 7610) and tender change took place at Swindon Works between 31st October and 19th December 1960. The engine was withdrawn in September 1962 from Old Oak Common depot (81A). Recorded mileage 1,339,619, service life 25 years, 2 months and 1 day. Disposal Cashmores, Great Bridge, December 1962. Unusually this locomotive was only ever allocated to a single depot.

Tender types principal fitted dates, Collett 4000g 10th July 1937, Hawksworth 4000g 1st July 1948, Collett 4000g 7th February 1950, Hawksworth 4000g 21st August 1957, Collett 4000g 21st April 1959, Hawksworth 4000g 21st May 1960, Collett 4000g 13th August 1960, Hawksworth 4000g 19th December 1960.

GWR 'Castle' class 4-6-0 No 5066 seen as WARDOUR CASTLE after arriving at Shrewsbury with the down 'Cambrian Coast Express', 1954. Note the non-stepped inside cylinder cover, two brackets for out of use lamps forward of the steam pipe and also the short fire iron compartment between the cab and trailing wheel splasher. *Cresselly Photos Collection*

Allocated Depot

| PDN Old Oak Common | 17/07/37 |

Wardour Castle is located at Wardour in Wiltshire, and is approximately 15 miles (24 km) west of Salisbury. The original castle was partially destroyed during the Civil War. The ruin is managed by English Heritage who have designated it as a 'Grade 1' listed building, and it is open to the public.

GWR 'Castle' class 4-6-0 No 5066 seen with double chimney as SIR FELIX POLE whilst approaching Bristol Temple Meads with a southbound North and West route service, in August 1960. Note the stepped inside cylinder cover. *Rail Photoprints Collection*

Sir Felix Pole (Felix John Clewett Pole 1887–1956) was the General Manager of the Great Western Railway from 1921 until 1929 when he left the company to become executive chairman of Associated Electrical Industries (AEI) and he held that post until 1945. Pole was born in Little Bedwyn, Wiltshire and he joined the GWR as a telegraph boy in 1891, when aged 14. Rapidly promoted he worked on the railways marketing campaigns. In 1912 he became head of the Staff and Labour Department, then Assistant General Manager in 1919 and was finally appointed General Manager in 1921. He was knighted in February 1924. Pole died in Reading in 1956 and he is buried at Little Bedwyn.

5067 ST. FAGANS CASTLE

Introduced into service in July 1937. Diagram HB boiler fitted. The locomotive's last 'Heavy Intermediate' overhaul including boiler (HB 6617) and tender change took place at Swindon Works between 25th February and 16th May 1960. The engine was withdrawn in September 1962 from Reading WR depot (81D). Recorded mileage 1,192,663, service life 24 years, 11 months and 22 days. Disposal Cashmores, Newport, June 1964.

Tender types principal fitted dates, Collett 4000g 10th July 1937, Hawksworth 4000g 5th June 1950, Collett 4000g 18th May 1951, Hawksworth 4000g 1st February 1952, Collett 4000g 17th February 1953, Hawksworth 4000g 17th December 1954, Collett 4000g 14th November 1956, Hawksworth 4000g 16th May 1960.

Allocated Depots

PDN Old Oak Common	21/07/37	BRD Bath Bristol Road	16/01/48	81D Reading WR	10/05/61
SDN Swindon	20/03/43	87G Carmarthen	20/06/58		

St. Fagans Castle is a former Elizabethan mansion in St Fagans, Cardiff, which dates from the late 1500s. The house and remaining medieval fortifications are Grade I listed. The grounds of St Fagans Castle now contain St Fagans National History Museum. The popular museum includes a collection of buildings which represent the architecture of Wales, including a nonconformist chapel (Unitarian), a village schoolhouse, a Toll road with toll booth, a cockpit, a pigsty, and a tannery.

GWR 'Castle' class 4-6-0 No 5067 ST. FAGANS CASTLE seen at Paignton, circa 1952. Note the advertising hoarding for the Westbourne Park Building Society, Newton Abbot branch. That company merged with the Leek & Moorlands Building Society in 1965 leading to a name change, becoming the Leek and Westbourne which later became the Britannia Building Society. *Rail Photoprints Collection*

5068 BEVERSTON CASTLE (Converted to double chimney)

Introduced into service in June 1938. Diagram HB boiler fitted. Double chimney with extended smokebox and 4-row superheater fitted during the locomotive's last 'Heavy General' overhaul which included boiler (HD 7671) and tender change, and took place at Swindon Works between 12th January and 15th March 1961. The engine was withdrawn in September 1962 from Oxford depot (81F). Recorded mileage 1,081,514, service life 24 years, 2 months and 30 days. Disposal Cashmores, Newport, December 1962.

Tender types principal fitted dates, Collett 4000g June 1938, Collett 4000g (8 wheeled) 16th April 1948, Collett 4000g 3rd November 1949, Hawksworth 4000g 26th October 1951, Collett 4000g 6th November 1953, Hawksworth 4000g 3rd October 1957.

Allocated Depots

BRD Bristol Bath Road	22/06/38	SDN Swindon	06/11/41
Brd Weston-super-Mare	15/11/40	81F Oxford	19/05/62
BRD Bath Bristol Road	01/02/41		

Beverston Castle, also known as Beverstone Castle was founded in 1229, it was constructed as a medieval stone fortress and is situated in the village of Beverston, Gloucestershire. Much of the castle is in a state of complete ruin but a portion of the structure was restored and that section is occupied. The castle, which saw action during the English Civil War, is in private ownership and the estate boasts exceptionally fine gardens which are open to the public between April and September.

GWR 'Castle' class 4-6-0 No 5068 BEVERSTON CASTLE is seen outside the works at Swindon in February 1959 following a 'Heavy Intermediate' overhaul. *Rail Photoprints Collection*

5069 ISAMBARD KINGDOM BRUNEL (Converted to double chimney)

Introduced into service in June 1938. Diagram HB boiler fitted. Double chimney and 4-row superheater fitted November 1958. The locomotive's last 'Heavy Intermediate' overhaul including boiler and tender change took place at Swindon Works between 1st December 1960 and 3rd February 1961. The engine was withdrawn in February 1962 from Laira depot (83D). Recorded mileage 1,217,505, service life 23 years and 8 months. Disposal Swindon Works, May 1962.

Tender types principal fitted dates, Collett 4000g 21st June 1938, Hawksworth 4000g 23rd June 1954, Collett 4000g 27th March 1957.

Allocated Depots

PDN Old Oak Common	21/06/38	PDN Old Oak Common	01/11/47	83D Laira	23/06/54
SDN Swindon	30/09/47	82A Bristol Bath Road	22/10/52		

The 1.15pm Paddington–Bristol runs through Sydney Gardens, Bath, behind GWR 'Castle' class 4-6-0 No 5069 ISAMBARD KINGDOM BRUNEL. On 15th September 1959 the engine was adorned with a headboard to commemorate the centenary of 'IKB'. In keeping with other 'Castle' class engine names, which do not include the word castle, this engine's nameplates are additionally inscribed with the words Castle Class below the main name. *Hugh Ballantyne Collection*

Isambard Kingdom Brunel, (1806–1859) Fellow of the Royal Society, perchance the name of no other man in history has ever been more closely linked with a railway company than his. The names of I.K. Brunel and the Great Western Railway will always be synonymously remembered. His working life was short in comparison to that of many other engineers, a factor which made his achievements all the more incredible.

He was born in Portsmouth, Hampshire to French civil engineer Mark Isambard Brunel and his English wife Sophia Kingdom on the 9th April 1806. His formal education took place at the University of Caen Lower Normandy (Université de Caen Basse-Normandie), and also in Paris. Brunel is described as an English mechanical and civil engineer, a simple job explanation, yet one describing a truly great man whose contribution to railway engineering in particular, and civil engineering in general is legendary and justifiably earned him worldwide recognition. He was a builder of dockyards, the Great Western Railway, steamships, bridges and tunnels.

All of Brunel's designs and developments were not necessarily successful, but they all mirrored his determination to find solutions to difficult engineering problems. His achievements included many firsts with perhaps the most notable being 'SS Great Britain' the first propeller-driven ocean-going iron ship.

For the GWR Brunel pioneered the building of their 'Broad Gauge' railway, with the metals placed at 7ft ¼ in apart he concluded that the passengers would enjoy a greater degree of comfort at speed. However, on the downside other 'Standard Gauge' (4ft 8½ in) railways could not connect directly with his system.

Brunel commenced building the GWR broad gauge system in 1838. Just over 25 years later the 'Gauge Commission' recommended that all UK railways should adopt the 'Standard Gauge' accordingly the GWR lines were converted to dual or standard gauge from 1864 onwards, with the final section of Brunel's broad gauge being converted over a single weekend in 1892, resulting in some 15 miles of temporary sidings at Swindon, all filled with redundant broad gauge locomotives and rolling stock

Brunel suffered a stroke in 1859, just before his iron sailing steam ship 'Great Eastern' set out on its maiden voyage, he died ten days later at the age of 53 and he is buried in Kensal Green Cemetery, London. In 2002, Brunel was placed second in a public poll to determine the '100 Greatest Britons'.

GWR 'Castle' class 4-6-0 No 5069 ISAMBARD KINGDOM BRUNEL is seen in 1947 at Old Oak Common depot in the company of sister engine No 5013 ABERGAVENNY CASTLE, circa 1947. Note the locomotive numbers on the buffer beam and the qualifying wording 'Castle Class' which is clearly seen beneath the main nameplate. *Mike Morant Collection*

GWR 'Castle' class 4-6-0 No 5069 ISAMBARD KINGDOM BRUNEL is seen in the Swindon scrap line in May 1962. *David Anderson*

5070 SIR DANIEL GOOCH

Introduced into service in July 1938. Diagram HB boiler fitted. The locomotive's last 'Heavy General' overhaul including boiler (HB 6654) and tender change took place at Swindon Works between 29th April and 24th October 1957. The engine was withdrawn in March 1964 from Old Oak Common depot (81A). Recorded mileage 1,139,354, service life 25 years, 8 months and 17 days. Disposal Birds, Risca, August 1964.

Tender types principal fitted dates, Collett 4000g July 1938, Hawksworth 4000g 17th May 1950, Collett 4000g 6th November 1951.

Allocated Depots

PDN Old Oak Common	03/07/38	SRD Stafford Road	18/03/40	Shrewsbury. Stored	07/09/62
BRD Bristol Bath Road	20/01/39	84G Shrewsbury	10/02/60	Old Oak Common. Reinstated	17/11/62

Sir Daniel Gooch, 1st Baronet (1816–1889) was an English railway and transatlantic cable engineer and politician who sat in the House of Commons from 1865 to 1885. He was the first 'Superintendent of Locomotive Engines' on the Great Western Railway from 1837 to 1864 and its Chairman from 1865 to 1889.

Gooch was born in Bedlington, Northumberland on 24th August 1816, the son of ironfounder John Gooch, and his wife Anna Longridge. He was some 10 years younger than the man who would eventually recruit him for the GWR, one I.K. Brunel.

In 1831 the Gooch family moved to Monmouthshire in South Wales when John Gooch accepted a managerial position at Tredegar Iron Works. Daniel received training at the works under ironmaster Thomas Ellis senior, a man who together with Sam Homfray and Richard Trevithick had pioneered steam railway locomotion. Gooch moved on to work and train in engineering techniques at several establishments including Robert Stephenson & Company, Vulcan Foundry and Robert Hawks & Co before being recruited by Brunel and joining the GWR at the age of 20.

GWR 'Castle' class 4-6-0 No 5070 SIR DANIEL GOOCH is seen passing West Ruislip with an up Birmingham–Paddington service, on 31st December 1955. *C. R. L. Coles (Dave Cobbe Collection)/Rail Photoprints*

Gooch's earliest days with the company were described as being a struggle in order simply to keep the miscellaneous collection of 7 ft 0¼ in broad gauge steam locomotives, ordered by Brunel, in working order. By later taking what he considered to be the best of those, the GWR 'Star Class' as a model, in partnership with Brunel he designed the successful 'Firefly' class of 2-2-2 express passenger locomotives, which were introduced in 1840. In a series of comparative trials, ordered by the Gauge Commissioners, 'Firefly' class locomotive IXION proved capable of speeds greater than its standard gauge challenger.

In 1840, Gooch was responsible for identifying the site of Swindon Works and with the backing of Brunel he convinced the GWR directors that the location which he had chosen, at the junction of the Cheltenham branch, was the right one. Building of the new works began soon after the GWR board gave their approval on 25th February 1841 and the work was officially completed on 2nd January 1843.

The first complete locomotive to be built at the works was the Gooch designed GREAT WESTERN of the 4-2-2 'Iron Duke' class. Locomotives of the class were by all accounts capable of achieving 70mph in service and whilst they were over time rebuilt and modified they did last in service to the end of the broad gauge era. Although the majority of the Gooch inspired designs were principally for the broad gauge he also designed a number of standard gauge engines between 1854 and 1864 for use on the GWR's then newly created 'Northern Division'. In total Gooch was associated with 18 classes of broad gauge locomotives between 1837 and 1862 (441 engines) and 6 classes of standard gauge locomotives between 1855 and 1862 (52 engines)

In 1864 Gooch resigned from his post of Locomotive Superintendent, although he continued as a member of the GWR Board until he left the company in order to become Chairman of the Telegraph Construction & Maintenance Company in 1865. In addition to being constituency MP for Cricklade (1865-1885) Baronet of Clewer (1866) he was also Deputy Lord Lieutenant of Berkshire and a Justice of the Peace.

Interestingly during a period as Chief Engineer of the Telegraph Construction Company (1865/66) he was instrumental in laying the first Atlantic telegraph cable, using Brunel's 'SS Great Eastern'.

Daniel Gooch died at Clewer Park, Berkshire on 24th August 1889, aged 73.

GWR 'Castle' class 4-6-0 No 5070 SIR DANIEL GOOCH is seen on shed at Shrewsbury in 1956. Those familiar with the location will recognize the top portion of a tower belonging to Shrewsbury Castle which is just visible above the engine. *Rail Photoprints Collection*

GWR 'Castle' class 4-6-0 No 5070 SIR DANIEL GOOCH is seen waiting to depart from Chippenham with a down Bristol service, in 1956. *Rail Photoprints Collection*

Preserved GWR 'Castle' class 4-6-0 No 5051 EARL BATHURST is seen in the display area at Barrow Hill Round House on 12th July 2003. *Fred Kerr*

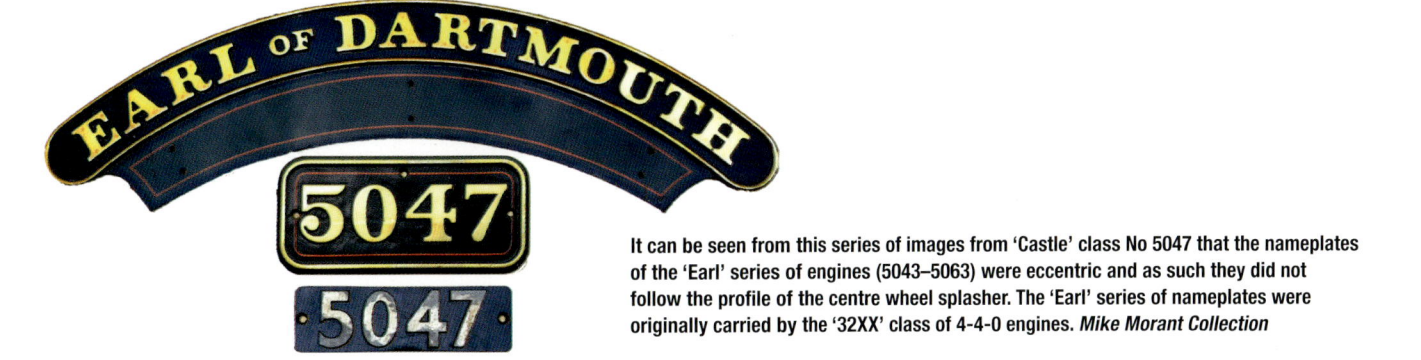

It can be seen from this series of images from 'Castle' class No 5047 that the nameplates of the 'Earl' series of engines (5043–5063) were eccentric and as such they did not follow the profile of the centre wheel splasher. The 'Earl' series of nameplates were originally carried by the '32XX' class of 4-4-0 engines. *Mike Morant Collection*

153

Preserved GWR 'Castle' class 4-6-0 No 5043 EARL OF MOUNT EDGCUMBE in Scotland, May 2012

No 5043 on the Forth Bridge, north on 27th May 2012. *Fred Kerr*

No 5043 proudly carrying 'The Caledonian' headboard is seen at Culross on 27th May 2012. Note the Chocolate and Cream stock, never a common sight in Scotland! *Fred Kerr*

No 5043 with Class 47 diesel No 47760 coupled inside is seen at North Queensferry station on 26th May 2012. Note the decoratively burnished faces of the locomotive's front buffers. *Fred Kerr*

GWR 'Castle' class 4–cylinder locomotives, Swindon Works 'Lot Numbers'

Nos 5043–5967 Lot 303 built 1936/37 (Average cost per engine £5799)
Nos 5068–5070 Lot 310 built 1938/39 (Average cost per engine £6344)

The so called 'Lion on a Bike' BR emblem was used on locomotives between 1950–56.

Chapter 5

LOCOMOTIVES 5071–5099

5071 CLIFFORD CASTLE renamed **SPITFIRE** September 1940 (Converted to double chimney)
Introduced into service in July 1938. Diagram HB boiler fitted. Double chimney and 4-row superheater fitted June 1959 (boiler HD 7683). The locomotive's last 'Heavy Intermediate' overhaul including boiler (HD 7677) and tender change took place at Swindon Works between 18th January and 8th March 1961. The engine was withdrawn in October 1963 from St Philips Marsh depot (82B). Recorded mileage 1,150,913, service life 25 years, 3 months and 15 days. Disposal Coopers Metals, Sharpness, May 1964.

Tender types principal fitted dates, Collett 4000g June 1938, Collett 4000g (8 wheeled) 7th June 1940, Collett 4000g 9th May 1942, Hawksworth 4000g 10th August 1950, Collett 4000g 3rd October 1951, Hawksworth 4000g 21st October 1953, Collett 4000g 28th March 1956, Hawksworth 4000g 8th March 1961, Collett 4000g 6th February 1962.

GWR 'Castle' class 4-6-0 No 5071 SPITFIRE is seen running into Exeter St David's with a down express, in August 1954. Note also the SR 'E1R' class 0-6-2T No 32135, one of several of the type which were often used on banking duties between Exeter St David's and Exeter Central. *Rail Photoprints Collection*

Allocated Depot

NA Newton Abbot	07/07/38	85A Worcester	20/03/58	85B Gloucester Horton Road	15/12/60
EXE Exeter	12/06/40	85B Gloucester Horton Road	20/05/58	82B St Philips Marsh	24/02/62
NA Newton Abbot	10/07/40	85A Worcester	16/09/59		

Spitfire – Supermarine Spitfire, was a British single-seat fighter aircraft designed for the RAF by Reginald Joseph Mitchell CBE, FRAeS, who was Chief Designer at the works of Supermarine Aviation during the 1930s. The aircraft was used by Great Britain and her allies during and after the Second World War. Powered by the legendary Rolls-Royce Merlin engine the Spitfire was built in many variants and was also the only British fighter aircraft to be in continuous production throughout the whole of the WWII period. With a top speed of 370 mph (595 km/h) the Spitfire was perceived by the public to be the main RAF fighter aircraft during the Battle of Britain (July–October 1940).

Supermarine Spitfire – Over 20,000 Spitfires were built and approximately 50 examples survived into preservation, including several in airworthy condition. This example is seen at RAF Abingdon in 1961. *David Anderson*

5072 COMPTON CASTLE renamed HURRICANE November 1940

Introduced into service in July 1938. Diagram HB boiler fitted. The locomotive's last 'Heavy General' overhaul including boiler (HC 7633) and tender change took place at Swindon Works between 14th July and 23rd September 1960. The engine was withdrawn in October 1962 from Stafford Road depot (84A). Recorded mileage 1,055,942, service life 24 years, 3 months and 23 days. Disposal Swindon Works, April 1963.

Tender types principal fitted dates, Collett 4000g July 1938, Hawksworth 4000g January 1952, Collett 4000g 20th May 1952, Hawksworth 4000g 2nd July 1953, Collett 4000g 13th January 1954, Hawksworth 4000g 4th August 1955, Collett 4000g 29th July 1958.

GWR 'Castle' class 4-6-0 No 5072 HURRICANE is seen at Chester in the summer of 1962. *Jim Carter/Rail Photoprints Collection*

Allocated Depots

NA Newton Abbot	07/07/38	84A Stafford Road	20/03/58
LDR Landore	03/47	86C Cardiff Canton	11/10/60
86C Cardiff Canton	05/12/55	84A Stafford Road	31/10/60
83D Laira	24/01/57		

Hurricane – The Hawker Hurricane was a British single-seat fighter aircraft used in WWII by Great Britain and her allies, in several variants. The Hurricane was designed by Hawker Aircraft Ltd during the 1930s, it had a maximum speed of 340 mph (547 km/h). The first 50 Hurricanes had reached RAF squadrons by the middle of 1938. During the Battle of Britain (July–October 1940), the Hurricanes were recognised by the Air Force as renowned fighter aircraft although in the public's perception of the battle Spitfire aircraft were the most prominent. The most important statistic however being that the Hurricane fighters accounted for approximately 60% of the RAF's air victories in the battle. There were some 14,533 Hurricanes built and reportedly 12 survive worldwide, with several being in airworthy condition.

Preserved Hurricane Mk1, RAF serial R4118, squadron code UP-W, UK civil registration G-HUPW, seen at the Royal International Air Tattoo, Fairford, Gloucestershire, in 2008. *Adrian Pingstone*

5073 CRANBROOK CASTLE renamed BLENHEIM November 1940 (Converted to double chimney)

Introduced into service in July 1938. Diagram HB boiler fitted. Double chimney and 4-row superheater fitted May 1959, (boiler HD 7686). The locomotive's last 'Heavy General' overhaul including boiler (HC 7687) and tender change took place at Swindon Works between 7th October and 30th November 1961. The engine was withdrawn in February 1964 from Cardiff East Dock depot (88A at that time). Recorded mileage 995,495, service life 25 years, 7 months and 13 days. Disposal Hayes Metals, Bridgend, June 1964.

Tender types principal fitted dates, Collett 4000g July 1938, Hawksworth 4000g 7th September 1953, Collett 4000g 30th November 1961.

GWR 'Castle' class 4-6-0 No 5073 BLENHEIM leaves Bristol Temple Meads station with an up express, in 1960. *Rail Photoprints Collection*

Allocated Depots

LA Laira	13/07/38	82A Bristol Bath Road	20/03/58	88A Cardiff Canton	11/09/61
SRD Stafford Road	12/38	83B Taunton	13/09/60	88A Cardiff East Dock	07/09/62
4A Shrewsbury	02/39				

Blenheim – The Bristol Blenheim was a British light fighter/bomber aircraft designed by Frank Barnwell and built by the Bristol Aeroplane Company and flown by the RAF and allies. The type carried a crew of three airmen, and was one of the first British aircraft to have all-metal stressed-skin, retractable landing gear and flaps, a powered gun turret and variable pitch propellers. In the *Battle of Britain* the Blenheim was no real match for the more advanced German Messerschmitt Bf 109 (often called Me 109) during daytime skirmishes, although it was more successful as a night fighter/bomber. The new aircraft's first flight took place in April 1935 and in the early years of WWII a total of 4,422 were built.

There are currently no airworthy Blenheim aircraft but examples do exist as static exhibits. The pictured example G-BPIV is under restoration at Duxford Airfield, Cambridge. *Blenheim Duxford Limited*

5074 DENBIGH CASTLE renamed HAMPDEN January 1941 (Converted to double chimney)

Introduced into service in July 1938. Diagram HB boiler fitted. Double chimney and 4-row superheater fitted during the locomotive's last 'Heavy General' overhaul, which also included boiler (HD 7648) and tender change took place at Swindon Works between 27th July and 30th September 1961. The engine was withdrawn in May 1964 from St Philips Marsh depot (82B). Recorded mileage 1,142,187, service life 25 years, 9 months and 5 days. Disposal Cashmores, Great Bridge, July 1964.

Tender types principal fitted dates, Collett 4000g July 1938, Hawksworth 4000g 3rd January 1951, Collett 4000g 18th September 1952, Hawksworth 4000g 23 April 1958, Collett 4000g 18th October 1961.

Allocated Depots

PDN Old Oak Common	31/07/38	Swindon Stored	22/02/51	87A Neath Court Sart	13/06/61
BRD Bristol Bath Road	01/39	Cardiff Canton Reinstated	02/07/54	87F Llanelly	14/07/62
Brd Weston-super-Mare	04/42	87E Landore	01/07/55	88L Cardiff East Dock	06/10/62
BRD Bristol Bath Road	10/06/42	86C Cardiff Canton	05/07/56	Cardiff East Dock Stored	04/03/63
NA Newton Abbot	24/08/45	81A Old Oak Common	12/56	St Philips Marsh Reinstated	05/11/63
BRD Bristol Bath Road	07/09/45	87E Landore	16/06/60		

GWR 'Castle' class 4-6-0 No 5074 HAMPDEN calls at Didcot with a 04.55 Fishguard–Paddington service, in 1960. Note the youthful enthusiasts, school raincoats and caps! Were you one of that trio? *Cresselley Photos*

Hampden – The Handley Page Hampden 'HP.52' was a Second World War British twin-engine medium bomber used by the RAF and allies. The Hampden was designed by Gustav Lachmann and built by Handley Page Ltd, 1430 Planes were built at the Handley Page factory at Radlett Airdrome, Hertfordshire in the period from 1936–1941. Hampdens took part in the first British night raid on Berlin and also operated as part of the first 1,000-plane raid on Cologne. The aircraft was nicknamed the 'Flying Suitcase' by aircrews because of the very cramped conditions which the crew members had to endure. The fuselage was in fact only wide enough for a single person, with the navigator sitting behind the pilot, access into the cockpit required folding down the seats, so once in place the crew had almost no room to move.

A Handley Page Hampden of No. 83 Squadron with members of the crew seen seated on a loaded bomb trolley, at RAF Scampton, Lincolnshire on 2nd October 1940. No Hampdens remain in flying condition, although two wrecks are in the process of being restored (2013). *Bomber Command*

5075 DEVIZES CASTLE renamed WELLINGTON October 1940

Introduced into service in August 1938. Diagram HB boiler fitted. The locomotive's last 'Heavy General' overhaul including boiler (HC 7643) and tender change took place at Swindon Works between 29th October and 22nd December 1960. The engine was withdrawn in September 1962 from St Philips Marsh depot (82B). Recorded mileage 1,068,502, service life 24 years, 1 months and 5 days. Disposal Cashmores, Newport, December 1962.

Tender types principal fitted dates, Collett 4000g 16th August 1938, Hawksworth 4000g 19th February 1948, Collett 4000g 13th January 1950, Hawksworth 4000g 6th October 1953, Collett 4000g 22nd December 1960.

GWR 'Castle' class 4-6-0 No 5075 WELLINGTON is seen at the end of its working life in the withdrawn locomotive line at St Philips Marsh (82B), in October 1962. Note that all 3 redundant locomotives still have their nameplates. *Rail Photoprints Collection*

Allocated Depots

SRD Stafford Road	16/08/38	84A Stafford Road	05/56	87A Neath Court Sart	25/07/61
SDN Swindon	28/03/49	83D Laira	04/58	88A Cardiff Canton	27/01/62
CHR Chester West	15/07/49	83C Exeter	18/06/59	82B St Philips Marsh	14/07/62

Wellington – Vickers Wellington long range medium bomber, usually crewed by six persons. These famous WWII bombers were designed by Rex Pierson in the mid 1930s at the aircraft division of Vickers Armstrong, Weybridge, Surrey. In the early years of WWII Wellingtons were used on night bombing raids, but they were later replaced on those duties as four engined heavy bombers became available. However, in May 1942 during the 1000 plus bomber raid on Cologne 599 out of the 1,046 aircraft total were Wellingtons. With Bomber Command, Wellingtons flew some 47,409 operations, 11,461 of the aircraft were built, of which 1,332 were reported lost in action. The Wellington was popularly known as the *Wimpy* by service personnel, after the portly J. Wellington Wimpy a Popeye cartoon character.

This preserved example is seen at RAF Abingdon in 1961. The Wellington was the only British bomber to be produced for the entire duration of the war, and was one of two bomber types named after Arthur Wellesley, 1st Duke of Wellington, the other being the Vickers Wellesley. There are two surviving aircraft based in the UK. *David Anderson*

5076 DRYSLLWYN CASTLE renamed GLADIATOR January 1941

Introduced into service in August 1938. Diagram HB boiler fitted. The locomotive's last 'Heavy Intermediate' overhaul including boiler (HB 6689) and tender change took place at Swindon Works between 23rd March and 17th May 1962. The engine was withdrawn in September 1964 from Southall depot (81C). Recorded mileage 1,121,080, service life 26 years and 22 days. Disposal Hayes Metals, Bridgend, December 1964.

Tender types principal fitted dates, Collett 4000g 25th August 1938, Hawksworth 4000g 29th May 1952, Collett 4000g 29th May 1953, Hawksworth 4000g 22nd December 1954, Collett 4000g 23rd February 1956, Hawksworth 4000g 5th April 1956, Collett 4000g 10th January 1957, Hawksworth 4000g 16th August 1957, Collett 4000g 31st March 1960, Hawksworth 4000g 17th May 1962, Collett 4000g 18th May 1963.

GWR 'Castle' Class 4-6-0 No 5076 GLADIATOR seen in the summer of 1961 with a train of cattle vans passing Foxhall Junction Didcot and taking the West Curve towards Didcot North. Only when developing the film did the photographer realise that the engine nameplate on the centre splasher was in fact a blank! *David Anderson*

Allocated Depots

EXE Exeter	25/08/38	BRD Weston-super-Mare	03/48	83D Laira	16/10/51
LDR Landore	12/38	BRD Bristol Bath Road	04/48	82A Bristol Bath Road	29/11/51
BRD Bristol Bath Road	02/39	81A Old Oak Common	07/02/51	81D Reading WR	31/03/60
BRD Weston-super-Mare	05/45	Swindon Stored	17/02/51	81A Old Oak Common	04/05/63
BRD Bristol Bath Road	07/45	Bristol Bath Road Reinstated	06/51	81C Southall	29/06/64

Gladiator – Gloster Gladiator (also Gloster SS.37) was a British biplane fighter aircraft dating from the 1930s which was designed by Henry Phillip Folland and built by the Gloster Aircraft Company Ltd from 1937 onwards. It was the RAF's last biplane fighter before being rendered obsolete by more modern fighter aircraft. The type, in two variants, which was used by the RAF and allies, also had two naval variants operated by the Fleet Air Arm (FAA). In the early days of WWII the Gladiators were often sent into combat against more formidable opponents, but nevertheless in the hands of skilled pilots they achieved a fair modicum of success. The biplanes saw action in almost all theatres of the war and notably several of these aircraft took part in the defence of Malta, the George Cross Island.

A Gloster Gladiator biplane is seen in flight with Royal Air Force pre-war markings, circa 1937. A total of 747 of these aircraft were built and several examples survive, including those included in the Gloucestershire Aviation Collection, Bedford and at RAF Museums Hendon and Cosford. *Royal Air Force*

5077 EASTNOR CASTLE renamed FAIREY BATTLE October 1940

Introduced into service in August 1938. Diagram HB boiler fitted. The locomotive's last 'Heavy General' overhaul including boiler (HC 7634) and tender change took place at Swindon Works between 5th November and 22nd December 1960. The engine was withdrawn in July 1962 from Llanelly depot (87F). Recorded mileage 1,089,166, service life 23 years, 11 months and 1 day. Disposal Hayes Metals, Bridgend, August 1962.

Tender types principal fitted dates, Collett 4000g 23rd August 1938, Hawksworth 4000g 18th April 1947, Collett 4000g 3rd September 1948, Hawksworth 4000g 12th August 1952, Hawksworth 3,800g (Self Weighing) 1st November 1952, Collett 4000g 14th May 1953, Hawksworth 4000g 30th January 1954, Collett 4000g 15th June 1954, Hawksworth 4000g 11th March 1959.

GWR 'Castle' class 4-6-0 No 5077 FAIREY BATTLE is seen in its final BR form, at Newport in April 1959. Note the rectangular hole cut into the side panel of the inside cylinder cover, presumably as an aid to inspection. *Norman Preedy Collection/Rail Photoprints*

Allocated Depots

PDN Old Oak Common	23/08/38	82C Swindon	12/08/52	87E Landore	07/56
TN Taunton	07/02/39	86C Cardiff Canton	22/09/52	87F Llanelly	13/06/61
86C Cardiff Canton	06/11/50	82A Bristol Bath Road	15/06/54		

Fairey Battle – This aircraft was a British single engine light bomber designed by Marcel Lobelle and built from 1936 onwards by the Fairey Aviation Company initially for the RAF, Battle aircraft had an operating crew of three. The Fairey Battle was powered by the same Rolls-Royce Merlin piston engines which gave other fighter aircraft of that era an edge in combat, however, the advantages of the Merlin engine were nullified by their poor power to weight ratio. The aircraft proved to be slow, limited in strike range and extremely vulnerable to both anti-aircraft fire and fighter attacks. By May 1940 the squadrons operating Fairey Battle bombers were reporting a high attrition rate, often in the region of 50% per mission and eventually the Battles were transferred to non-combat duties.

RAF Fairey Battle light bomber K7650/63M of No 63 Squadron RAF Benson is pictured in flight, November 1939, the three crew members can be seen. The original order called for the building of 2,419 aircraft but that was cut short as production ceased in September 1940 when only 2,185 of the aircraft had been built. *Royal Air Force*

5078 LAMPHEY CASTLE renamed BEAUFORT January 1941 (Converted to double chimney)

Introduced into service in May 1939. Diagram HB boiler fitted. Double chimney and 4-row superheater fitted during the locomotive's last 'Heavy Casual' overhaul which included boiler (HD 7689) and tender change, and took place at Swindon Works between 10th August and 11th December 1961. The engine was withdrawn in November 1962 from Neath Court Sart depot (87A). Recorded mileage 1,038,165, service life 23 years, 6 months and 5 days. Disposal Swindon Works, April 1963.

Tender types principal fitted dates, Collett 4000g May 1939, Hawksworth 4000g 29th October 1952, Collett 4000g 22nd May 1953, Hawksworth 4000g 17th March 1954, Collett 4000g 5th January 1956, Hawksworth 4000g 11th December 1961.

Allocated Depots

LA Laira	15/05/39	NA Newton Abbot	01/42	87E Landore	03/10/60
PZ Penzance	01/41	86C Cardiff Canton	24/07/58	87A Neath Court Sart	13/06/61
LA Laira	01/07/41	82A Bristol Bath Road	02/12/58	Neath Court Sart Stored	11/12/61
TN Taunton	10/41	82B St Philips Marsh	16/09/60		

GWR 'Castle' class 4-6-0 No 5078 BEAUFORT is seen at Taunton station with 'The Devonian' up service, July 1955. During the BR steam era 'The Devonian' inter-regional trains operated between Bradford (Forster Square) and Paignton during the summer only 1949-52 but daily Monday–Saturday from the summer of 1953, until 1st May 1967 when the northern departure station became Bradford Exchange. *David Anderson*

Beaufort – The Bristol Beaufort was a British twin engined torpedo bomber built by the Bristol Aeroplane Company and introduced in 1933. Beauforts first saw service with Royal Air Force Coastal Command and then the Royal Navy Fleet Air Arm from 1940. They were used as torpedo bombers, conventional bombers and mine-layers until 1942 when they were removed from front line service and were found alternative use as trainer aircraft until being declared obsolete by the RAF in 1945. Beauforts saw their most extensive use with the Royal Australian Air Force in the Pacific theatre, where they were used until the very end of the war. With the exception of six examples delivered from England, Australian Beauforts were locally constructed under licence. Just over 2000 of the aircraft were delivered including the 700 built in Australia.

The Australian Beauforts were built at a plant in Fisherman's Bend, Melbourne, Victoria and also at a new factory at Mascot, New South Wales. To speed up the process drawings, jigs and tools and complete parts for six airframes were supplied by Bristol. The bulk of Australian-built Beauforts used locally available materials. In this 1943 image a batch is seen under construction at the Fisherman's Bend, Melbourne plant. There are 5 preserved examples, 3 are in Australia. *Royal Australian Air Force*

5079 LYDFORD CASTLE renamed LYSANDER January 1941

Introduced into service in May 1939. Diagram HB boiler fitted. Converted to oil burning 24th January 1947 to 7th October 1948, cab roof vent fitted. The locomotive's last 'Heavy General' overhaul including boiler (HC 7612) and tender change took place at Swindon Works between 14th December 1957 and 20th January 1958. The engine was withdrawn in May 1960 from Landore depot (87E). Recorded mileage 1,008,175, service life 20 years, 11 months and 17 days. Disposal Swindon Works, June 1960.

Tender types principal fitted dates, Collett 4000g 19th May 1939, Collett 4000g (Oil) 24th January 1947, Collett 4000g 7th October 1948, Hawksworth 4000g 26th May 1954, Collett 4000g 20th January 1958.

GWR 'Castle' class 4-6-0 No 5079 LYSANDER is seen at Exeter St. Davids with a down express, in August 1954. Southern Railway Maunsell 'N' class 2-6-0 No 31831 stands at the other platform. *Rail Photoprints Collection*

Allocated Depots

PDN Old Oak Common	19/05/39	SDN Swindon	24/01/47	NA Newton Abbot	01/11/47
CDF Cardiff Canton	13/11/40	LA Laira	03/47	87E Landore	22/04/60
LDR Landore	03/41				

Lysander – Westland Lysander was a British army co-operation and liaison aircraft designed in 1936 by Arthur Davenport and Teddy Petter and produced by Westland Aircraft. There were 1,786 Lysander aircraft built and they were powered by Bristol Mercury air-cooled radial engines. These aircraft were used immediately before and during the Second World War by the RAF and allies. After becoming obsolete in their army co-operation role, the aircraft's exceptional short field take off and landing performances enabled them to be used on clandestine missions operating to small, unprepared airstrips behind enemy lines to place or recover agents, particularly in occupied France (with the help of the French Resistance). Like other British army air co-operation aircraft it was given the name of a mythical or legendary leader, in this case the Spartan general Lysander.

In August 1941 a new squadron, No. 138 (Special Duties), was formed to undertake missions behind enemy lines. Amongst its aircraft were Lysander Mk IIIs. A number of Lysanders are preserved worldwide. This airworthy RAF example is seen at RAF Abingdon in 1961. *David Anderson*

5080 OGMORE CASTLE renamed DEFIANT January 1941. Preserved

Introduced into service in May 1939. Diagram HB boiler fitted. The locomotive's last 'Heavy Casual' overhaul including tender change took place at Swindon Works between 2nd August and 7th September 1961. The engine was withdrawn in April 1963 from Llanelly depot (87F). Recorded mileage 1,117,030, service life 23 years, 10 months and 17 days. Sold to Woodham Brothers, Barry in October 1963.

Tender types principal fitted dates, Collett 4000g May 1939, Hawksworth 16th March 1953, Hawksworth 3,800g (Self Weighing) 11th July 1953, Hawksworth 4000 5th September 1963, Collett 4000g 28th April 1954, Hawksworth 4000g 15th May 1959, Collett 4000g 17th February 1961.

Allocated Depots

PDN Old Oak Common	25/05/39	CDF Cardiff Canton	20/03/41	87E Landore	12/55
CDF Cardiff Canton	08/40	SDN Swindon	16/08/49	87F Llanelly	07/09/61
SDN Swindon	09/01/41	CDF Cardiff Canton	13/09/49	Llanelly Stored	01/05/62

Preserved GWR 'Castle' class 4-6-0 No 5080 DEFIANT seen whilst crossing the picturesque Berwyn Viaduct on the extremely scenic Llangollen Railway in North Wales. In addition to hauling service trains, during a May 1996 visit, the locomotive was used on several 'Driver Experience Trains'. This is one such run on which the pupil was fortunate to have long serving LR driver Gordon Francis rostered as his instructor. The locomotive carries GWR livery, note the number stencilled on the front buffer beam, the TYS Tyseley shed marking on the side plating over the bogie, but also the out of period BR overhead power cable warning stickers no doubt a hangover from the engine's mainline charter days. *Keith Langston*

GWR 'Castle' class 4-6-0 No 5080 DEFIANT spent eleven years in Barry scrapyard before being purchased by the Birmingham Railway Museum Trust and was the 62nd departure from there. At the end of 1985, an intensive programme of restoration began to transform Defiant into a working locomotive once again capable of hauling main line trains at express speeds over BR tracks.

No 5080 returned to the main line on 11th June 1988, its first mainline duty as a preserved engine was to haul a train from Tyseley to Didcot, bearing the familiar 'Red Dragon' headboard.

Since then, No 5080 DEFIANT has visited numerous preserved railways including the Gloucestershire & Warwickshire, Great Central, Llangollen and the Mid Hants railways. Following the introduction of the popular Drive-A-Loco footplate experience courses many fortunate enthusiasts got to experience the thrill of driving this famous 'Castle' class engine during its visits around the country. The locomotive was withdrawn from service in 1997 pending an overhaul and it is currently on static display in the recreated Oxford Rewley Road LMS Station at the Buckinghamshire Railway Centre, Quainton (2013).

Preserved GWR 'Castle' class No 5080 DEFIANT seen at the Llangollen Railway in May 1996. Keith Langston

Defiant – The Boulton Paul Defiant was a twin seat British interceptor aircraft that served with the Royal Air Force and allies during the Second World War. The Defiant was designed by John Dudley North and first flew in 1937. It was built by Boulton Paul Aircraft from 1939 onwards. There were 1064 Defiants built in several variants and was designated a 'turret fighter', without any forward-firing guns. The plane was powered by the famous Rolls-Royce Merlin V12 engine. The concept of a 'turret fighter' related directly to the successful First World War-era Bristol F.2 Fighter. However, their lack of forward armament proved to be a major weakness in daylight combat and its potential was better realised when it switched to a night combat role. Amongst RAF pilots the type earned the nickname 'Daffy'.

A pair of No 264 Squadrons Boulton Paul Defiant 'turret fighters' are seen in this wartime image, taken from the Squadron Leader's aircraft. There were 1,064 Defiants built in several variants and there is a single surviving complete example N1671 which was formerly attached to No 307 Polish Night Fighter Squadron at Kirton In Lindsey, Lincolnshire. That aircraft is displayed at RAF Museum Hendon (2013). Royal Air Force

GWR 'Castle' class No 5080 Nameplate. Keith Langston

Newly restored preserved GWR 'Castle' class 4-6-0 No 5080 DEFIANT, with 'The Red Dragon' headboard is seen on Hatton Bank during the engines triumphant return to mainline steam duties, 11th May 1988. The Red Dragon service between London and Carmarthen is known in Welsh as 'Y Ddraig Goch'. A similarly named train runs in the present day (2014). *Malcolm Ranieri*

5081 PENRICE CASTLE renamed LOCKHEED HUDSON January 1941

Introduced into service in June 1939. Diagram HB boiler fitted. The locomotive's last 'Heavy Intermediate' overhaul including boiler (HC 7626) and tender change took place at Swindon Works between 17th July and 14th September 1961. The engine was withdrawn October 1963 from Cardiff East Dock depot (88L). Recorded mileage 1,208,003, service life 24 years, 4 months and 18 days. Disposal Hayes Metals, Bridgend, June 1964.

    Tender types principal fitted dates, Collett 4000g May 1939, Hawksworth 4000g 3rd November 1948, Collett 4000g 23rd May 1950, Hawksworth 3,800g (Self Weighing) 26th September 1962, Collett 4000g 1st November 1952, Hawksworth 4000g 19th April 1956, Collett 4000g 16th December 1957, Hawksworth 4000g 14th September 1961.

GWR 'Castle' class 4-6-0 No 5081 LOCKHEED HUDSON is seen on shed at Swindon (82C) on 24th April 1956. Note Hawksworth tender No 4105 which was coupled with this engine 5 days before this picture was taken. *Transport Treasury*

Allocated Depots

SRD Stafford Road	03/06/39	PDN Old Oak Common	02/49	87J Fishguard Loaned	09/03/61
PDN Old Oak Common	17/01/45	85A Worcester	10/12/54	88A Cardiff Canton	10/05/61
NA Newton Abbot	13/01/49	86C Cardiff Canton	02/08/60	88L Cardiff East Dock	07/09/62

Lockheed Hudson – The Lockheed Hudson was perhaps an unusual choice to be included in the 'Castle' class aircraft of WWII listings, particularly when famous British built aircraft such as Lancaster bombers, Mosquito fighters and Meteor jet fighters were not included. The Lockheed Hudson was an American light bomber and coastal patrol twin engined aircraft designed by Clarence 'Kelly' Johnson and built in the period 1938-43 by the Lockheed Aircraft Corporation, for the RAF and allies. A total of 2.941 of these aircraft were built and several examples are preserved including one such in RAAF colours which is kept at RAF Museum, Hendon. The Hudson served throughout the war, mainly with Coastal Command but also in transport and training roles as well as delivering agents into occupied territory. They were also used extensively with the Royal Canadian Air Force's anti-submarine squadrons.

Royal Australian Air Force survivor A16-112, a preserved Lockheed Hudson III was pictured at Point Cook, Australia in February 2008. *Phil Vabre*

5082 POWIS CASTLE renamed SWORDFISH January 1941

Introduced into service in June 1939. Diagram HB boiler fitted. The locomotive's last 'Heavy Intermediate' overhaul including boiler (HC 7625) and tender change took place at Swindon Works between 10th October and 3rd December 1960. The engine was withdrawn July 1962 from Old Oak Common depot (81A). Recorded mileage 1,161,413, service life 23 years and 16 days. Disposal Cashmores, Great Bridge, December 1962.

Tender types principal fitted dates, Collett 4000g June 1939, Hawksworth 4000g 21st March 1951, Collett 4000g 1st March 1954, Hawksworth 4000g 3rd November 1956, Collett 4000g July 1957.

GWR 'Castle' class 4-6-0 No 5082 SWORDFISH is seen on shed at Oxford in the company of sister engine No 7008 SWANSEA CASTLE, in May 1961. *David Anderson*

Allocated Depots

BRD Bristol Bath Road	16/06/39	BRD Bristol Bath Road	05/44	81A Old Oak Common	07/11/52
Brd Weston-super-Mare	04/44				

Swordfish – The Fairey Swordfish was a torpedo bomber biplane designed by the Fairey Aviation Company and built between 1936-44. They were used by the Fleet Air Arm of the Royal Navy during the Second World War. Originating in the 1930s, the Swordfish, nicknamed 'Stringbag' by the aircrews, was an outdated design by the start of the war in 1939, but remarkably continued to fly in front-line combat service until VE Day (Victory in Europe). It was initially operated primarily as a fleet attack aircraft; during its later years it was used as an anti-submarine and training aircraft. The Swordfish achieved some spectacular successes, notably the sinking of one and damaging of two other battleships of the Italian Navy in the Battle of Taranto, and also taking part in the action which crippled the famous German battleship Bismarck.

A preserved Royal Navy Fairey *Swordfish Mk. II* (serial number LS326) seen in flight during 2012. This aircraft is today operated by the Royal Navy Historic Flight. There was a total of 2,391 of the type built in several variants and there are at least 7 surviving aircraft worldwide and 3 of those are in the UK. *Tony Hisgett*

5083 BATH ABBEY rebuilt from 'Star' class No **4063**

Introduced into service as a 'Star' class in November 1922 and rebuilt as a 'Castle' in June 1937. Diagram HB boiler fitted. Converted to oil burning 6th December 1946 until 15th January 1947, roof vent fitted. The locomotive's last 'Heavy General' overhaul including boiler change (HC 7621) took place at Swindon Works between 19th March and 22nd May 1957. The engine was withdrawn January 1959 from Worcester depot (85A). Recorded 'Castle' mileage 1,001,686 (total 1,322,834), service life as a 'Castle' 21 years 6 Months and 10 days (total 36 years 2 months and 7 days). Disposal Swindon Works, January/February 1959.

Tender types principal fitted dates, Collett 4000g 12th June 1937, Collett 4000g (Oil) 6th December 1946, Collett 4000g 15th January 1947, Hawksworth 4000g 20th September 1951, Collett 4000g 1st July 1953, Hawksworth 4000g 6th May 1955.

GWR 'Castle' class 4-6-0 No 5083 BATH ABBEY is seen when newly rebuilt at Swindon Works in June 1937. *Rail Photoprints Collection*

Allocated Depots

LDR Landore	28/06/37	SDN Swindon	06/12/46	SDN Swindon	21/07/48
NEA Neath Court Sart	02/10/37	BRD Bristol Bath Road	29/08/47	85A Worcester	06/56
LDR Landore	24/11/37				

GWR 'Castle' class 4-6-0 No 5083 BATH ABBEY seen westbound at Langley Crossing (east of Chippenham) circa 1957. *Rail Photoprints Collection*

Bath Abbey – The Abbey Church of Saint Peter and Paul, in the City of Bath, is an Anglican parish church and former Benedictine monastery. The Abbey was founded in the 7th century, reorganised in the 10th century and then rebuilt in both the 12th and 16th centuries. During the 1860s Sir George Gilbert Scott carried out major restoration work on what is claimed to be one of the finest examples of Perpendicular Gothic architecture, it is Grade 1 listed.

5084 READING ABBEY rebuilt from 'Star' class No **4064** (Converted to double chimney)

Introduced into service as a 'Star' class in December 1922 and rebuilt as a 'Castle' in March 1937. The rebuild included new front section frames (straight replacing 'joggled'). Diagram HB boiler fitted. Double chimney and 4-row superheater fitted October 1958, with boiler HD 7678. The locomotive's last 'Heavy General' overhaul including boiler change (HD 7676) took place at Swindon Works between 4th May and 1st July 1960. The engine was withdrawn July 1962 from Old Oak Common depot (81A). Recorded 'Castle' mileage 1,188,386 (total 2,017,118), service life as a 'Castle' 26 years 3 Months and 18 days (total 40 years 7 months and 2 days). Disposal Cashmores, Newport, December 1962.

Tender types principal fitted dates, Collett 4000g April 1937, Hawksworth 3800g (Self Weighing) 17th March 1952, Collett 4000g 20th March 1952, Hawksworth 4000g 22nd August 1952, Collett 4000g 17th June 1954, Hawksworth 4000g 19th October 1956, Collett 4000g 22nd October 1958.

GWR 'Castle' class 4-6-0 No 5084 READING ABBEY hurries towards Box Tunnel as it passes Corsham with the down 'Merchant Venturer', circa 1959. There is no headboard carried on this occasion. Right up to the present time (2014) this service operates between London–Bristol–Penzance. In the steam era the service terminated at Weston-super-Mare. The train is named after the 'Society of Merchant Venturers' an organisation which was formed in Bristol during the 13th century. Alan Sainty Collection

Allocated Depots

BRD Bristol Bath Road	04/37	BRD Bristol Bath Road	02/43	81A Old Oak Common	15/07/55
WEY Weymouth GWR	10/37	SDN Swindon	21/05/48	82C Swindon	01/09/55
BRD Bristol Bath Road	11/37	82A Bristol Bath Road	22/08/52	81A Old Oak Common	19/10/56
Brd Weston-super-Mare	15/01/43	82C Swindon	02/11/52		

GWR 'Castle' class 4-6-0 No 5084 READING ABBEY is seen passing Stoke Gifford (Bristol) with a down South Wales Express, in 1960. Rail Photoprints Collection

Reading Abbey – The ruins of Reading Abbey stand in the centre of the town of the same name. The abbey was founded by King Henry 1st circa 1121, and was largely destroyed in 1538 during Henry VIII's Dissolution of the Monasteries. The last abbot, Hugh Cook Faringdon, was subsequently tried and convicted of high treason and hanged, drawn and quartered in front of the Abbey Church. Between 1785 and 1786, the old hall was dismantled and replaced on the same site by buildings which collectively now form Reading Town Hall.

5085 EVESHAM ABBEY rebuilt from 'Star' class No 4065

Introduced into service as a 'Star' class in December 1922 and rebuilt as a 'Castle' in July 1939. Diagram HB boiler fitted. The locomotive's last 'Heavy Intermediate' overhaul including boiler change (HB 6675) took place at Swindon Works between 3rd March and 26th April 1961. The engine was withdrawn February 1964 from St Philips Marsh depot (82B). Recorded 'Castle' mileage 1,214,357 (total 2,112,594), service life as a 'Castle' 24 years 7 Months (total 41 years 2 months and 1 days). Disposal Hayes Metals, Bridgend, June 1964.

Tender types principal fitted dates, Collett 4000g July 1939, Hawksworth 4000g 10th January 1947, Collett 4000g 25th November 1948, Hawksworth 4000g 14th June 1952, Collett 4000g 15th April 1954, Hawksworth 4000g 11th July 1959, Collett 4000g 10th May 1961.

Allocated Depots

PDN Old Oak Common	13/07/39	St Philips Marsh Stored	13/02/62	87F Llanelly Loan	09/02/63
82A Bristol Bath Road	10/52	81D Reading Reinstated	11/08/62	82B St Phillips Marsh	09/03/63
82B St Philips Marsh	16/09/60	87A Neath Court Sart	03/11/62		

Evesham Abbey – The ruins of the abbey, founded between 700 and 710AD stand in the town of the same name. The abbey was founded was founded by Saint Egwin between 700 and 710 A.D. following an alleged vision of the Virgin Mary by a swineherd by the name of Eof. According to the monastic history, Evesham came through the Norman Conquest unusually well. However, only one section of walling survives from the actual abbey, although fragments of the chapter house, the bell tower and the gateway remain. Simon de Montfort (1208–1265) is buried beneath the high altar of the ruined abbey; the spot is marked by an altar-like memorial monument which was dedicated by the Archbishop of Canterbury in 1965.

The last up 'Bristolian' (4.30pm Bristol–Paddington) booked for steam power waits to leave Bristol Temple Meads behind recently ex works GWR 'Castle' class 4-6-0 No 5085 EVESHAM ABBEY, on 12th June 1959. The Bristolian London Paddington–Bristol Temple Meads service first ran in 1935 and in modern times (2014) a similar named service still operates. *Hugh Ballantyne/Rail Photoprints*

5086 VISCOUNT HORNE rebuilt from 'Star' class No 4066

Introduced into service as a 'Star' class in December 1922 and rebuilt as a 'Castle' in December 1937. Diagram HB boiler fitted. The locomotive's last 'Heavy General' overhaul took place at Swindon Works between 27th March and 11th May 1953. New boiler (HB6600) fitted during a later visit, February 1957. The engine was withdrawn in November 1958 from Swindon depot (82C). Recorded 'Castle' mileage 1,060,762 (total 1,871,501), service life as a 'Castle' 20 years 10 months and 13 days, (total 35 years, 11 months and 11 days). Disposal Swindon Works, December 1958.

Tender types principal fitted dates, Collett 4000g 13th December 1937, Hawksworth 4000g 31st July 1952, Collett 4000g 11th May 1953, Hawksworth 4000g 19th February 1957.

Allocated Depots

SRD Stafford Road	28/12/37	4A Shrewsbury	03/08/42	82C Swindon	30/12/54
4A Shrewsbury	03/38	Bletchley Stored	26/09/50	85A Worcester	09/02/55
SRD Stafford Road	29/11/39	85A Worcester Reinstated	06/11/50	82C Swindon	03/10/58

Viscount Horne – Robert Stevenson Horne, 1st Viscount Horne of Slamannan GBE, PC, KC (1871–1940) was a Scottish businessman, advocate and politician. He served under David Lloyd George as Minister of Labour between 1919 and 1920, as President of the Board of Trade between 1920 and 1921 and as Chancellor of the Exchequer between 1921 and 1922. He served as chairman of the Great Western Railway Company in 1934 and in 1937 he was ennobled as Viscount Horne of Slamannan. As a bachelor, Horne led a colourful life and reportedly enjoyed lots of female company, earning him the tag 'Scots cad' from Prime Minister Baldwin. On his death in September 1940 the Viscountcy became extinct.

GWR 'Castle' class 4-6-0 No 5086 VISCOUNT HORNE is seen approaching Didcot with a lengthy down express, circa 1952. *Rail Photoprints Collection*

5087 TINTERN ABBEY rebuilt from 'Star' class No **4067**

Introduced into service as a 'Star' class in January 1923 and rebuilt as a 'Castle' in December 1940. Diagram HB boiler fitted. The locomotive's last 'Heavy General' overhaul including boiler (HC 7609) and tender change took place at Swindon Works between 16th September and 22nd November 1961. The engine was withdrawn in August 1963 from Llanelly depot (87F). Recorded 'Castle' mileage 1,088,932 (total 2,029,151), service life as a 'Castle' 22 years 7 Months and 29 days (total 40 years 7 months and 1 days). Disposal Cohens, Morriston, January 1964.

Tender types principal fitted dates, Collett 4000g November 1940, Hawksworth 4000g 12th December 1946, Collett 4000g 24th February 1949, Hawksworth 4000g 26th September 1952, Collett 4000g 30th January 1954, Hawksworth 4000g 16th October 1956, Collett 4000g 30th April 1958, Hawksworth 4000g 5th September 1959.

GWR 'Castle' class 4-6-0 No 5087 TINTERN ABBEY is seen leaving Chippenham with a Paddington–Bristol service, in November 1956, note Hawksworth 4000g tender. *Rail Photoprints Collection*

Allocated Depots

PDN Old Oak Common	13/12/40	SDN Swindon (test plant)	04/04/49	87A Neath Court Sart	09/07/62
SDN Swindon (test plant)	10/02/49	PDN Old Oak Common	02/05/49	87F Llanelly	13/08/62
PDN Old Oak Common	24/02/49	87F Llanelly	11/01/62		

GWR 'Castle' class 4-6-0 No 5087 TINTERN ABBEY is seen at Old Oak Common in May 1954, note Collett 4000g tender. *Rail Photoprints Collection*

Tintern Abbey – This ruined abbey is situated in the village of Tintern in Monmouthshire and stands on the banks of the River Wye. The Abbey was founded by Walter de Clare the then Lord of Chepstow in 1131. Tintern was only the second Cistercian foundation in Britain and the first of that order to be established in Wales. The impressive ruins and its location have inspired poets and artists, William Wordsworth wrote 'Lines written a few miles above Tintern Abbey', Alfred, Lord Tennyson's poem 'Tears, Idle Tears' and Allen Ginsberg's 'Wales Visitation'. It has been the subject of several paintings by J. M. W. Turner. The Grade 1 listed building was the setting for the 1969 Flirtations 'Nothing But a Heartache' video and also the 1988 Iron Maiden video 'Can I Play with Madness'.

5088 LLANTHONY ABBEY rebuilt from 'Star' class No 4068 (Converted to double chimney)

Introduced into service as a 'Star' class in January 1923 and rebuilt as a 'Castle' in March 1939. The rebuild included new front section frames (straight replacing 'joggled'). The locomotive's last 'Heavy General' overhaul including boiler (HB 6678) and tender change took place at Swindon Works between 12th May and 21st June 1956. Double chimney and 4-row superheater fitted June 1958 (boiler HB 7652). The engine was withdrawn in September 1962 from Stafford Road depot (84A). Recorded 'Castle' mileage 1,047,932 (total 1,879,955), service life as a 'Castle' 23 years, 6 months and 14 days (total 39 years, 8 months and 21 days). Disposal Swindon Works, March 1963.

Tender types principal fitted dates, Collett 4000g February 1939, Hawksworth 4000g 2nd March 1953, Collett 4000g 21st June 1956.

GWR 'Castle' class 4-6-0 No 5088 LLANTHONY ABBEY, coupled with a Hawksworth 4000g tender and the 'Lion on a Bike' motif is seen passing Bentley Heath, on 11th July 1953. Rail Photoprints Collection

Allocated Depots

SALOP Shrewsbury	07/03/39	84F Stourbridge Junction	29/11/61	84A Stafford Road	02/01/62
SRD Stafford Road	08/03/42				

GWR 'Castle' class 4-6-0 No 5088 LLANTHONY ABBEY is seen coupled with a Collett 4000g tender displaying the 'Ferret and Dartboard' motif, near Hatton with an up express, circa 1959. Rail Photoprints Collection

Llanthony Abbey – Also known as Llanthony Priory, is a partly ruined former Augustinian priory in the secluded Vale of Ewyas, a steep sided once glaciated valley within the Black Mountains area of the Brecon Beacons National Park in Monmouthshire. The Grade 1 listed structure is in the care of Cadw, and the grounds are open to the public. Renewed building took place around 1325 and included a new gatehouse. On Palm Sunday, April 4th 1327, the deposed King Edward II stayed at the Priory on his way from Kenilworth Castle to Berkeley Castle, where he was alleged to have been murdered.

5089 WESTMINSTER ABBEY rebuilt from 'Star' class No 4069

Introduced into service as a 'Star' class in January 1923 and rebuilt as a 'Castle' in November 1939. Diagram HB boiler fitted. The locomotive's last 'Heavy General' overhaul including boiler (HB 6626) and tender change took place at Swindon Works between 7th May and 3rd July 1959. The engine was withdrawn in November 1964 from Oxley depot (2B). Recorded 'Castle' mileage up to the end of 1963, 1,158,893 (total 2,097,247), service life as a 'Castle' 25 years (total 41 years 10 months). Disposal Cashmores, Great Bridge, February 1965.

Tender types principal fitted dates, Collett 4000g 1st November 1939, Hawksworth 4000g 22nd December 1950, Collett 4000g 30th January 1954.

Allocated Depots

LDR Landore	01/11/39	CDF Cardiff Canton	14/04/49	83D Laira	04/56
PDN Old Oak Common	07/48	87E Landore	04/54	84A Stafford Road	20/05/58
SDN Swindon	31/03/49	83A Newton Abbot	25/10/55	2B Oxley	09/09/63

Westminster Abbey is formally titled the Collegiate Church of St Peter at Westminster, it is a large, mainly Gothic, church in the City of Westminster, London, located just to the west of the Palace of Westminster. It is one of the most notable religious buildings in the United Kingdom and is the traditional place of coronation and burial for English and, later, British monarchs.

Reading on a filthy day as GWR 'Castle' 4-6-0 No 5089 WESTMINSTER ABBEY runs in with an up express, circa 1957. *Norman Preedy Collection/Rail Photoprints*

5090 NEATH ABBEY rebuilt from 'Star' class No 4070

Introduced into service as a 'Star' class in February 1923. In March 1937 the newer style 'Modified' outside steam pipes were fitted before the engine was rebuilt as a 'Castle' in April 1939. Diagram HB boiler fitted. The locomotive's last 'Heavy Intermediate' overhaul including boiler (HB 6685) and tender change took place at Swindon Works between 24th August and 19th October 1960. The engine was withdrawn in May 1962 from Old Oak Common depot (81A). Recorded 'Castle' mileage 1,161,961 (total 2,058,275), service life as a 'Castle' 23 years and 30 days (total 39 years 4 months). Disposal Cashmores, Newport, December 1962.

Tender types principal fitted dates, Collett 4000g 22nd April 1939, Hawksworth 4000g 19th October 1953, Collett 4000g 24th April 1957, Hawksworth 4000g 28th January 1959, Collett 4000g 19th October 1960.

Allocated Depots

LA Laira	01/05/39	85A Worcester	11/52	81A Old Oak Common	19/10/60
86C Cardiff Canton	10/52	82A Bristol Bath Road	20/03/58		

Neath Abbey – was a Cistercian monastery, and it is located near the present-day town of Neath in South Wales. It was once the largest abbey in the Principality. Substantial ruins can still be seen, and they are in the care of Cadw. The accomplished Tudor historian John Leland described Neath Abbey 'the fairest abbey of all Wales.' The site has also been used during location filming for several episodes of the 'Dr Who' TV series.

Oiling around is taking place before GWR 'Castle' class 4-6-0 No 5090 NEATH ABBEY departs from Oxford with a Worcester-Paddington service in July 1954. *David Anderson*

5091 CLEEVE ABBEY rebuilt from 'Star' class No 4071

Introduced into service as a 'Star' class in February 1923. The engine was rebuilt as a 'Castle' in December 1938. Diagram HB boiler fitted. Converted to oil burning 31st August 1946 until 5th October 1948, roof vent fitted. The locomotive's last 'Heavy Intermediate' overhaul including boiler (HC 7601) and tender change took place at Swindon Works between 27th March and 25th May 1962. The engine was withdrawn in October 1964 from Tyseley depot (2A). Recorded 'Castle' mileage up to the end of 1963, 1,082,935 (total 1,921,723), service life as a 'Castle' 25 years 9 Months and 15 days (total 41 years 8 months and 2 days). Disposal Cashmores, Great Bridge, November 1964.

Tender types principal fitted dates, Collett 4000g 10th December 1938, Churchward 3500g (Oil) 2nd October 1946, Collett 4000g (Oil) 24th February 1947, Collett 4000g 5th November 1948, Hawksworth 4000g 27th October 1949, Collett 4000g 16th May 1950, Hawksworth 4000g 3rd February 1954, Collett 4000g 9th March 1954, Hawksworth 4000g 9th June 1958, Collett 4000g 22nd April 1961.

Allocated Depots

BRD Bristol Bath Road	18/12/38	84G Shrewsbury	04/54	87F Llanelly	13/06/61
WEY Weymouth GWR	04/39	84K Chester West	09/55	88A Cardiff Canton	11/09/61
BRD Bristol Bath Road	06/39	83C Exeter	06/57	88L Cardiff East Dock	07/09/62
SDN Swindon	30/06/47	87G Carmarthen	09/57	85A Worcester	13/04/64
84G Shrewsbury	05/53	87E Landore	12/06/58	2A Tyseley	16/06/64
82C Swindon	03/02/54				

Cleeve Abbey is a medieval monastery located near the village of Washford, in Somerset. It is a Grade I listed building which has been scheduled as an ancient monument. The abbey was founded in the late 12th century as a house for monks of the austere Cistercian order. Over its 350-year monastic history Cleeve was undistinguished amongst the abbeys of its order, frequently ill-governed and often financially troubled. In 1536 Cleeve was closed by Henry VIII in the course of the 'Dissolution of the Monasteries' and the abbey was converted into a country house.

GWR 'Castle' class 4-6-0 No 5091 CLEEVE ABBEY is seen on a fitted freight at Cardiff in June 1961. *Rail Photoprints Collection*

5092 TRESCO ABBEY rebuilt from 'Star' class No **4072** (Converted to double chimney)

Introduced into service as a 'Star' class in February 1923. The engine was rebuilt as a 'Castle' in April 1938. Diagram HB boiler fitted. Double chimney and 4-row superheater fitted during the locomotive's last 'Heavy General' overhaul which included boiler (HD 9611) and tender change, and took place at Swindon Works between 31st August and 27th October 1961. The engine was withdrawn in July 1963 from Cardiff East Dock depot (88L). Recorded 'Castle' mileage 1,143,594 (total 1,968,877), service life as a 'Castle' 25 years 2 months and 24 days (total 40 years, 4 months and 30 days). Disposal Cashmores, Newport, October 1964.

Tender types principal fitted dates, Collett 4000g 7th April 1938, Hawksworth 4000g 28th January 1950, Collett 4000g 31st August 1950, Hawksworth 4000g 27th January 1955, Collett 4000g 2nd March 1956.

Allocated Depots

GLO Gloucester Horton Road	07/04/38	WOS Worcester	11/46	82A Bristol Bath Road	20/03/58
WOS Worcester	07/43	81A Old Oak Common	27/01/55	86C Cardiff Canton	02/08/60
SDN Swindon	31/07/46	81D Reading WR	02/58	88L Cardiff East Dock	07/09/62

Tresco Abbey – The remains of a former Benedictine abbey founded in 964 AD are located on the island of Tresco in the Isles of Scilly, although the majority of what can be seen is actually ruins from the Priory of St Nicholas, founded in 1114. Some 17 acres of beautiful gardens, which were established by the nineteenth-century proprietor of the islands Augustus Smith, surround the site. The famous Valhalla Collection, of 30 maritime figureheads from the days of sailing ships, is displayed to dramatic effect within the gardens. Public access is allowed.

GWR 'Castle' class 4-6-0 No 5092 TRESCO ABBEY is seen approaching Bristol Temple Meads with a Manchester–Penzance service (via the North and West route), during May 1959. *Rail Photoprints Collection*

5093 UPTON CASTLE

Introduced into service in June 1939. Diagram HB boiler fitted. The engine was fitted with a heavy cadmium whistle chain in August 1954. The locomotive's last 'Heavy Intermediate' overhaul including boiler and tender change took place at Swindon Works between 24th November 1961 and 25th January 1962. The engine was withdrawn in September 1963 from Old Oak Common depot (81A). Recorded mileage 1,145,221, service life 24 years, 3 months and 5 days. Disposal Swindon Works, October 1963.

Tender types principal fitted dates, Collett 4000g 17th June 1939, Hawksworth 4000g 26th June 1953, Collett 4000g 10th August 1954, Hawksworth 4000g January 1956, Collett 4000g 4th June 1956, Hawksworth 4000g 13th August 1960.

GWR 'Castle' class 4-6-0 No 5093 UPTON CASTLE is seen with a Paddington–Worcester service at Oxford station in February 1963. Rail Photoprints Collection

Allocated Depots

PDN Old Oak Common	26/06/39	SDN Swindon	26/12/41	81A Old Oak Common	12/53
CDF Cardiff Canton	08/40	LDR Landore	02/42	87F Llanelly	07/01/61
NPT Ebbw Jct, Newport	02/41	81A Old Oak Common	06/52	81A Old Oak Common	27/01/61
LDR Landore	03/41	83C Exeter	09/53		

GWR 'Castle' class 4-6-0 No 5093 UPTON CASTLE is seen preparing to leave Paddington station with a Worcester service in February 1963. Rail Photoprints Collection

Upton Castle is a small 13th century castle described variously as a knight's holding and fortified mansion, which stands on a creek of the Carew river near to Tenby, Pembrokeshire. The castle was modernized in the 18th century and today is on private grounds which are not open to the public, however the adjacent Upton Castle Gardens are accessible.

5094 TRETOWER CASTLE (Converted to double chimney)

Introduced into service in June 1939. Diagram HB boiler fitted. Double chimney and 4-row superheater fitted during the locomotive's last 'Heavy General' overhaul which included boiler (HD 7673) and tender change, and took place at Swindon Works between 25th April and 30th June 1960. The engine was withdrawn in September 1962 from St Philips Marsh depot (82B). Recorded mileage 948,540, service life 23 years, 2 months and 29 days. Disposal Cashmores, Newport, December 1962.

Tender types principal fitted dates, Collett 4000g 17th June 1939, Hawksworth 4000g 26th June 1953, Collett 4000g 10th August 1954, Hawksworth 4000g January 1956, Collett 4000g 4th June 1956, Hawksworth 4000g 19th February 1958, Collett 4000g 12th February 1960, Hawksworth 4000g 13th August 1960.

GWR 'Castle' class 4-6-0 No 5094 TRETOWER CASTLE seen at Oxford, on 22nd August 1959. The fireman can be seen trimming the coal. *Alan Sainty Collection*

Allocated Depots

NA Newton Abbot	23/06/39	82F Weymouth GWR	06/51	82C Swindon	25/06/58
LA Laira	04/06/43	82A Bristol Bath Road	07/51	85B Gloucester Horton Road	16/10/58
NA Newton Abbot	09/02/44	82C Swindon	31/07/56	82A Bristol Bath Road	30/06/60
82A Bristol Bath Road	06/07/50	85B Gloucester Horton Road	21/08/56	82B St Philips Marsh	16/09/60

GWR 'Castle' class 4-6-0 No 5094 TRETOWER CASTLE passing Wootton Bassett Junction with the 08.30 (SO) Bristol to Paddington service, on 25th March 1961. *Hugh Ballantyne/Rail Photoprints*

Tretower Castle is a 12th century Welsh fortification in the Powys village of the same name, originally founded as a motte and bailey castle. In the early 14th century residential buildings were constructed away from the original fortifications forming what is today Tretower Court. Administered by Cadw, the ruins are open to the public.

5095 BARBURY CASTLE (Converted to double chimney)

Introduced into service in July 1939. Diagram HB boiler fitted. Double chimney fitted November 1958 (boiler HD 7656). The locomotive's last 'Heavy General' overhaul including boiler (HD 7673) and tender change took place at Swindon Works between 14th June and 8th September 1960. The engine was withdrawn in August 1962 from Shrewsbury depot (89A). Recorded mileage 1,122,493, service life 23 years, 1 month and 10 days. Disposal Swindon Works, March 1963.

Tender types principal fitted dates, Collett 4000g July 1939, Hawksworth 4000g 4th December 1954, Collett 4000g 28th March 1955, Hawksworth 4000g 18th January 1957, Collett 4000g 14th November 1958, Hawksworth 4000g 8th September 1960.

GWR 'Castle' class 4-6-0 No 5095 BARBURY CASTLE is seen leaving Oxford with a Birmingham service in the summer of 1961. Oxford shed can be seen to the right. *David Anderson*

Allocated Depots

LA Laira	06/07/39	86C Cardiff Canton	18/01/57	86C Cardiff Canton	24/06/58
81A Old Oak Common	16/02/51	84G Shrewsbury	12/06/58	84G Shrewsbury	08/09/60

Barbury Castle is an Iron Age hill fort situated in Wiltshire, England. It is one of several such forts found along the ancient Ridgeway route. The site lies within the Wessex Downs 'Area of Outstanding Natural Beauty', and is managed as a country park by Swindon Borough Council. Barbury Hill is a local vantage point, which, weather conditions permitting, commands a view across to the Cotswolds and the River Severn. The Old Ridgeway (ancient roadway) runs close by and the modern Ridgeway track crosses through the castle site. Public access is permitted.

GWR 'Castle' class 4-6-0 No 5095 BARBURY CASTLE, with double chimney, is seen at Shrewsbury in June 1960. *Rail Photoprints Collection*

5096 BRIDGWATER CASTLE

Introduced into service in July 1939. Diagram HB boiler fitted. The locomotive's last 'Heavy General' overhaul including boiler (HC 7639) took place at Swindon Works between 19th October and 21st December 1961. The engine was withdrawn in June 1964 from Worcester depot (85A). Recorded mileage 1,103,607, service life 24 years, 11 months and 7 days. Disposal Cohens, Morriston, December 1964.

Tender types principal fitted dates, Collett 4000g July 1939, Hawksworth 4000g 22nd June 1955, Collett 4000g 18th November 1955, Hawksworth 4000g 10th January 1957, Collett 4000g 23rd August 1957, Hawksworth 4000g 9th October 1959.

GWR Castle' class 4-6-0 No 5096 BRIDGWATER CASTLE is seen in pristine ex works condition standing outside Reading shed, in September 1957. *Alan Sainty Collection*

Allocated Depots

BRD Bristol Bath Road	08/07/39	Brd Weston-super-Mare	02/05/47	BRD Bristol Bath Road	01/50
Brd Weston-super-Mare	05/40	BRD Bristol Bath Road	18/07/47	83B Taunton	13/09/60
BRD Bristol Bath Road	06/40	Brd Weston-super-Mare	12/47	88A Cardiff Canton	20/09/61
Brd Weston-super-Mare	07/42	BRD Bristol Bath Road	12/47	88L Cardiff East Dock	07/09/62
BRD Bristol Bath Road	08/42	NPT Ebbw Jct, Newport	22/11/49	85A Worcester	13/04/64

GWR Castle' class 4-6-0 No 5096 BRIDGWATER CASTLE is seen passing Patchway with a down Swansea express, perchance to wonder if the precariously fixed 'Train Indicator Board' ever made it to the train's destination! November 1959. *Norman Preedy Collection/Rail Photoprints*

Bridgwater Castle was a 13th century fortification in the Somerset town of the same name. During the later part of the 17th century John Harvey built a mansion on the summit of the site and in the 1720s much of that site was built on to create Castle Street. In modern times Kings Square is said to approximately cover the site of the former castle.

5097 SARUM CASTLE (Converted to double chimney)

Introduced into service in July 1939. Diagram HB boiler fitted. Double chimney and 4-row superheater fitted during the locomotive's last 'Heavy General' overhaul which included boiler (HD 9606) and tender change, and took place at Swindon Works between 25th May and 12th July 1961. The engine was withdrawn in March 1963 from Cardiff East Dock depot (88L). Recorded mileage 993,804, service life 23 years, 7 months and 19 days. Disposal Cashmores, Newport, June 1965.

Tender types principal fitted dates, Collett 4000g July 1939, Hawksworth 4000g 8th September 1952, Collett 4000g 7th December 1953, Hawksworth 4000g 22nd February 1957, Collett 4000g 2nd June 1959.

GWR 'Castle' class 4-6-0 No 5097 SARUM CASTLE is seen leaving Hereford with a Midlands-West Country service in May 1959. *David Anderson*

Allocated Depots

4A Shrewsbury	17/07/39	4A Shrewsbury	03/41	88A Cardiff Canton	16/09/60
SRD Stafford Road	01/02/41	82A Bristol Bath Road	02/06/59	88L Cardiff East Dock	07/09/62

GWR 'Castle' class 4-6-0 No 5097 SARUM CASTLE is seen at Cardiff East Dock in July 1963, after being withdrawn. The engine is in the company of other redundant locos which include '43xx' class No 7303. The 3-wheeler car looks a little the worse for wear! *Rail Photoprints Collection*

Sarum Castle – Old Sarum is the location of the earliest settlement of Salisbury. The site contains evidence of human habitation as early as 3000 BC. Old Sarum is mentioned in some of the earliest records in the country, and it is located on a hill about two miles north of modern Salisbury. It was originally an Iron Age hill fort strategically placed on the junction of two trade routes and adjacent to the River Avon. It is an English Heritage property and open to the public.

5098 CLIFFORD CASTLE (Converted to double chimney)

Introduced into service in May 1946. Diagram HC boiler fitted. Double chimney and 4-row superheater fitted January 1959 (boiler HD 7679). The locomotive's last 'Heavy General' overhaul including boiler (HD 9612) and tender change took place at Swindon Works between 10th October and 4th December 1961. The engine was withdrawn in June 1964 from Reading WR depot (81D). Recorded mileage 826,525, service life 18 years, 1 month and 16 days. Disposal Cohens, Morriston, December 1964.

Tender types principal fitted dates, Collett 4000g 16th May 1946, Hawksworth 4000g 5th January 1951, Collett 4000g 13th December 1955, Hawksworth 4000g 30th January 1959.

Double chimney GWR 'Castle, Class 4-6-0 No 5098 CLIFFORD CASTLE stands at Bath Spa with a Paddington–Bristol parcels working, on 10th August 1963. *Hugh Ballantyne/Rail Photoprints*

Allocated Depots

SRD Stafford Road	05/46	Swindon Testing Plant	30/05/49	87F Llanelly	09/02/63
EXE Exeter	09/46	LA Laira	01/07/49	81A Old Oak Common	06/05/63
PZ Penzance	10/48	83A Newton Abbot	27/01/62	81D Reading WR	13/04/64
LA Laira	11/03/49	87G Carmarthen	11/08/62		

GWR 'Castle' class 4-6-0 No 5098 CLIFFORD CASTLE is seen at Bristol Temple Meads station, in 1962. *Rail Photoprints Collection*

Clifford Castle is a castle in the village of the same name, the ruins lie on a 4 acre site four miles to the north of Hay-on-Wye in Herefordshire. In 1070 an early motte and bailey castle was built on a cliff overlooking a ford on the River Wye, by William Fitzpond. Clifford was the home of Walter Fitz Richard's daughter Rosamund Clifford, who was famously known as The Fair Rosamund, and was the mistress of Henry II (12th century). A branch of the GWR ran just to the north of the castle, between it and the river.

5099 COMPTON CASTLE

Introduced into service in May 1946. Diagram HC boiler fitted. The locomotive's last 'Heavy General' overhaul including boiler (HC 7621) and tender change took place at Swindon Works between 6th May and 26th June 1961. The engine was withdrawn in February 1963 from Gloucester Horton Road depot (85B). Recorded mileage 863,411, service life 16 years, 8 months and 15 days. Disposal RA Kings, Norwich, September 1963.

Tender types principal fitted dates, Collett 4000g 16th May 1946, Hawksworth 4000g 18th May 1953, Collett 4000g 11th July 1953, Hawksworth 4000g 26th May 1955, Collett 4000g 27th November 1957, Hawksworth 4000g 26th June 1961.

GWR 'Castle' class 4-6-0 No 5099 COMPTON CASTLE, with Hawksworth 4000g tender, is seen passing Stoke Gifford with the up 'The Red Dragon', in 1960. The engine is carrying the 3rd style of 'The Red Dragon' headboard (introduced in 1956) which was surmounted by a disc containing a dragon emblem. *Rail Photoprints Collection*

Allocated Depots

Depot	Date	Depot	Date	Depot	Date
PDN Old Oak Common	25/05/46	81A Old Oak Common	20/11/56	85B Gloucester Horton Road	06/10/62
SDN Swindon	24/02/47	82A Bristol Bath Road	12/06/58	85B Gloucester Horton Road Stored	12/11/62
PDN Old Oak Common	05/47	86C Cardiff Canton	26/08/58		
CDF Cardiff Canton	05/48	85A Worcester	20/02/62		

GWR 'Castle' class 4-cylinder locomotives, Swindon Works 'Lot Numbers'

Nos 5071–5082 Lot 310 built 1938/39 (Average cost per engine £6344)
Nos 5083–5092 re-built 'Star' class engines, Lot 317 built 1937/40 (Average cost per engine £6114)
Nos 5093–5097 Lot 324 built 1939 (Average cost per engine £6502)
Nos 5098–5099 Lot 357 built 1946 (Average cost per engine £9749)

The GWR Roundel or 'Shirt button' monogram was used during the period 1934–1942.

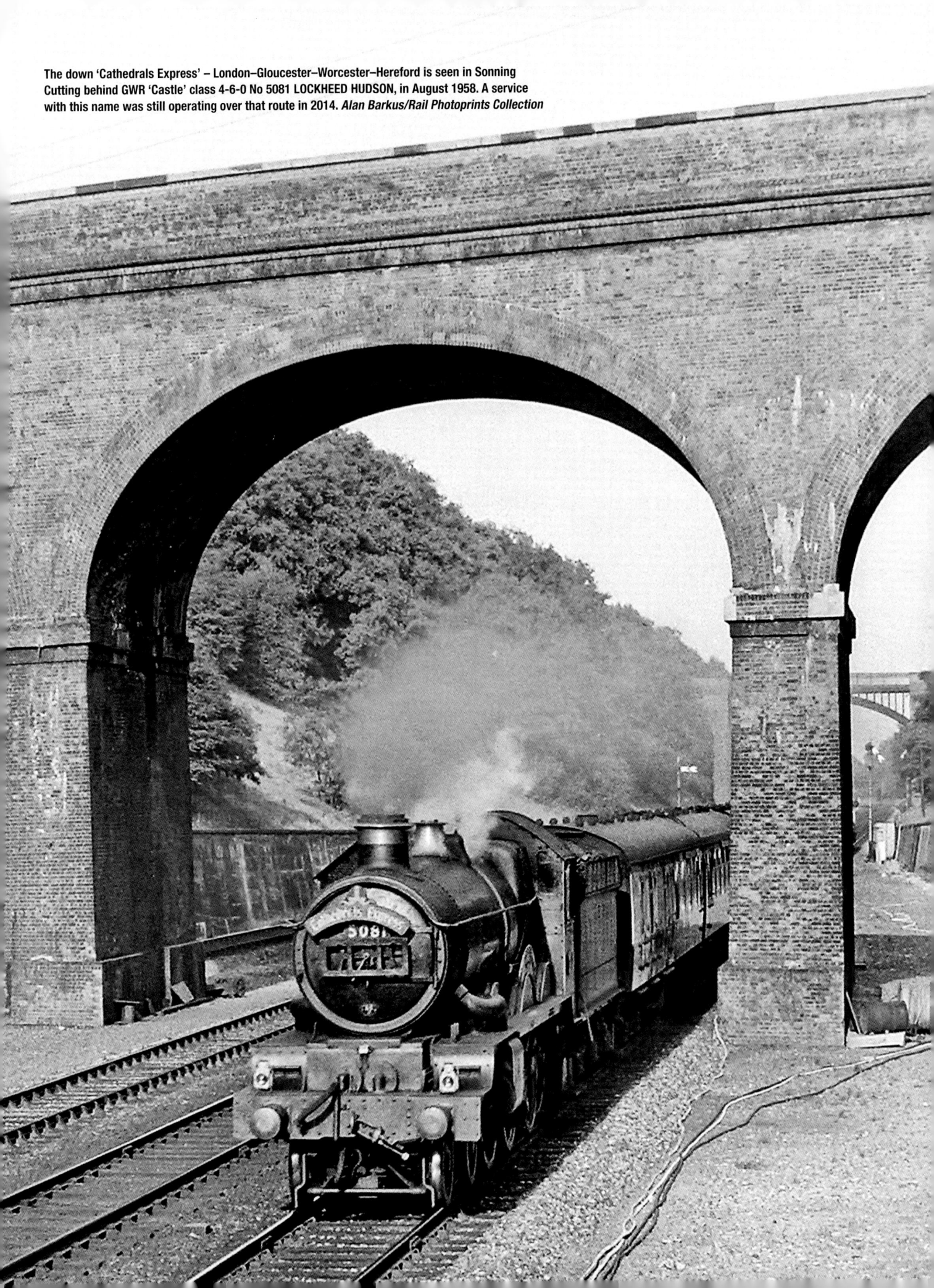

The down 'Cathedrals Express' – London–Gloucester–Worcester–Hereford is seen in Sonning Cutting behind GWR 'Castle' class 4-6-0 No 5081 LOCKHEED HUDSON, in August 1958. A service with this name was still operating over that route in 2014. *Alan Barkus/Rail Photoprints Collection*

Chapter 6

LOCOMOTIVES 7000–7037

7000 VISCOUNT PORTAL

Introduced into service in May 1946. Diagram HC boiler fitted. The locomotive's last 'Heavy General' overhaul including boiler (HC 7641) and tender change took place at Swindon Works between 17th March and 15th May 1959. The engine was withdrawn in December 1963 from Worcester depot (85A). Recorded mileage 824,873, service life 17 years, 7 months and 3 days. Disposal Cashmores, Great Bridge, June 1964.

Tender types principal fitted dates, Collett 4000g 25th May 1946, Hawksworth 4000g 17th November 1948, Collett 4000g 22nd August 1950, Hawksworth 4000g 25th April 1952, Collett 4000g 28th July 1953, Hawksworth 4000g 7th April 1954, Collett 4000g 26th October 1955.

GWR 'Castle' class 4-6-0 No 7000 VISCOUNT PORTAL with a Collett 4000g tender is seen entering Newton Abbot with the up 'Torbay Express', 1959. The 'Torbay Express' London–Torquay–Paignton service was introduced by the GWR as one of its premier holiday trains. A similarly named service still operates in the present day (2014). Note the stepped inside cylinder cover. *Rail Photoprints Collection*

Allocated Depots

NA Newton Abbot	25/05/46	85A Worcester	14/08/62	85A Worcester	22/03/63
85B Gloucester Horton Road	15/05/59	85B Gloucester Horton Road	30/08/62		

Viscount Portal – Wyndham Raymond Portal, 1st Viscount Portal PC GCMG DSO MVO (1885–1949) was a British politician. In 1919, following a distinguished military career Portal became chairman of the family's banknote paper mill company, Portals Limited. In 1935 he was made chairman of the Bacon Development Board, and in April 1939 he became regional commissioner for Wales under the Civil Defence Scheme. In 1940 he became the chairman of the Coal Production Council, and he served in government as Additional Parliamentary Secretary to the Ministry of Supply from 1940–1942, and as Minister of Works and Planning from 1942–1944. In 1945, he became the last chairman of the Great Western Railway, and Lord Lieutenant of Hampshire from 1947. He was president of the organising committee for the 1948 London Olympic Games.

GWR 'Castle' class 4-6-0 No 7000 VISCOUNT PORTAL with Hawksworth 4000g tender is seen passing Parsons Tunnel signalbox and running along the sea wall near Teignmouth, 1957. Note the un-stepped inside cylinder cover. *John Day Collection/Rail Photoprints*

7001 DENBIGH CASTLE renamed **SIR JAMES MILNE** in February 1948 (Converted to double chimney)

Introduced into service in May 1946. Diagram HC boiler fitted. Double chimney and 4 row superheater fitted during the locomotive's last 'Heavy General' overhaul which included boiler (HD 7693) and tender change, and took place at Swindon Works between 16th July and 19th September 1960. The engine was withdrawn in September 1963 from Oxley depot (2B). Recorded mileage 838,604, service life 17 years, 3 months and 17 days. Disposal Cohens, Morriston, April 1964.

Tender types principal fitted dates, Collett 4000g May 1946, Hawksworth 4000g 22nd June 1955, Collett 4000g 22nd March 1958, Hawksworth 21st February 1959, Collett 4000g October 1959, Hawksworth 4000g 26th March 1960, Collett 4000g 19th September 1960.

This trio of GWR 'Castle' class 4-6-0 engines, seen being prepared for duty at Wolverhampton Stafford Road depot on 24th August 1963, shows No 7001 SIR JAMES MILNE in the company of No 5026 CRICCIETH CASTLE and No 7006 LYDFORD CASTLE. Note the dilapidated condition of the 84A running shed. Hugh Ballantyne/Rail Photoprints

Allocated Depots

CDF Cardiff Canton	31/05/46	83D Laira	11/07/53	84A Stafford Road	18/08/61
PDN Old Oak Common	09/04/48	81A Old Oak Common	13/07/53	2B Oxley	09/09/63

GWR 'Castle' class 4-6-0 No 7001 SIR JAMES MILNE is seen at Oxford. The locomotive's double chimney is seen to good effect in this 1961 image. Note the Hawksworth coach beyond the locomotive. David Anderson

Sir James Milne (1883–1958). James Milne joined the Great Western Railway in 1904 as an engineering graduate. He worked in the company's head office and gained operational experience whilst at the same time concerning himself with the statistical facts of railway operation. In 1919 he became Director of Statistics at the then newly created Ministry of Transport. He left that post in 1922 and returned to the GWR to take up the post of Assistant General Manager, becoming General Manager in 1929; he was knighted in 1932. Milne was occupied with counteracting the problems of declining freight traffic on many of the inherited South Wales lines which coupled with the general effects of the economic depression greatly affected the profitability of the company. In addition to instituting cost cutting measures Milne also looked to the future by involving the GWR in a programme of road transport expansion, additionally he maintained an interest in the Channel Island air services operated from Croydon by Jersey Airways in 1945. During World War II Milne served as deputy-chairman of the controlling Railway Executive. Whilst serving as the last General Manager of the GWR he was privy to the government's railway nationalisation plans. Milne openly opposed nationalisation, but nevertheless was offered the chairmanship of the Railway Executive, which he duly turned down.

GWR 'Castle' class 4-6-0 No 7001 SIR JAMES MILNE is seen with steam to spare at Standish Junction in June 1962. *Rail Photoprints Collection*

GWR 'Castle' class 4-6-0 No 7001 SIR JAMES MILNE is seen backing onto stock before working an up train from Wolverhampton in September 1962. A superb portrait of a double chimney Collett 'Castle' class locomotive in its final form. *Rail Photoprints Collection*

7002 DEVIZES CASTLE (Converted to double chimney)

Introduced into service in June 1946. Diagram HC boiler fitted. Double chimney and 4-row superheater fitted during the locomotive's last 'Heavy General' overhaul which included boiler (HD 7667) and tender change, and took place at Swindon Works between 15th May and 10th July 1961. The engine was withdrawn in March 1964 from Worcester depot (85A). Recorded mileage 837,626, service life 17 years, 9 months and 4 days. Disposal Cashmores, Great Bridge, June 1964.

Tender types principal fitted dates, Collett 4000g 6th June 1946, Hawksworth 4000g February 1950, Collett 4000g 14th December 1963.

GWR 'Castle' class 4-6-0 No 7002 DEVIZES CASTLE is seen at Oxford on 3rd March 1961, whilst waiting to depart with an up Worcester–Paddington train. Note that the driver has his oil can in hand and that there are no less than 10 railway workers in this busy image. *David Anderson*

Allocated Depots

LDR Landore	06/06/46	87E Landore	12/06/58	85A Worcester	26/11/58
87G Carmarthen	10/56				

GWR 'Castle' class 4-6-0 No 7002 DEVIZES CASTLE is seen in pristine condition standing adjacent to the turntable at Swindon Works in September 1956. Note the BR 'Lion on a Bike' emblem and the Landore shed plate. *Rail Photoprints Collection*

Devizes Castle was a medieval fortification in the town of Devizes, Wiltshire. The first motte and bailey castle on this site was built in 1080 by Osmund, Bishop of Salisbury. That castle burnt down in 1113 and was rebuilt in stone by Roger, Bishop of Salisbury circa 1120. He occupied it under King Henry I and later under King Stephen. It then remained the property of the Crown and it was used as a prison by King Henry II and King Henry III. It went on to become the property of Catherine of Aragon, the first wife of Henry VIII. The present castle structure is a Victorian era building in the castellated Neo Norman/Gothic design which was built in the 19th century by the Leach family. In 2013 the structure housed modern flats and was not open to the public.

7003 ELMLEY CASTLE (Converted to double chimney)

Introduced into service in June 1946. Diagram HC boiler fitted. Double chimney and 4-row superheater fitted during the locomotive's last 'Heavy General' overhaul which included boiler (HD 7691) and tender change, and took place at Swindon Works between 24th March and 7th June 1960. The engine was withdrawn in August 1964 from Gloucester Horton Road depot (85B). Recorded mileage 773,642, service life 18 years, 1 month and 28 days. Disposal Cashmores, Newport, December 1964.

Tender types principal fitted dates, Collett 4000g 13th June 1946, Hawksworth 4000g 24th May 1954, Collett 4000g 7th June 1960.

GWR 'Castle' class 4-6-0 No 7003 ELMLEY CASTLE coasts downhill from Whiteball Tunnel past Marlands with a 13 coach train, in August 1952. *Rail Photoprints Collection*

Allocated Depots

LDR Landore	13/06/46	85B Gloucester Horton Road	16/06/60	85B Gloucester Horton Road	22/06/64
82A Bristol Bath Road	02/12/58	82B St Philips Marsh	13/04/64		

GWR 'Castle' class 4-6-0 No 7003 ELMLEY CASTLE, now with double chimney is seen at Westbury depot in June 1963. *Rail Photoprints Collection*

Elmley Castle – The ruins of an important Norman and medieval castle, from which the village derives its name, are located in the deer park, just over half a mile south on Bredon Hill. The castle is supposed to have been built for Robert Despenser in the years following the Norman Conquest. After his death (post 1098) it descended to his heirs, the powerful Beauchamp family. The family later became Earls of Warwick and the family coat of arms, the ragged staff, is to be found inscribed on the ancient font that stands in the parish church of Elmley.

7004 EASTNOR CASTLE (Converted to double chimney)

Introduced into service in June 1946. Diagram HC boiler fitted. Double chimney and 4-row superheater fitted February 1958 (to existing boiler HC 7610). The locomotive's last 'Heavy General' overhaul including boiler (HD 7690) and tender change took place at Swindon Works between 28th March and 4th May 1960. The engine was withdrawn in August 1964 from Reading WR depot (81D). Recorded mileage 876,349, service life 17 years, 6 months and 27 days. Disposal Swindon Works, February 1964.

Tender types principal fitted dates, Collett 4000g 19th June 1946, Hawksworth 4000g 14th January 1955, Collett 4000g 19th June 1956.

Allocated Depots

GLO Gloucester Horton Road	13/06/46	PDN Old Oak Common	01/49	81D Reading WR	22/06/64
CDF Cardiff Canton	30/09/48	85A Worcester	05/07/60		

GWR 'Castle' class 4-6-0 No 7004 EASTNOR CASTLE is seen on shed at Worcester (85A) on a very cold February day in 1963, note the icicles on the tender framing, steps and motion bracket. The post war 'Castle' class build modifications included continuing the cab window handrail upwards forward of the window frame from loco No 5088 onwards, and that can clearly be seen in this image.
Rail Photoprints Collection

Eastnor Castle is a 19th-century mock or revival castle, two miles from the town of Ledbury in Herefordshire, close by the village of Eastnor. It was founded by John Cocks, 1st Earl Somers as his stately home and continues to be inhabited by his descendants. Currently in residence in 2013 were the family of James Hervey-Bathurst, the grandson of Arthur Somers-Cocks, 6th Baron Somers. The castle is a Grade I listed building. The grounds are the location of the Land Rover vehicle test track, accordingly each June the castle is host to the Land Rover World Event.

7005 LAMPHEY CASTLE renamed SIR EDWARD ELGAR in August 1957

Introduced into service in June 1946. Diagram HC boiler fitted. The locomotive's last 'Heavy Intermediate' overhaul including boiler (HC 7604) and tender change took place at Swindon Works between 15th August and 12th October 1962. The engine was withdrawn in September 1964 from Southall depot (81C). Recorded mileage 869,370 service life 18 years, 2 months and 13 days. Disposal Cohens, Morriston January 1964.

Tender types principal fitted dates, Collett 4000g 25th June 1946, Hawksworth 4000g 29th January 1950, Collett 4000g 26th July 1951, Hawksworth 4000g 18th March 1954, Collett 4000g 7th April 1955, Hawksworth 4000g 10th August 1960, Collett 4000g 12th October 1962.

Allocated Depots

WOS Worcester	25/06/46	81C Southall	08/64

Sir Edward Elgar, 1st Baronet, OM, GCVO (1857–1934) was an English composer, many of whose works have entered the British and international classical concert repertoire. Among his best-known compositions are orchestral works including the *Enigma Variations*, the *Pomp and Circumstance Marches*, concertos for violin and cello, and two symphonies. Elgar was born in the small village of Lower Broadheath, outside Worcester. The year 1957 was Elgar's centenary year and BR renamed No 7005 (appropriately then a Worcester allocated engine) to mark the occasion.

Lamphey Castle – the medieval bishops of St David's, in Pembrokeshire built for themselves a magnificent retreat away from worries of Church and State. Their palace was improved over two centuries, though it was mainly the work of Henry de Gower, Bishop of St David's from 1328 to 1347, who built the splendid Great Hall. The ruins are administered by Cadw (Welsh Historic Monuments) and are open to the public.

The 'Bobby' looks out from his signalbox as GWR 'Castle' class 4-6-0 No 7005 SIR EDWARD ELGAR arrives at Ledbury station with the Hereford portion of the 1.45 service from Paddington, on 11th July 1959. *Hugh Ballantyne/Rail Photoprints*

7006 LYDFORD CASTLE (Converted to double chimney)

Introduced into service in June 1946. Diagram HC boiler fitted. Double chimney and 4-row superheater fitted during the locomotive's last 'Heavy General' overhaul which included boiler (HD 7692) and tender change, and took place at Swindon Works between 23rd March and 3rd June 1960. The engine was withdrawn in December 1963 from Old Oak Common depot (81A). Recorded mileage 789,052 service life 17 years, 5 months and 18 days. Disposal Birds, Risca August 1964.

Tender types principal fitted dates, Collett 4000g 28th June 1946, Hawksworth 4000g 18th May 1950, Collett 4000g 27th May 1952, Hawksworth 4000g 25th May 1953, Collett 4000g 24th January 1955, Hawksworth 4000g 13th August 1955, Collett 4000g 3rd June 1960.

Plenty of activity to be seen in this study, as GWR 'Castle' class 4-6-0 No 7006 LYDFORD CASTLE waits to depart from Oxford station with a down Paddington–Worcester service on 2nd March 1961. Note that the rear nearside sandbox can be clearly seen located between the cab steps and trailing driving wheel. *David Anderson*

Allocated Depots

4A Shrewsbury	28/06/46	85B Gloucester Horton Road	28/05/51	86C Cardiff Canton	22/09/59
CDF Cardiff Canton	06/48	81A Old Oak Common	26/02/58	85A Worcester	05/07/60
GLO Gloucester Horton Road	25/08/48	83D Laira	03/58	81A Old Oak Common	19/03/62
SDN Swindon	20/01/50				

GWR 'Castle' class 4-6-0 No 7006 LYDFORD CASTLE is seen at Oxford station with an up Paddington service on 8th May 1961. This image shows the engine's (some may say incongruous) double chimney to good effect. Note also the mechanical lubricator located behind the offside steam pipe. *David Anderson*

Lydford Castle is a medieval castle in the Devonian town of the same name. The first castle in Lydford, sometimes termed the Norman Fort, was a small ringwork built in a corner of the Anglo-Saxon fortified burh in the years after the Norman Conquest. It was intended to help control Devon following the widespread revolt against Norman rule in 1068. The Norman fort was abandoned by the middle of the 12th century. The second castle in Lydford was constructed in 1195. The structure has been described as 'the earliest example of a purpose-built gaol' in England and the English Heritage owned site is open to the public.

7007 OGMORE CASTLE renamed GREAT WESTERN in January 1948

This was the last express passenger engine built at Swindon by the Great Western Railway. (Converted to double chimney)

Introduced into service in July 1946. Diagram HC boiler fitted. Double chimney and 4-row superheater fitted during the locomotive's last 'Heavy General' overhaul which included boiler (HD 9604) and tender change, and took place at Swindon Works between 13th April and 5th June 1961. The engine was withdrawn in February 1963 from Worcester depot (85A). Recorded mileage 851,649 service life 16 years, 7 months and 8 days. Disposal Cashmores, Great Bridge January 1964.

Tender types principal fitted dates, Collett 4000g 1st July 1946, Hawksworth 4000g 27th January 1950, Collett 4000g 3rd July 1951, Hawksworth 4000g 16th January 1953, Collett 4000g 11th September 1963, Hawksworth 4000g 4th June 1954, Collett 4000g 23rd January 1958, Hawksworth 4000g 21st February 1959, Collett 4000g 11th September 1959.

Allocated Depots

| SRD Stafford Road | 01/07/46 | PDN Old Oak Common | 09/48 | WOS Worcester | 02/50 |

Great Western – 'Castle' class locomotive No 7007 which was originally named OGMORE CASTLE was renamed GREAT WESTERN on 1st January 1948 when British Railways (and British Railways Western Region) came into being and the Great Western Railway (GWR) ceased to exist.

GWR 'Castle' class 4-6-0 No 7007 GREAT WESTERN is seen at Oxford station in 1959. Note the GWR crest on the centre wheel splasher below the nameplate, also the mechanical lubricator behind the modified style outside steampipe. *David Anderson*

GWR 'Castle' class 4-6-0 No 7007 GREAT WESTERN nameplate photographed at Reading. *Martyn Hunt/Rail Photoprints Collection*

GWR 'Castle' class 4-6-0 No 7007 GREAT WESTERN receiving attention outside Laira shed, circa 1960. *Keith Langston Collection/Rail Photoprints*

Selected GWR Milestones

1835 – 31st August. Great Western Railway Act received Royal Assent. The railway's first engineer Isambard Kingdom Brunel was given approval to construct his broad gauge network.

1837 – In July an Act was obtained for the London terminus at Paddington and one month later Daniel Gooch became Superintendent of Locomotive Engineers.

1841 – On 30th June the line from London to Bristol was completed.

1842 – On 13th June HRH Queen Victoria became the first reigning monarch to travel by rail, journeying from Slough to Paddington.

1843 – Swindon Works was brought into regular use on 2nd January.

1859 – Formal opening of the Royal Albert Bridge by the Prince Consort, allowing trains to travel from Plymouth to Truro. Brunel died on 15th September.

1864 – Was the year that Joseph Armstrong took over the post of Superintendent of Locomotive Engineers following the resignation of Gooch.

1868 – On 1st June the conversion from Broad Gauge to Narrow Gauge (standard gauge) tracks began. The last broad gauge trains left Paddington and Penzance simultaneously at 10.15am on 20th May 1892.

1892 – First corridor train with full lavatory facilities ran between Paddington and Birkenhead on 7th March. In May 1896 the first dining cars were introduced on Paddington – Plymouth and Cardiff express services.

1902 – Six-coupled 4-6-0 locomotives were introduced.

1904 – On 9th May locomotives CITY OF TRURO and DUKE OF CONNAUGHT achieved the record speed of 102.3mph.

1908 – Britain's first Pacific (4-6-2) locomotive THE GREAT BEAR was introduced.

1906 – First AWS installation was completed, on the Henley Branch.

1923 – The first 'Castle' class 4-6-0 No 4073 CAERPHILLY CASTLE was introduced, followed by the 'King' class 4-6-0s in 1927.

1924 – Their Royal Highnesses King George V and Queen Mary visited Swindon Works in the April of that year.

1932 – On 6th June 'Castle' class No 5006 TREGENNA CASTLE set a world record start to stop speed record with the 'Cheltenham Flyer' 81.6mph Swindon-Paddington.

1935 – Centenary year, saw the introduction of 'The Bristolian' from 9th September.

1948 – The 5th March was the date of the last meeting of the board of the Great Western Railway Co.

7008 SWANSEA CASTLE

This was the first of the class built at Swindon by British Railways (BR).

Introduced into service in May 1948. Diagram HC boiler fitted. Double chimney and 4-row superheater fitted June 1959 (boiler HD 7682). The locomotive's last 'Heavy Intermediate' overhaul including boiler (HD 7660) and tender change took place at Swindon Works between 9th August and 10th October 1962. The engine was withdrawn in September 1964 from Old Oak Common depot (81A). Recorded mileage 483,663 (up to 28th December 1963) service life 16 years, 4 months and 1 day. Disposal Birds, Risca February 1965.

Tender types principal fitted dates, Hawksworth 4000g 12th May 1948, Collett 4000g 10th November 1954, Hawksworth 4000g 21st March 1956, Collett 4000g 11th September 1956.

Allocated Depots

OXF Oxford	12/05/48	81F Oxford	01/55	81A Old Oak Common	09/03/63
82C Swindon	10/11/54				

Swansea Castle was founded by Henry de Beaumont in 1106 as the head of the Lordship of Gower, in Wales. In the 18th and 19th centuries parts of the castle were variously used as a market, a town hall, a drill hall and a prison. The Castle remains are now so hemmed in by modern buildings and roads that it is hard to imagine its original surroundings, or indeed the original form of the 13th century fortification. What is visible now is only a small part of what was the latest castle to be built on the site. Building work, in the 20th century, led to further demolition and what little remains of the once strategically important castle can be viewed from the road.

BR/WR 'Castle' class 4-6-0 No 7008 SWANSEA CASTLE is seen ex works after receiving a double chimney in June 1959. *Rail Photoprints Collection*

7009 ATHELNEY CASTLE

Introduced into service in July 1948. Diagram HC boiler fitted. The locomotive's last 'Heavy General' overhaul including boiler (HC 7642) took place at Swindon Works between 27th April and 27th June 1961. The engine was withdrawn in March 1963 from Old Oak Common depot (81A). Recorded mileage 671,920, service life 14 years, 8 months and 20 days. Disposal Cashmores, Newport August 1965.

Tender types principal fitted dates, Hawksworth 4000g 27th May 1948, Collett 4000g 27th June 1951, Hawksworth 4000g 25th May 1954, Collett 4000g 28th June 1955, Hawksworth 7th January 1958, Collett 4000g 10th June 1958.

Allocated Depots

LDR Landore	07/48	81A Old Oak Common	05/07/61	85B Gloucester Horton Road	03/11/62
87G Carmarthen	27/06/61	85A Worcester	24/02/62	81A Old Oak Common	22/03/63

Athelney Castle – The Isle of Athelney near Bridgwater in Somerset is the site of the lowest known Hillfort in the United Kingdom. There is evidence of Iron Age and Bronze age occupation, as well as Athelney being the place famous for King Alfred's stand against the Viking invaders (and the legend of him burning his cakes). Very little earthworks remains, however, pedestrian access to the Hillfort site and King Alfred's monument is possible.

BR/WR 'Castle' class 4-6-0 No 7009 ATHELNEY CASTLE is seen at Swindon station on 12th August 1962. *Rail Photoprints Collection*

7010 AVONDALE CASTLE (Converted to double chimney)

Introduced into service in July 1948. Diagram HC boiler fitted. Double chimney and 4-row superheater fitted during the locomotive's last 'Heavy General' overhaul which included boiler (HD 7996) and tender change, and took place at Swindon Works between 8th September and 28th October 1960. The engine was withdrawn in January 1964 from Reading WR depot (81D). Recorded mileage 662,192, service life 15 years, 8 months and 9 days. Disposal Hayes, Bridgend June 1964.

Tender types principal fitted dates, Hawksworth 4000g 9th June 1948, Collett 4000g 28th April 1950, Hawksworth 4000g 8th May 1956, Collett 4000g 3rd November 1956.

Running wrong line BR/WR 'Castle' class 4-6-0 No 7010 AVONDALE CASTLE (in single chimney form) arrives at Bath Spa with the 12.30 (Sun) Paddington–Bristol service, on 28th February 1960. The reason for the wrong line running was ongoing permanent way repairs and the 'gang' can be seen to the right of the train. *Hugh Ballantyne/Rail Photoprints*

Allocated Depots

| OXF Oxford | 07/1948 | 81A Old Oak Common | 10/52 | 81D Reading WR | 10/03/64 |

BR/WR 'Castle' class 4-6-0 No 7010 AVONDALE CASTLE, now with double chimney is seen at Shrewsbury, in November 1960. *Rail Photoprints Collection*

Avondale Castle – The official lists of castles in England and Wales does not contain the name Avondale Castle, neither does the name appear to be associated with any stately homes which may stand on the site of former castles. Gayler's Castle Strathaven, is a Scheduled Ancient Monument in South Lanarkshire Scotland which is alternatively known as Avondale Castle.

7011 BANBURY CASTLE

Introduced into service in July 1948. Diagram HC boiler fitted. The locomotive's last 'Heavy General' overhaul including boiler (HC 7617) and tender change took place at Swindon Works between 5th October and 22nd November 1962. The engine was withdrawn in February 1965 from Oxley depot (2B). Recorded mileage 748,635 (up to 28th December 1963), service life 16 years, 7 months and 14 days. Disposal Cashmores, Great Bridge May 1965.

Tender types principal fitted dates, Hawksworth 4000g 17th June 1948, Collett 4000g 1st June 1950, Hawksworth 4000g 10th September 1961, Collett 4000g 12th December 1952, Hawksworth 4000g 16th February 1955, Collett 4000g 15th May 1957, Hawksworth 4000g April 1958, Collett 4000g 23rd December 1960, Hawksworth 4000g 22nd November 1962.

Worcester allocated (85A) BR/WR 'Castle' class 4-6-0 No 7011 BANBURY CASTLE is seen being turned at Southall (81C) depot in 1964. Note that the smokebox number plate had already been removed. *Gordon Edgar Collection /A. E. Durrant/Rail Photoprints*

Allocated Depots

BRD Bristol Bath Road	07/48	85A Worcester	23/12/60	85A Worcester	27/01/64
84C Banbury	21/10/59	81D Reading WR	22/11/62	2B Oxley	20/06/64
86C Cardiff Canton	04/04/60				

BR/WR 'Castle' class 4-6-0 No 7011 BANBURY CASTLE is seen leaving Oxford with an up train, in July 1961. *David Anderson*

Banbury Castle was a medieval castle that stood near the centre of the Oxfordshire town of the same name. The castle was built in 1135 by Alexander, Bishop of Lincoln, in a motte and bailey design. King Stephen confiscated the castle in 1139, but it was returned to the bishop later that year and mostly remained in the hands of later bishops until 1547. Nothing can now be seen of Banbury Castle, whose location is marked by Castle Street.

7012 BARRY CASTLE

Introduced into service in August 1948. Diagram HC boiler fitted. The locomotive's last 'Heavy General' overhaul including boiler (HC 7612) and tender change took place at Swindon Works between 11th August and 19th October 1960. The engine was withdrawn in November 1964 from Oxley depot (2B). Recorded mileage 667,408 (up to 28th December 1963), service life 16 years and 3 months. Disposal Cashmores, Great Bridge February 1965.

Tender types principal fitted dates, Hawksworth 4000g August 1948, Collett 4000g 12th May 1950, Hawksworth 4000g 27th April 1951, Collett 4000g 31st January 1952.

BR/WR 'Castle' class 4-6-0 No 7012 BARRY CASTLE has just passed Aynho troughs at the head of the 'Pines Express' (nameboard not carried), the 09.35 Bournemouth West–Manchester service, on 15th April 1963. The 'Pines Express' was a named passenger train that ran daily between Manchester and Bournemouth (1910 to 1967). It is believed to have been named after the pine tress growing in the Bournemouth area. *Hugh Ballantyne/Rail Photoprints*

Allocated Depots

LDR Landore	08/48	87G Carmarthen	22/09/59	84A Stafford Road	13/06/61
82C Swindon	14/04/50	81A Old Oak Common	31/10/60	2B Oxley	20/06/64
87E Landore	12/05/50				

BR/WR 'Castle' class 4-6-0 No 7012 BARRY CASTLE, then a Stafford Road engine is seen at Oxford (81F) in January 1965. *David Anderson*

Barry Castle is a small Grade II listed ruined two-storey gatehouse with the adjacent walls of a hall located in the Romilly district of the Glamorgan town of the same name. The originally Norman castle was really little more than a small fortified manor house, which was the seat of the de Barry family built in the 13th and 14th centuries to replace an earlier earthwork. During the 14th century the castle was strengthened by the addition of a large hall and gatehouse on its south side, and it is those ruins which can be seen today.

7013 Renamed **WINDSOR CASTLE** in February 1952, originally named **BRISTOL CASTLE** (Converted to double chimney)

Introduced into service in July 1948. Diagram HC boiler fitted. Double chimney, 4-row superheater and 'Davies & Metcalf patent lubricator' fitted May 1958. The locomotive's last 'Heavy General' overhaul including boiler (HD 7657) took place at Swindon Works between 2nd March and 6th May 1960. The engine was withdrawn in September 1964 from Gloucester Horton Road depot (85B). Recorded mileage 712,286 (up to 28th December 1963), service life 16 years 2 months and 1day. Disposal Cox & Danks, Park Royal June 1965.

Tender types principal fitted dates, Collett 4000g 31st August 1948, Hawksworth 4000g 9th November 1948, Collett 4000g 14th June 1949, Hawksworth 4000g 24th January 1950, Collett 4000g 21st February 1951, Hawksworth 4000g 5th January 1954, Collett 4000g 16th March 1955.

This locomotive assumed the identity of No 4082 WINDSOR CASTLE in February 1952. No 4082 was driven by HRH King George VI from Swindon Works to Swindon station during an official visit in 1924, and therefore that engine was deemed an appropriate one to haul his funeral train in 1952. However, No 4082 (a single chimney engine) needed more repair work than could be achieved in the time available, and so No 7013 (later to become a double chimney engine) took its identity. The planned swap back never happened and the two locomotives, although strikingly different in appearance, worked out their days in the guise of each other.

Allocated Depots

PDN Old Oak Common	07/48	85A Worcester	06/05/60	81A Old Oak Common. Reinstated	28/09/63
85A Worcester	25/04/52	Worcester Stored	08/63	85B Gloucester Horton Road	24/08/64
81A Old Oak Common	09/57				

Windsor Castle is a royal residence at Windsor in the English county of Berkshire. See the details for locomotive No 4082.

Bristol Castle was a Norman castle built for the defence of Bristol. Remains can be seen today in Castle Park near the Broadmead Shopping Centre, and includes the remains of the 'sally port'. The first castle built at Bristol was of a timber motte and bailey style which was possibly erected on the command of William the Conqueror, who effectively owned Bristol. The Domesday Book has mention of the fortification. Little remains of the castle proper but the castle moat (which was covered over in 1847) still exists and is mainly navigable by boat, flowing as it does under Castle Park and into the city's famous Floating Harbour. The western section is a dry ditch and a 'sally port' into the moat survives near St Peter's Church.

The original GWR 'Castle' class 4-6-0 No 7013 BRISTOL CASTLE is seen passing Bentley Heath on 13th May 1950. This locomotive changed identities with No 4082 in February 1952 when that locomotive was required to head the Funeral train of King George VI. As previously mentioned No 7013 received the name and number plates and effectively became No 4082 WINDSOR CASTLE, and the plates were never changed back. King George VI died on 6th February 1952 at Sandringham and was buried at St George's Chapel, Windsor Castle, on 15th February 1952, following a State Funeral in the Chapel. His daughter, HRH The Princess Elizabeth, had been proclaimed Queen Elizabeth II on 8th February 1952. *Rail Photoprints Collection*

GWR 'Castle' class 4-6-0 No 7013 BRISTOL CASTLE (formerly locomotive 4082) is seen with a down 'Cathedrals Express' working at Oxford in 1962. Note the double chimney, pipe smoking driver and young admirers. *David Anderson*

GWR 'Castle' class 4-6-0 No 7013 BRISTOL CASTLE is again seen at Oxford station on this occasion with a Worcester–Paddington service on 18th March 1961. Note that the smokebox reservoir associated with the Davies & Metcalf patent lubricator can be clearly identified. *David Anderson*

7014 CAERHAYS CASTLE (Converted to double chimney)

Introduced into service in July 1948. Diagram HC boiler fitted. Double chimney and 4-row superheater fitted February 1959 to existing boiler (HD7645) 'Davies & Metcalf patent lubricator' also fitted. The locomotive's last 'Heavy General' overhaul including boiler (HD 9603) and tender change took place at Swindon Works between 14th March and 5th May 1961. The engine was withdrawn in February 1965 from Tyseley depot (2A). Recorded mileage 765,282 (up to 28th December 1963), service life 16 years 6 months and 10 days. Disposal Cashmores, Great Bridge May 1965.

Tender types principal fitted dates, Hawksworth 4000g 16th July 1948, Collett 4000g 14th June 1950, Hawksworth 4000g 6th January 1954, Collett 4000g 13th May 1957, Hawksworth 4000g 3rd December 1960, Collett 4000g 5th May 1961.

Allocated Depots

SDN Swindon	21/07/48	82B St Philips Marsh	03/10/60	2B Oxley	09/09/63
BRD Bristol Bath Road	08/48	81A Old Oak Common	08/08/61	2A Tyseley	27/06/64
87E Landore	16/09/60	84A Stafford Road	15/06/62		

Caerhays Castle is a semi-castellated manor house, which is Norman in appearance and located near to St Michael Caerhays in Cornwall (the translation of *caerhays* into modern English is 'enclosed castle'). The exterior was built of rough stone quarried from the surrounding countryside. Parts of the original manor remain, including the ancient chapel as well as an old walkway to the sea which retains the name of the Watchhouse Walk. Such walkways allowed castles to be supplied by sea during times of siege. The adjacent gardens host the largest collection of magnolias in England, and the castle and grounds are open from February to June.

BR/WR 'Castle' class 4-6-0 No 7014 CAERHAYS CASTLE is seen passing Thingley Sidings, near Chippenham with a down Bristol service, in 1959. Note the smokebox mounted reservoir associated with the Davies & Metcalf lubricator. *Norman Preedy Collection/Rail Photoprints*

7015 CARN BREA CASTLE (Converted to double chimney)

Introduced into service in September 1948. Diagram HC boiler fitted. Double chimney and 4-row superheater fitted during the locomotive's last 'Heavy General' overhaul which included boiler change (HD 7681) and tender change, took place at Swindon Works between 26th March and 28th May 1959. The engine was withdrawn in April 1963 from Old Oak Common depot (81A). Recorded mileage 636,439, service life 14 years 7 months and 5 days. Disposal, sold to Coopers Metals, Sharpness and then resold to Cashmores, Newport April 1964.

Tender types principal fitted dates, Hawksworth 4000g September 1948, Collett 4000g 13th February 1952, Hawksworth 4000g 12th January 1954, Collett 4000g 14th November 1956.

Allocated Depots

SDN Swindon	09/48	84A Stafford Road	28/05/59	Shrewsbury Stored	07/09/62
82A Bristol Bath Road	11/55	84G Shrewsbury	04/11/59	81A Old Oak Common. Reinstated	15/06/62

Carn Brea Castle on Carn Brea near Redruth in Cornwall is a 14th-century Grade II listed granite stone building which was extensively remodeled in the 18th century as a hunting lodge in the style of a castle, for the Basset family. In 2013 the building was in private use as a restaurant.

BR/WR 'Castle. Class 4-6-0 No 7015 CARN BREA CASTLE seen approaching Saltford with the morning Swindon running in turn (10.05 Bristol to Bath Spa), the train will lay over on the centre road at Bath Spa before heading on to Swindon, November 1957 this working followed a 'Heavy Intermediate' overhaul. *Hugh Ballantyne/Rail Photoprints*

7016 CHESTER CASTLE

Introduced into service in September 1948. Diagram HC boiler fitted. The locomotive's last 'Heavy Intermediate' overhaul including boiler (HC 7624) and tender change, place at Swindon Works between 9th July and 29th September 1960. The engine was withdrawn in November 1962 from Cardiff East Dock depot (then 88L). Recorded mileage 672,533, service life 14 years 2 months and 26 days. Disposal Hayes/Birds, Bridgend April 1964.

Tender types principal fitted dates, Hawksworth 4000g September 1948, Collett 4000g 10th July 1954, Hawksworth 4000g 6th October 1958.

BR/WR 'Castle' class 4-6-0 No 7016 CHESTER CASTLE seen arriving at Swansea with the down 'South Wales Pullman' on 16th April 1959. *S.Rickard-J and J Collection*

Allocated Depots

CDN Cardiff Canton	09/48	86C Cardiff Canton	09/57	88A Cardiff Canton	11/09/61
82C Swindon	18/12/50	87G Carmarthen	22/09/59	88L Cardiff East Dock	07/09/62
87E Landore	20/09/56	87F Llanelly	05/07/61		

Chester Castle is in the city of Chester, Cheshire. It is sited at the southwest extremity of the area bounded by the city walls. The castle site overlooks the River Dee. The first castle was built in 1070 by Hugh Lupus, first Earl of Chester. In the castle complex are the remaining parts of the medieval castle together with neoclassical buildings built between 1788 and 1813. Parts of the castle are used today as Crown Courts and a military museum. The site is a popular tourist attraction.

BR/WR 'Castle' class 4-6-0 No 7016 CHESTER CASTLE seen with a down fitted freight at Rumney on 10th Oct 1954. *S.Rickard-J and J Collection*

7017 G.J. CHURCHWARD

Introduced into service in September 1948. Diagram HC boiler fitted. The locomotive's last 'Heavy Intermediate' overhaul including boiler (HC 6698) took place at Swindon Works between 16th December 1960 and 9th February 1961. The engine was withdrawn in February 1963 from Old Oak Common depot (81A). Recorded mileage 724,589, service life 14 years 5 months and 9 days. Disposal R.A. Kings, Norwich January 1964.

Tender types principal fitted dates, Hawksworth 4000g September 1948, Collett 4000g 18th December 1952, Hawksworth 4000g 27th February 1954, Collett 4000g 22nd February 1955, Hawksworth 4000g 23rd April 1955, Collett 4000g December 1961.

Allocated Depots

SDN Swindon	09/48	CDF Cardiff Canton	12/48	Old Oak Common. Stored	12/11/62
PDN Old Oak Common	11/48	81A Old Oak Common	09/07/54		

G.J. Churchward – George Jackson Churchward CBE (1857–1933) was Chief Mechanical Engineer of the Great Western Railway (GWR) from 1902 until his retirement on 31st December 1921. He was regarded by many as the father of modern Great Western locomotive design, his influence was undoubtedly far-reaching.

Churchward was born in Stoke Gabriel, Devon, into a family whose ancestors had been squires of that region since 1457, and was educated at Totnes Grammar School. His railway career began at the Newton Abbot works of the South Devon Railway where he served as an apprentice from 1873 to 1876. He later moved to the GWR's Swindon works being apprenticed there under Joseph Armstrong between 1876 and 1877, he then joined the company as an employee at the end of his apprenticeship. At Swindon he progressively rose from draughtsman through several positions, which included a spell as Carriage Works Manager, until in 1897 when he was appointed Chief Assistant to William Dean. After serving five years as Chief Assistant, he then succeeded Dean as Locomotive Superintendent in 1902.

During his tenure at Swindon Works Churchward presided over the introduction of the 2-2-0 Railmotors (112 built-1904) and 20 classes of steam locomotives which included in 1908 the Great Bear Pacific, 'City' class 4-4-0s (1903), the 'Saint'(1903) and 'Star' (1907) classes of 4-6-0s from which Collett's 'Castle' class engines were derived, the 'County' class 4-4-0 and 4-4-2Ts (1904/5), and the '4200' class 2-8-0Ts and '4300' class 2-6-0s (1910/11). His last introduction was the '4700' 2-8-0 class, an example of which was in 2014 the subject of an ongoing 'New Build' project. Between 1902 and 1919 Churchward introduced a total of 1,254 locomotives and 112 Railmotors. Preserved examples of Churchward engines total 20 and include 'City' class No 3440 CITY OF TRURO and 'Star' class 4-6-0 No 4003 LODE STAR.

Churchward's Pacific (4-6-2) No 111 THE GREAT BEAR was the only locomotive of that wheel arrangement ever to be built by the GWR. While being over 50 per cent more powerful than the 4-6-0 'Star' class it was also a third heavier and thus was restricted to the Paddington-Bristol route. The GWR route availability code of No 111 was Red and although the locos tractive effort (27,800lbf) actually placed it within power classification 'D' the engine was given a rating of 'Special' on account of its weight characteristics and that was indicated by a black + on the cabside red disc.

During a 1913 upgrade the loco was given a new Swindon No 3 superheater. Commentators of the time concluded that the Pacific although up to all the tasks it was asked to perform in traffic was never really pushed to the limits. Occasional reports suggested that the loco could in certain circumstances be a poor steamer. As a test bed locomotive Churchward and his team would almost certainly have desired to take the development of the 4-6-2 wide firebox locomotive further, but they were not asked by the GWR management to do so.

In January 1924 the loco was listed as being in need of heavy repairs and subsequently withdrawn from traffic by the GWR. The amount of available work was not considered to be sufficient to justify repairing the Pacific and so it was alternatively converted into a Castle Class (4073) 4-6-0. Churchward (by that time in retirement) was said to have been very upset by its demise.

Churchward Pacific THE GREAT BEAR which became GWR 'Castle' class 4-6-0 No 111 VISCOUNT CHURCHILL. *Image reproduced by kind permission of the Great Western Society*

Honours included being Chairman of New Swindon Urban District Council in 1897 and later becoming the first mayor of Swindon in 1900, being appointed President of the Association of Railway Locomotive Engineers (ARLE) in 1917, being awarded a C.B.E. in 1918, and in 1920 being made the First Honorary Freeman of the Borough of Swindon.

After retiring Churchward (who had never married) continued to live in a GWR owned house sited near to the mainline at Swindon. On 19th December 1933, with reportedly failing eyesight and poor hearing, he was inspecting what he observed to be a defectively bedded sleeper on the down through line when he was struck and killed by a Paddington to Fishguard express, ironically hauled by Collett locomotive No 4085 'BERKELEY CASTLE'!

BR/WR 'Castle' class 4-6-0 No 7017 G. J. CHURCHWARD approaches Corsham and Box Tunnel with a down Paddington–Bristol service, in 1960. Note the diamond shaped plate on the signal post informing footplate crews that track circuiting is in use. *Rail Photoprints Collection*

7018 DRYSLLWYN CASTLE (Converted to double chimney)

Introduced into service in June 1949. When first modified to a double chimney engine in May 1956 the original HC boiler with three row superheater was retained, also the lubrication setting was raised to 50% higher than the rest of the class. In July and August 1956 the engine was tested with the dynamometer car, first on the Paddington–Torquay service and then on the Bristol–Paddington service. The locomotive's last 'Heavy General' overhaul including boiler (HD 9610) and tender change took place at Swindon Works between 16th August and 9th October 1961. The engine was withdrawn in September 1963 from Old Oak Common depot (81A). Recorded mileage 614,259, service life 14 years 3 months and 17 days. Disposal Cashmores, Great Bridge June 1964.

Tender types principal fitted dates, Hawksworth 4000g June 1949, Collett 4000g 3rd May 1951, Hawksworth 4000g 17th March 1955, Collett 4000g 13th January 1960.

BR/WR 'Castle' class 4-6-0 No 7018 DRYSLLWYN CASTLE is seen as a single chimney engine running through Swindon station with the up 'South Wales Pullman' on 10th August 1955. Rail Photoprints Collection

Allocated Depots

LDR Landore	06/49	82A Bristol Bath Road	26/05/56	81A Old Oak Common	09/10/61
82C Swindon Testing Plant	11/48	82B St Philips Marsh	16/09/60		

BR/WR 'Castle' class 4-6-0 No 7018 DRYSLLWYN CASTLE is seen as a double chimney engine in the shed yard at Old Oak Common (81A) in August 1962. On 28th April 1958 this engine whilst working the up 'Bristolian' had reportedly passed Little Somerford at 100mph, arriving at London Paddington in 94 minutes. Rail Photoprints Collection

Drysllwyn Castle is a native Welsh castle, sited on a hill roughly halfway between Llandeilo and Carmarthen. The circa 1197 fortification occupies a majestic hilltop location above the river Tywi and valley, it commands a place of great affection in the minds and traditions of the Welsh people. The site is forever associated with the princes of Deheubarth (Kingdom of Deheubarth). The castle eventually fell to the English Crown from 1287, thereafter serving as an administrative centre. By the end of the Middle Ages the castle had fallen into disuse and become ivy-clad ruins. The Cadw managed site is open to the public.

7019 FOWEY CASTLE (Converted to double chimney)

Introduced into service in June 1949. Diagram HC boiler fitted. Double chimney and 4-row superheater fitted June 1958 to existing boiler (HD7669). The locomotive's last 'Heavy General' overhaul including boiler (HD 7674) and tender change took place at Swindon Works between 10th June and 19th August 1960. The engine was withdrawn in February 1965 from Oxley depot (2B). Recorded mileage 680,454 (up to 28th December 1963) service life 14 years 3 months and 17 days. Disposal Cashmores, Great Bridge April 1965.

Tender types principal fitted dates, Hawksworth 4000g 27th May 1949, Collett 4000g 12th April 1951, Hawksworth 4000g 30th October 1951, Collett 4000g 21st January 1953, Hawksworth 4000g 14th October 1954, Collett 4000g 10th December 1957.

Single chimney BR/WR 'Castle' class 4-6-0 No 7019 FOWEY CASTLE is seen passing Filton Junction with the up 'Bristolian' on 19th May 1959. *Hugh Ballantyne/Rail Photoprints*

Allocated Depots

| BRD Bristol Bath Road | 06/49 | 84A Stafford Road | 09/11/61 | 2B Oxley | 09/09/63 |

Double chimney BR/WR 'Castle' class 4-6-0 No 7019 FOWEY CASTLE is seen at Oxley (2B) having recently received attention at Stafford Road depot, May 1964. *Brian Robbins/Rail Photoprints Collection*

Fowey Castle – Otherwise known as St Catherine's Castle, is a small Device fort commissioned by Henry VIII. It is a two-storey building built to protect Fowey Harbour in Cornwall. A twin battery of 64-pounder rifled muzzle-loading guns was added on a lower terrace in the 19th century. One emplacement was modified in WWII to mount a 4.7″ naval gun inside a concrete shelter, but that was later removed in order to restore the Victorian gun races. The English Heritage managed site is open to the public.

7020 GLOUCESTER CASTLE (Converted to double chimney)

Introduced into service in June 1949. Diagram HC boiler fitted. Double chimney and 4-row superheater fitted during the locomotive's last 'Heavy General' overhaul including boiler (HD 7678) and tender change, which took place at Swindon Works between 24th November 1960 and 3rd February 1961. The engine was withdrawn in September 1964 from Southall depot (81C). Recorded mileage 610,143 (up to 28th December 1963) service life 15 years and 3 months. Disposal Hayes Metals, Bridgend December 1964.

Tender types principal fitted dates, Hawksworth 4000g 31st May 1949, Collett 4000g 5th June 1951, Hawksworth 4000g 10th December 1952, Collett 4000g 19th August 1954, Hawksworth 4000g 4th August 1955, Collett 4000g 8th November 1956, Hawksworth 4000g 28th February 1961.

BR/WR 'Castle' class 4-6-0 No 7020 GLOUCESTER CASTLE is seen in very grimy condition, but nevertheless the still in service double chimney engine is receiving attention. The location is Didcot depot (81E) in May 1962. *David Anderson*

Note that the GWR/BRWR often used a three-character frame mounted on the locomotive smokebox in which the train reporting number could be displayed. The 3ft wide frame had provision for displaying three digits, each 16 inches in height. In this instance 'X' denotes an excursion working and '86' the relevant destination code.

Allocated Depots

CDN Cardiff Canton	06/49	81A Old Oak Common	21/12/56	Old Oak Common. Reinstated	11/09/61
82C Swindon	08/11/56	Old Oak Common. Stored	13/02/62	81C Southall	07/09/62

'Changing times' BR/WR 'Castle' class 4-6-0 No 7020 GLOUCESTER CASTLE faces an unidentified 'Western' class diesel hydraulic locomotive in the new shed at Old Oak Common (81A), in August 1962. *Rail Photoprints Collection*

Gloucester Castle was a castle in the city of the same name. The original fortification was of motte and bailey construction and dated from early Norman times. A stone castle was later constructed and that was in full repair until the mid 15th century. The building later reverted to being a goal and that structure was demolished circa 1790, and in modern times there are no castle remains to be seen.

7021 HAVERFORDWEST CASTLE (Converted to double chimney)

Introduced into service in June 1949. Diagram HC boiler fitted. Double chimney and 4-row superheater fitted during the locomotive's last 'Heavy General' overhaul including boiler (HD 9613) and tender change, which took place at Swindon Works between 28th September and 23rd November 1961. The engine was withdrawn in September 1963 from Llanelly depot (87F). Recorded mileage 673,231, service life 14 years 3 months and 9 days. Disposal Cashmores, Great Bridge May 1964.

Tender types principal fitted dates, Hawksworth 4000g 8th June 1949, Collett 4000g 6th August 1953, Hawksworth 4000g 26th December 1953, Collett 4000g 25th February 1956.

Allocated Depots

LDR Landore	06/49	87E Landore	02/51	87E Landore	18/06/61
87G Carmarthen	06/50	87G Carmarthen	11/57	87F Llanelly	09/09/63

Haverfordwest Castle is located in the town centre at Haverfordwest, Pembrokeshire. The castle was established during Norman times circa 1120 and constructed in a naturally defensive position at the end of a strong, isolated ridge. However, much of the architecture remaining today dates from around 1290. For centuries the castle remained an English stronghold. Pembrokeshire records indicate that there was an Iron Age hill fort on the site of the castle; although there is no physical evidence to suggest that structure was at the location of the Norman ruins. Today the castle is operated by the Pembrokeshire Coast National Park Authority and it is open to the public.

BR/WR 'Castle' class 4-6-0 No 7021 HAVERFORDWEST CASTLE is seen calling at Newport with the 3.45 Paddington–Fishguard service, on 30th August 1961. *Hugh Ballantyne/Rail Photoprints*

7022 HEREFORD CASTLE (Converted to double chimney)

Introduced into service in June 1949. Diagram HC boiler fitted. Double chimney and 4-row superheater fitted January 1958 to existing boiler (HD 7672). The locomotive's last 'Heavy Intermediate' overhaul including boiler (HD 7684) and tender change, took place at Swindon Works between 24th October and 18th December 1961. The engine was withdrawn in June 1965 from Gloucester Horton Road depot (85B). Recorded mileage 733,069 (up to 28th December 1963) service life 15 years 11 months and 26 days. Disposal Hayes/Birds, Bridgend October 1965.

Tender types principal fitted dates, Hawksworth 4000g 15th June 1949, Collett 4000g 18th January 1955, Hawksworth 4000g 18th December 1961.

Allocated Depots

CDF Cardiff Canton	07/49	86C Hereford	30/11/63	85B Gloucester Horton Rd	25/10/64
83D Laira	23/01/58	85A Worcester	13/04/64		

Hereford Castle was a fortification in the city of the same name. It was founded circa 1052, and was one of the earliest castles in England. The castle is thought to have been destroyed when the Welsh sacked Hereford in 1055, but it was rebuilt during the following decade. During the Owain Glyndŵr rebellion from 1400 to 1411 King Henry IV based himself at the castle. During the Civil War Herefordshire was very much a Royalist stronghold but the castle does not appear to have played a significant part. The castle was dismantled during the 1650s with some of the stones being used for other buildings in the city. The area of Castle Green and Castle Pool mark the former castle site.

In superb condition Worcester based BR/WR 'Castle' class 4-6-0 No 7022 HEREFORD CASTLE is seen at its then home shed of 85A on 4th July 1964. *Norman Preedy/Rail Photoprints*

7023 PENRICE CASTLE (Converted to double chimney)

Introduced into service in July 1949. Diagram HC boiler fitted. Double chimney and 4-row superheater fitted May 1958 to existing boiler (HD7666) The locomotive's last 'Heavy General' overhaul including boiler (HD 7662) and tender change, which took place at Swindon Works between 23rd April and 21st June 1960. The engine was withdrawn in February 1965 from Oxley depot (2B). Recorded mileage 730,636 (up to 28th December 1963) service life 15 years 7 months and 14 days. Disposal Cashmores, Great Bridge May 1965.

Tender types principal fitted dates, Hawksworth 4000g 24th June 1949, Collett 4000g 11th September 1952, Hawksworth 4000g 18th October 1954, Collett 4000g 25th August 1955.

Allocated Depots

CDN Cardiff Canton	07/49	85A Worcester	02/08/60	2B Oxley	27/06/64

Penrice Castle on the Gower Peninsula, South Wales is the 13th century successor to a strong ringwork to the southeast, known as the Mountybank. It was built by the de Penrice family who were originally given land for their part in the Norman conquest of Gower. In the late 1770s a mansion was built adjacent to the castle ruins, which in modern times is the property of the Methuen-Campbell family, who are direct descendants of the de Penrice family. The castle is on private land, but a public footpath allows viewing of parts of the ruins.

BR/WR 'Castle' class 4-6-0 No 7023 PENRICE CASTLE is seen departing Oxford station with the up 'Cathedrals Express' on 11th March 1961. Note bottom left the railwayman with his pushbike arriving for work. *David Anderson*

7024 POWIS CASTLE (Converted to double chimney)

Introduced into service in July 1949. Diagram HC boiler fitted. Double chimney and 4-row superheater fitted March 1959, together with boiler HD7663. The locomotive's last 'Heavy General' overhaul including boiler (HD 7695) and tender change took place at Swindon Works between 8th September and 20th October 1960. The engine was withdrawn in February 1965 from Oxley depot (2B). Recorded mileage 731,344 (up to 28th December 1963) service life 15 years 7 months and 1 day. Disposal Cashmores, Newport May 1965.

Tender types principal fitted dates, Hawksworth 4000g 30th June 1949, Collett 4000g 2nd January 1953.

Allocated Depots

| PDN Old Oak Common | 07/49 | 84A Stafford Road | 18/08/61 | 2B Oxley | 09/09/63 |

Powis Castle is a medieval castle, fortress and grand country mansion located near the town of Welshpool, in Powys, Mid Wales. The residence of the Earl of Powis, the castle is known for its extensive, attractive formal gardens, terraces, parkland, deerpark and landscaped estate. The property is under the care of the National Trust.

BR/WR 'Castle' class 4-6-0 No 7024 POWIS CASTLE stands at Bristol Temple Meads after arrival with the last booked steam hauled down 'Bristolian' (08.45 Paddington–Bristol) 12/6/59. Note the mechanical lubricator in the final forward position. *Hugh Ballantyne/Rail Photoprints*

7025 SUDELEY CASTLE

Introduced into service in August 1949. Diagram HC boiler fitted. The locomotive's last 'Heavy General' overhaul including boiler change (HD 7630) took place at Swindon Works between 12th April and 16th June 1960. The engine was withdrawn in September 1964 from Worcester depot (85A). Recorded mileage 685,916 (up to 28th December 1963) service life 15 years 1 months and 7 days. Disposal Cohens, Morriston November 1964.

Tender types principal fitted dates, Hawksworth 4000g 4th August 1949, Collett 4000g 20th October 1959.

Allocated Depots

| PDN Old Oak Common | 08/49 | 84G Shrewsbury | 02/08/60 | 85A Worcester | 06/10/62 |

Sudeley Castle is a located in the Cotswolds, near to Winchcombe in Gloucestershire. The present structure was built in the 15th century, possibly on the site of a 12th-century castle. The castle has a notable garden, which is designed and maintained to a very high standard. The chapel, St. Mary's Sudeley, is the burial place of Queen Catherine Parr (1512–1548), the sixth wife of King Henry VIII. Sudeley is also one of the few castles left in England that is still a residence. Accordingly the castle is only open to visitors on specific dates and at those times the private family quarters are closed to the public. It is a Grade I listed building (1960).

BR/WR 'Castle' class 4-6-0 No 7025 SUDELEY CASTLE waits at Chester before working south, 2-6-4T 42210 waits in the wings, circa 1962. *Alan Bryant ARPS /Rail Photoprints*

7026 TENBY CASTLE

Introduced into service in August 1949. Diagram HC boiler fitted. The locomotive's last 'Heavy General' overhaul including boiler change (HD 7611) took place at Swindon Works between 22nd October and 10th December 1958. The engine was withdrawn in October 1964 from Tyseley depot (2A). Recorded mileage 636,668 (up to 28th December 1963) service life 15 years 1 months and 30 days. Disposal Cashmores, Great Bridge April 1965.

Tender types principal fitted dates, Hawksworth 4000g 16th August 1949, Collett 4000g 14th January 1957.

BR/WR 'Castle' class 4-6-0 No 7026 TENBY CASTLE, with Collett 4000g tender and stepped inside cylinder cover, is seen approaching Twerton Tunnel with the 10.35 (So) Weston-super-Mare to Paddington service, on 30th June 1962. Note the reversed headboard from a previous, or for a future working? *Hugh Ballantyne/Rail Photoprints*

Allocated Depots

Unallocated	08/49	85B Gloucester Horton Road	07/09/62	2B Oxley	09/09/63
SRD Stafford Road	11/49	84A Stafford Road	12/11/62	2A Tyseley	27/06/64

BR/WR 'Castle' class 4-6-0 No 7026 TENBY CASTLE is seen at Stafford Road (84A) in 1955. Note the Hawksworth 4000g tender without a logo and also the mechanical lubricator in the original position and un-stepped inside cylinder cover. *Rail Photoprints Collection*

Tenby Castle is a fortification which stands on a headland separated by an isthmus from the town of Tenby, Pembrokeshire. It was founded by the Normans during their invasion of West Wales in the 12th century. A stone tower was built on the headland's highest point which was protected by a curtain wall. The walls had a gateway and several small towers on the landward side. A lesser sea wall surrounded the remainder of the site and the beach area to the west. There is public access to the site.

7027 THORNBURY CASTLE Preserved

Introduced into service in September 1949. Diagram HC boiler fitted. The locomotive's last 'Heavy General' overhaul including boiler change (HD 7615) took place at Swindon Works between 16th February and 25th April 1960. The engine was withdrawn in August 1963 from Reading WR depot (81D). Recorded mileage 728,843 service life 14 years 3 months and 26 days. Sold to Woodham Brothers, Barry. Tender types principal fitted dates, Hawksworth 4000g 26th August 1949, Collett 4000g 27th March 1954, Hawksworth 4000g 18th May 1954, Collett 4000g 13th September 1955.

BR/WR 'Castle' class 4-6-0 No 7027 THORNBURY CASTLE is seen newly arrived at Platform 6 Paddington station, in May 1962. *R. A. Whitfield/Rail Photoprints*

Allocated Depots

Stored Swindon	02/09/49	82C Swindon	17/10/51	85A Worcester	25/04/60
LA Laira	11/49	81A Old Oak Common	09/11/51	81D Reading WR	31/08/63

BR/WR 'Castle' class 4-6-0 No 7027 THORNBURY CASTLE. The locomotive arrived at Woodham's scrapyard Barry during May 1964. No 7027 remained at that location until August 1972 when having been rescued it became the 23rd departure from Barry. The hulk was first moved to the then Birmingham Railway Museum before being sold to pop music mogul Pete Waterman O.B.E., thus becoming one of the locomotives in the 'Waterman Railways Heritage Trust'. In 2014 the engine was still in an un-restored condition and stored adjacent to the Crewe Heritage Centre. One set of name and number plates for the 7027 are reportedly mounted on a wall of the main hall of The Castle School in Thornbury, South Gloucestershire. *Keith Langston Collection*

Thornbury Castle is a castle in Thornbury, South Gloucestershire, the building of which began in 1511 as a home for Edward Stafford, 3rd Duke of Buckingham. It is not a true castle, but rather an early example of a Tudor country house, with minimal defensive attributes. It is now a Grade I listed building and a luxury hotel and restaurant.

In happier times BR/WR 'Castle' class 4-6-0 No 7027 THORNBURY CASTLE is seen ex overhaul at Swindon Works, in May 1956. *Hugh Ballantyne/Rail Photoprints*

The so called 'Lion on a Bike' BR logo as seen on the tender of No. 7027.

7028 CADBURY CASTLE (Converted to double chimney)

Introduced into service in May 1950. Diagram HC boiler fitted. Double chimney and 4-row superheater fitted October 1961 during the locomotive's last 'Heavy Intermediate' overhaul including boiler (HD 7683) and tender change, which took place at Swindon Works between 4th September and 31st October 1961. The engine was withdrawn in December 1963 from Llanelly depot (87F). Recorded mileage 624,626 service life 13 years 6 months and 27 days. Disposal Balborough Metals, Briton Ferry August 1964.

Tender types principal fitted dates, Hawksworth 4000g 19th May 1950, Collett 4000g 23rd February 1952, Hawksworth 4000g 29th October 1959, Collett 4000g 24th January 1961.

Allocated Depots

87E Landore	06/50	87F Llanelly	31/10/61	87F Llanelly. Reinstated	09/07/62
87G Carmarthen	10/56	88C Barry Stored	01/05/62	97F Llanelly. Stored	09/09/63
87E Landore	06/57				

Cadbury Castle is a Bronze and Iron Age hill fort in the parish of South Cadbury, Somerset. The site has long been thought to have associations with the legendary King Arthur. It is located 5 miles (8.0 km) north east of Yeovil and stands on the summit of Cadbury Hill, situated on the southern edge of the Somerset Levels.

Landore based BR/WR 'Castle' class 4-6-0 No 7028 CADBURY CASTLE is seen approaching Westerleigh Junction with a South Wales–Paddington service, in 1959. *Norman Preedy Collection/Rail Photoprints*

7029 CLUN CASTLE (Converted to double chimney) Preserved Introduced into service in May 1950

Diagram HC boiler fitted. Double chimney and 4-row superheater fitted October 1959 (boiler HD7664). The locomotive's last 'Heavy General' overhaul including boiler (HD 7675) and tender change, took place at Swindon Works between 1st May and 2nd July 1962. The engine was withdrawn in December 1965 from Gloucester Horton Road depot (85B). Recorded mileage 618,073 (up to 28th December 1963) service life 15 years 7 months. The locomotive was displayed at Allerton Shed (then 8J) open day on 26th July 1969.

Tender types principal fitted dates, Hawksworth 4000g 25th May 1950, Collett 4000g 12th May 1952, Hawksworth 4000g 24th March 1954, Collett 4000g 19th April 1958, Hawksworth 4000g 7th October 1959, Collett 4000g 23rd November 1960.

BR/WR 'Castle' class 4-6-0 No 7029 CLUN CASTLE is seen at Foxhall Junction, Didcot on 3rd April 1965. The train depicted is a Warwickshire Railway Society special to Swindon. *David Anderson*

Allocated Depots

83A Newton Abbot	05/50	81A Old Oak Common	02/07/62	85B Gloucester Horton Road	05/10/64

CLUN CASTLE represents the final development of the 4-6-0 'Castle' class incorporating all the modifications made by British Railways during the 1950s. No 7029 was the last Castle to remain in BR service, and hauled the last official steam train out of Paddington (to Banbury) on 11th June 1960.

On 9 May 1964 the 'Great Western' special train ran between Paddington and Plymouth and the return leg was rostered for loco No 7029 CLUN CASTLE, an engine which proved to be more than equal to the task. Observers reported that as No 7029 neared the summit of Whiteball 'she still had enough steam in hand to lift the safety valves'. The loco then raced down Wellington Bank reaching 94 mph, before the driver had to brake to 80mph through Wellington Station. Clear of the station precincts CLUN CASTLE accelerated again to an official 96mph, a speed some onboard observers actually clocked at 97mph! However No 7029 was denied the magic 'ton' with the special train having to slow to 80mph, because of the governing speed restriction through Taunton station. The engine continued to run superbly maintaining high speeds all the way to Bristol Temple Meads and, to the great delight of several hundred welcoming enthusiasts, arrived there 9¾ minutes early.

The great performance had impressed a man with the strongest of railway connections, one John Trounson a West Country mining engineer who was the fifth cousin to none other than steam pioneer Richard Trevithick. Mr Trounson, who was a passenger on the train, enlisted the help of fellow traveller Mr John Southern of Dobwalls Forest Railway fame and the pair subsequently started a No 7029 preservation fund, which helped to kick start the eventual purchase and preservation of CLUN CASTLE.

Since preservation, the engine has travelled widely on excursions and to Open Days in all parts of the UK. During 1985, CLUN CASTLE played a prominent part in the Great Western Railway 150th Anniversary celebrations by hauling main line trains to destinations in South Wales and Cornwall. The locomotives last 'certificate' ran out at the end of 2001, and the engine now awaits overhaul to mainline condition at its Tyseley Locomotive Works home base. A comprehensive account of No 7029's history and future prospects can be found at http://www.tyseleylocoworks.co.uk/tlw/7029.htm

Clun Castle is a ruined Norman fortification in the Shropshire township of the same name. The castle was established by the Norman lord Robert de Say, and went on to become an important Marcher lord castle in the 12th century. Clun originally played a key part in protecting the region from Welsh attack. Today the castle is classed as a Grade I listed building and also as a Scheduled Monument. It is owned by the Duke of Norfolk, who also holds the title of Baron Clun, and is managed by English Heritage; accordingly public access is allowed.

BR/WR 'Castle' class 4-6-0 No 7029 CLUN CASTLE is seen at Birmingham Snow Hill station with the SLS (Midland Area) 'Farewell To The Castle Class Tour', the 24th January 1965. *Rail Photoprints Collection*

This superb 2008 image of the preserved BR/WR 'Castle' class 4-6-0 No 7029 CLUN CASTLE shows the pleasing lines of the Collett design to great effect, (Collett 4000g tender). The locomotive has the benefit of British Railways final modifications which included a Diagram HD boiler with a 4-row superheater, double chimney and mechanical lubricator. The 1950 built engine has enjoyed a very successful life in preservation and in 2010 a new appeal was launched in order to put No 7029 back into steam once again. *Phil Neale*

BR/WR 'Castle' class 4-6-0 No 7029 CLUN CASTLE leads sister preserved 'Castle' class 4-6-0 No 5051 running as DRYSLLWYN CASTLE. The Collett pair are seen heading north through Tiverton Junction station with SLOA's 'Great Western Limited' Plymouth to Bristol special on 1st September 1985. *John Chalcraft/ Rail Photoprints Collection*

'Castles in the Night'. An evocative study of two Tyseley based preserved 'Castle' class engines seen on shed. No 7029 CLUN CASTLE (BR/WR) with a Collett 4000g tender and No 5043 EARL OF MOUNT EDGCUMBE (GWR) with a Hawksworth 4000g tender. *Phil Neale*

7030 CRANBROOK CASTLE (Converted to double chimney) Introduced into service in June 1950

Diagram HC boiler fitted. Double chimney and 4-row superheater fitted May 1959 (boiler HD7661). The locomotive's last 'Heavy Intermediate' overhaul including boiler (HD 7689) and tender change, took place at Swindon Works between 18th March and 11th May 1961. In May 1962 this engine carried out return high speeds runs on the Paddington-Wolverhampton service, twice reaching a speed of 103mph during the return journey. The engine was withdrawn in February 1963 from Old Oak Common depot (81A). Recorded mileage 637,339, service life 12 years 8 months and 4 days. Disposal R.A. Kings, Norwich December 1963. The engine was only ever allocated to one depot.

Tender types principal fitted dates, Hawksworth 4000g 5th June 1950, Collett 4000g 30th June 1952, Hawksworth 4000g 5th September 1957, Collett 4000g July 1959, Hawksworth 4000g 11th May 1961.

Allocated Depot

| 81A Old Oak Common | 05/50 | 81A Old Oak Common. Reinstated | 01/05/62 |
| 81A Old Oak Common. Stored | 13/02/62 | | |

Cranbrook Castle is the site of an Iron Age Hill fort overlooking the Teign valley in Devon. Public access is allowed.

BR/WR 'Castle' class 4-6-0 No 7030 CRANBROOK CASTLE runs through Sydney Gardens as it approaches Bath Spa with a Paddington–Bristol/Weston-super-Mare service, on 14th September 1958. *Hugh Ballantyne/Rail Photoprints*

7031 CROMWELL'S CASTLE

Introduced into service in June 1950. Diagram HC boiler fitted. The locomotive's last 'Heavy General' overhaul including boiler (HC 6699) and tender change, took place at Swindon Works between 30th November 1961 and 9th February 1962. The engine was withdrawn in July 1963 from Worcester depot (85A). Recorded mileage 749,715, service life 13 years 1 month and 15 days. Disposal Cashmores, Newport June 1964.

Tender types principal fitted dates, Hawksworth 4000g 20th June 1950, Collett 4000g 24th April 1952, Hawksworth 4000g 27th April 1955, Collett 4000g 13th August 1955, Hawksworth 4000g 24th April 1956, Collett 4000g 31st January 1957.

Allocated Depots

83D Laira	06/50	83D Laira	24/03/59	85A Worcester	24/03/62
83B Taunton	31/01/57	82C Swindon	05/01/60		

Cromwell's Castle is a 17th-century fortification on the island of Tresco in the Isles of Scilly, built by Sir Robert Blake in 1651 after the Parliamentary invasion of the Isles. It was named for Oliver Cromwell, who was Lord Protector of England. Standing on a rocky promontory guarding the lovely anchorage between Bryher and Tresco, this round tower is one of the few surviving Cromwellian fortifications in Britain. In the 21st century, the castle is controlled by English Heritage and operated as a tourist attraction.

*Left: Two Collett designed locos sit in the depths of Worcester shed – Mixed Traffic 0-6-0 No 2246 (left) and 'Castle class' 4-6-0 No 7031 (right) in February 1963. **Rail Photoprints Collection***

Below: BR/WR 'Castle' class 4-6-0 No 7031 CROMWELL'S CASTLE is seen at speed on the 'Didcot Avoiding Line' (east) in this 1960s image. David Anderson

7032 DENBIGH CASTLE (Converted to double chimney) Introduced into service in June 1950

Diagram HC boiler fitted. Double chimney and 4-row superheater fitted during the locomotive's last 'Heavy General' overhaul which included boiler (HD 7694) and tender change, and took place at Swindon Works between 27th July and 27th September 1960. The engine was withdrawn in September 1964 from Old Oak Common depot (81A). Recorded mileage 666,374 (up to 28th December 1963) service life 14 years 1 month and 26 days. Disposal Birds, Risca February 1965.

Tender types principal fitted dates, Hawksworth 4000g 23rd June 1950, Collett 4000g 13th March 1952, Hawksworth 4000g 18th April 1955, Collett 4000g 26th March 1956, Hawksworth 4000g 3rd April 1957, Collett 4000g 7th November 1958.

BR/WR 'Castle' class 4-6-0 No 7032 DENBIGH CASTLE is seen leaving Didcot with an up perishable goods/parcels working in 1961. *David Anderson*

Allocated Depots

| 82C Swindon | 07/50 | 81A Old Oak Common | 10/07/50 |

BR/WR 'Castle' class 4-6-0 No 7032 DENBIGH CASTLE is seen at Old Oak Common (81A), on 21st April 1963. *Martyn Hunt/Rail Photoprints Collection*

Denbigh Castle was a fortress built following the 13th-century conquest of Wales by Edward I. The castle, which stands on a rocky promontory above the Welsh market town of Denbigh, was built upon an earlier Welsh stronghold. A planned town (*bastide*) was laid out at the same time as the castle in an attempt by Edward I to pacify the Welsh. The castle is managed by Cadw, the Welsh heritage agency tasked with looking after historic buildings and monuments. The ruins are open to the public. Denbigh was served by the Vale of Clywd Railway, later the LNWR, and LMS.

7033 HARTLEBURY CASTLE (Converted to double chimney) Introduced into service in July 1950

Diagram HC boiler fitted. Double chimney and 4-row superheater fitted July 1959 (boiler HD 7685). The locomotive's last 'Heavy General' overhaul which included boiler (HD 7669) and tender change, and took place at Swindon Works between 6th February and 11th April 1961. The engine was withdrawn in February 1963 from Old Oak Common depot (81A). Recorded mileage 605,219, service life 12 years 7 month and 10 days. Disposal Cashmores, Great Bridge June 1964.

Tender types principal fitted dates, Hawksworth 4000g 4th July 1950, Collett 4000g 27th February 1952, Hawksworth 4000g 19th November 1957, Collett 4000g July 1959.

BR/WR 'Castle' class 4-6-0 No 7033 HARTLEBURY CASTLE is seen at Old Oak Common (81A) in June 1960. *Ian Turnbull/Rail Photoprints*

Allocated Depots

| 81A Old Oak Common | 07/50 | 82C Swindon | 27/03/52 | 81A Old Oak Common | 28/04/52 |

'The end is nigh!' Shorn of name and number plates BR/WR 'Castle' class 4-6-0 No 7033 HARTLEBURY CASTLE is seen in rundown condition at Shrewsbury depot pending the locomotive's last trip to Cashmores Great Bridge, Tipton. *Rail Photoprints Collection*

Hartlebury Castle is a Grade I listed building in Worcestershire, which was built in the mid-13th century as a fortified manor house on land given to the Bishop of Worcester by King Burgred of Mercia. It is located near Stourport and part of the building now houses the Worcestershire County Museum. The castle grounds include a cider mill and a transport display that features vehicles including a fire engine, hansom cab, bicycles, carts and a collection of Gypsy caravans.

7034 INCE CASTLE (Converted to double chimney) Introduced into service in August 1950

Diagram HC boiler fitted. Double chimney and 4-row superheater fitted December 1959 (boiler HD 7655). The locomotive's last 'Heavy General' overhaul which included boiler (HD 9614) and tender change, and took place at Swindon Works between 19th October and 28th November 1961. The engine was withdrawn in June 1965 from Gloucester Horton Road depot (85B). Recorded mileage 616,584 (up to 28th December 1963), service life 14 years 10 months. Disposal Hayes/Birds, Bridgend October 1965.

Tender types principal fitted dates, Hawksworth 4000g 1st August 1950, Collett 4000g 12th June 1952.

Allocated Depots

82A Bristol Bath Road	08/50	82B St Philips March	16/09/60	85B Gloucester Horton Road	11/12/61

Ince Castle is three miles from Saltash in Cornwall. It is not a castle in the conventional sense but a manor house built of brick, circa 1642, at the start of the English Civil War. The structure is located at the end of a very attractive peninsula surrounded by the river Lynher, and it is opposite Antony House and gardens. The present owners are Simon Lennox-Boyd, 2nd Viscount Boyd of Merton and his wife Alice. The attractive house and gardens are only occasionally open to the public.

A very grimy BR/WR 'Castle' class 4-6-0 No 7034 INCE CASTLE heads west through Dawlish Warren, on 16th September 1953. *Rail Photoprints Collection*

7035 OGMORE CASTLE (Converted to double chimney) Introduced into service in August 1950

Diagram HC boiler fitted. Double chimney and 4-row superheater fitted during the locomotive's last 'Heavy General' overhaul which included boiler (HD 7650) and tender change, and took place at Swindon Works between 27th November 1959 and 29th January 1960. The engine was withdrawn in June 1964 from Old Oak Common depot (81A). Recorded mileage 580,346 (up to 28th December 1963), service life 13 years 9 months and 1 day. Disposal Swindon Works, August 1965.

Tender types principal fitted dates, Hawksworth 4000g 9th August 1950, Collett 4000g 13th October 1952, Hawksworth 4000g 22nd March 1954, Collett 4000g 26th July 1955, Hawksworth 4000g 16th November 1955, Collett 4000g 1st October 1956, Hawksworth 4000g 23rd June 1959, Collett 4000g 29th January 1960.

Allocated Depots

84G Shrewsbury	09/50	82C Swindon	19/11/56	85B Gloucester Horton Road	29/02/60
85B Gloucester Horton Road	09/53	82A Bristol Bath Road	01/12/56	81F Oxford	12/11/62
82A Bristol Bath Road	01/10/56	87E Landore	16/02/59	81A Old Oak Common	04/03/63

Ogmore Castle is located near the village of Ogmore-by-Sea, south of the town of Bridgend in Glamorgan. It is situated on the south bank of the River Ewenny and the east bank of the River Ogmore. Ogmore was one of three castles built in the area in the early 12th century, the others being Coity Castle and Newcastle Castle. The ghost 'Y Ladi Wen' (the White Lady–Eng Lady Wen) purportedly guarded the castle's treasure. Public access is allowed.

BR/WR 'Castle' class 4-6-0 No 7035 OGMORE CASTLE is seen passing Old Oak Common Junction on 22nd August 1962. *Rail Photoprints Collection*

7036 TAUNTON CASTLE (Converted to double chimney)

Introduced into service in August 1950. Diagram HC boiler fitted. Double chimney and 4-row superheater fitted August 1959 (boiler HD 7684). The locomotive's last 'Heavy General' overhaul which included boiler (HD 9605) and tender change took place at Swindon Works between 25th April and 15th June 1961. The engine was withdrawn in September 1963 from Old Oak Common depot (81A). Recorded mileage 617,653, service life 13 years 9 days. Disposal Cashmores, Great Bridge June 1964.

Tender types principal fitted dates, Hawksworth 4000g 17th August 1950, Collett 4000g 2nd July 1952, Hawksworth 4000g 23rd November 1955, Collett 4000g 15th June 1961.

BR/WR 'Castle' class 4-6-0 No 7036 TAUNTON CASTLE arrives at Swindon with a special from Birmingham, which ran in conjunction with the RCTS 'Farewell to the M & SWJ'. The motive power for which, GWR '4300' class 2-6-0 No 5306 can be seen to the right of the signal box, 10th September 1961. *Rail Photoprints Collection*

Allocated Depots

81A Old Oak Common	09/50	84A Stafford Road. Stored	07/09/62	81A Old Oak Common. Reinstated	06/10/62
84A Stafford Road	14/07/62				

Yatton Station on a rainy 7th September 1963. BR/WR 'Castle' class No 7036 TAUNTON CASTLE arrives with the 09.45 (So) Paddington–Weston Super Mare service, whilst Ivatt 'Class 2' 2-6-2T No 41245 takes water at the head of the 1.45 service to Witham. This was probably the last steam hauled Paddington–Weston-super-Mare service, as it ran on the last Saturday of that year's Summer timetable. *Hugh Ballantyne/Rail Photoprints*

Taunton Castle was built to defend the Somerset town of the same name. It has origins in the Anglo Saxon period and was later the site of a priory. The current heavily reconstructed buildings are the inner ward, and they now house the Museum of Somerset and additionally the Somerset Military Museum.

7037 SWINDON

Introduced into service in August 1950. Diagram HC boiler fitted. This was the last of the 'Castle' class locomotives to be built. The locomotive's last 'Heavy General' overhaul which included boiler (HC 7603) and tender change took place at Swindon Works between 18th June and 25th August 1960. The engine was withdrawn in March 1963 from Old Oak Common depot (81A). Recorded mileage 519,885 (lowest of the class) service life 12 years 7 months and 1 day (marginally the shortest of the class). Disposal Cashmores, Newport August 1965.

Tender types principal fitted dates, Hawksworth 4000g 28th August 1950, Collett 4000g 12th November 1952, Hawksworth 4000g 10th December 1952, Collett 4000g 4th March 1954, Hawksworth 4000g 31st October 1959, Collett 4000g 25th August 1960.

Allocated Depots

82C Swindon	08/50	82C Swindon. Reinstated	08/11/50	81A Old Oak Common	06/09/60
82C Swindon. Stored	09/09/50				

Swindon – The locomotive was named in recognition of the Wiltshire town and its famous GWR-BR/WR locomotive works where all 171 of the 'Castle' class 4-6-0 engines were built, between August 1923 and August 1950. The naming ceremony was carried out by HRH Princess Elizabeth.

Swindon's pride and joy BR/WR 'Castle' class 4-6-0 No 7037 SWINDON on shed at 82C, during 1956. *R.S. Wilkins/Rail Photoprints*

GWR/BR 'Castle' class 4-cylinder locomotives, Swindon Works 'Lot Numbers'

Nos 7000–7007 Lot 357 built 1946 (Average cost per engine £9749)
Nos 7008–7027 Lot 367 built 1948/49 British Railways (Average cost per engine £10,765)
Nos 7028–7037 Lot 375 built 1950 British Railways (Average cost per engine £11,643)

General Specification

Power Classification	6P reclassified 7P in 1951 (GWR Power Class D)
GWR Route availability	Red
Introduced	1923–1947 GWR and 1948–1950 BR
Designer	C.B. Collett
Driving Wheel Diameter	6 feet 8½ inches
Bogie Wheel Diameter	3 feet 2 inches
Boiler Type	'Number 8', variously Diagram HA, HB, HC and HD
Boiler Diameter	Minimum 5 feet 1 15/16 inches, Maximum 5 feet 9 inches
Boiler Length	14 feet 10 inches
Boiler Pressure	225 psi Superheated
Grate Area	29.36 square feet
Cylinders	4 x 16 inch diameter and 26th inch stroke
Tractive Effort	31625lbf (pounds)
Valve Gear	Inside Walschaert with rocking shafts (piston valves)
Tender Coal Capacity	6 tons (some earlier locomotives 7 ton)
Tender Water Capacity	4000 gallons (some earlier locomotives 3500 gallons)
Total Weight	126 tons 11cwts
Overall Length	65 feet 3 inches

Swindon Locomotive Works

Swindon Locomotive Works was built in 1842 for the Great Western Railway on a site which soon grew to cover an area of 140 acres. The works was situated adjacent to the London–Bristol and South Wales mainline. The expanding works caused a 'Railway Village' to be built around the site. That collection of workers houses was complimented by a school, swimming baths, church, lending library and hospital. The highest number of employees was recorded as being 5,758 in the Locomotive Works and a further 4,157 in the Carriage Wagon and Stores departments (total 9,915).

Swindon Works Milestones

1846 – First phase of the building work completed. The first locomotive built using some bought in component parts. The first locomotive built entirely at Swindon appeared, 7 feet 0¼ inch gauge 2-2-2 GREAT WESTERN.
1855 – First Standard Gauge locomotive produced.
1891 – Last Broad Gauge locomotives built, abolition of the Broad Gauge followed in 1892.
1897 – The first 4-6-0 built in England, No 36.
1902 – The famous 'A' Shop was completed.
1908 – First Pacific built in Britain, No 111 THE GREAT BEAR.
1924 – Royal visit by King George V and Queen Mary.
1948 – Became part of the British Transport Commission (BTC) on Nationalisation.
1950 – Royal visit by HRH Princess Elizabeth who named 'Castle' class 4-6-0 No 7037, as SWINDON.
1951 – First BR Standard locomotive completed, 'Class 4' 4-6-0 No 75000.
1955 – Last GWR type locomotive completed, 0-6-0PT No 1669.
1960 – Last steam locomotive built, '9F' class 2-10-0 No 92220 EVENING STAR. The 5,720th standard gauge steam locomotive to be built at the works.
1986–87 – Closure of the works, and sale of the site.

On the Works No. 2

GWR 'Castle' class 4-6-0 No 7003 ELMLEY CASTLE is seen in June 1956 following a 'Heavy General' overhaul. *Rail Photoprints Collection*

GWR 'Castle' class 4-6-0 No 7005 is seen as LAMPHEY CASTLE following a February 1957 'Heavy Intermediate' overhaul. Locomotive renamed SIR EDWARD ELGAR in August 1957. *Keith Langston Collection*

BR/WR 'Castle' class 4-6-0 No 7021 HAVERFORDWEST CASTLE is seen during December 1959 in the company of GWR 'Hall 4900' class 4-6-0 No 6936 BRECCLES HALL. This image illustrates well the basic exterior differences in the appearance of the two Collett classes. The 'Castle' class locomotive had visited for a 'Heavy General' overhaul. *Hugh Ballantyne/Rail Photoprints*

BR/WR 'Castle' class 4-6-0 No 7016 CHESTER CASTLE is seen during an August 1960 visit on the occasion of the locomotives last 'Heavy Intermediate' overhaul during which the single chimney locomotive was fitted with replacement boiler HC 7624. GWR 'Hall 4900' class 4-6-0 No 5926 GROTRIAN HALL can also be identified. *Keith Langston Collection/Rail Photoprints.co.uk*

BR/WR 'Castle' class 4-6-0 No 7019 FOWEY CASTLE is seen in April 1964 during an unclassified visit, the locomotive was withdrawn 11 months later. Note the 2B Oxley shed plate and the adjacent LMS 'Stanier' Mogul BR No 42954 which was withdrawn in February 1967. *Hugh Ballantyne/Rail Photoprints*

Rail Photoprints

for the best in editorial photo files and images of Steam and Modern traction, in the UK and further afield

GWR 'Castle' class No 5085 EVESHAM ABBEY on Dainton Bank 30/07/60. *Image number HB770*

www.railphotoprints.zenfolio.com

THE RAIL PHOTOPRINTS COLLECTION

Over 20,000 files already uploaded and more added every day

The Great Western Society Limited

Didcot Railway Centre, Didcot, Oxfordshire, OX11 7NJ

www.didcotrailwaycentre.org.uk

The GWS are the owners of 'Castle' class locomotives No 4079 PENDENNIS CASTLE and No 5051 EARL BATHURST. No 5051, which is currently on display at the Didcot Railway Centre, was purchased by them from the Mynors family in 1987. The Rio Tinto Company in Australia (Hamersley Iron) gifted No 4079 to the society, on the condition that they paid for its removal, and in 2000 the engine was repatriated to the UK. In 2014 PENDENNIS CASTLE was the subject of an ongoing restoration project, which when completed will see the 1924 Swindon built engine return to the mainline in full working order. You can become part of that project by making a donation which will help to complete that work and thereafter help to maintain the locomotive.

In the first instance contact Richard Croucher, GWS Ltd Chairman at The Didcot Railway Centre, Didcot, Oxfordshire OX11 7NJ, or simply check out the web sites at www.didcotrailwaycentre.org.uk also www.gwsmainline.org/

Opposite: Preserved GWR 'Castle' class 4-6-0 No 5043 EARL OF MOUNT EDGCUMBE is seen at Tyseley Locomotive Works depot on 25th October 2009. *Brian Wilson*

A re-creation of 'The Mayflower' 1Z27, 07.15 Paddington–Plymouth, passing Marlands on the climb to Whiteball behind preserved GWR 'Castle' class 4-6-0 5051 EARL BATHURST, on 26th March 2005. The inaugural titled run of 'The Mayflower' took place on 17th June 1957 with the last taking place on 12th June 1965. Note the crested design of headboard depicting the famous Pilgrim Fathers ship. *John Chalcraft/www.railphotoprints.co.uk*